Understanding and shaping public administration: The IDHEAP model

Understanding and shaping public administration: The IDHEAP model

Edited by
Nils Soguel
Pirmin Bundi
Tobias Mettler
Sophie Weerts

EPFL PRESS

Unless otherwise stated, the figures presented in this book were designed by the authors of the papers in which they appear.

General management: Lucas Giossi
Editorial and sales management: Sylvain Collette and May Yang.
Promotion and distribution: Manon Reber
Production manager: Christophe Borlat
Editorial: Alice Micheau-Thiébaud and Jean Rime
Graphic design: Kim Nanette
Accounting: Daniela Castan
Logistics: Émile Razafimanjaka

www.epflpress.org

First edition, 2025

EPFL Press is an imprint of the foundation of the Presses polytechniques et universitaires romandes.
Print edition: ISBN 978-2-88915-915-679-5
ebook (PDF): ISBN 978-2-8323-2291-8, doi.org/10.55430/UASPATIM

Printed in France

In memory of Andreas Ladner

Summary

The IDHEAP model of public administration: an overview

Nils Soguel, Pirmin Bundi, Tobias Mettler, Sophie Weerts

1 The importance of the IDHEAP model of public administration

1.1 The IDHEAP model and public administration

The running of public organizations and public policies is becoming ever more complex. Systematic globalization, new technological developments as well as crises of all kinds are placing totally new demands on the actors of public administration. Political and administrative decisions are subject to almost-live commenting on social media. The resulting impression is that everybody is an expert in political intervention and can question the activity of public administration. While this is not in itself a bad thing, it does create new challenges for current and future managers of public administration.

The goal of the *model* put forward by the Swiss Graduate School of Public Administration of the University of Lausanne (or IDHEAP, the acronym of its French designation "Institut de hautes études en administration publique") is to define the main dimensions, challenges and issues facing public administration using a structure that is as coherent as possible. This structure, like that of any model, describes a complex reality in a simplified, illustrative, pragmatic manner (Stachowiak 1973). Simplification of this kind aids the understanding of phenomena, clarifying the relationships between the various elements of public administration. The model places public administration—the action of public managers—in a global perspective. It also proposes a series of concepts, norms and instruments that contribute to that action.

The IDHEAP model seeks to understand public administration as a process of action, movement and transformation. This is why we define *public administration* as all the measures and activity that directly or indirectly contribute to the accomplishment of public tasks. This definition is a *functional definition*. Thus the contributions feeding into the model understand public administration as a set of measures and activities. When using the expression "public administration", they emphasize this functional dimension.

To avoid the risks of confusion, the model and the contributions that address its underlying principles do not use the term "public administration" in the meaning of its *institutional definition*. In an institutional definition, a public administration is the set of legal and physical persons who accomplish this activity (of public administration). Defined in this institutional manner, then, the public administration of a community or country is made up of public powers and their implementing agencies, which are entities instituted by political decisions that exercise legislative, judicial or executive power over the territory of the community or country in question. Where the institutional dimension is meant, the model and the articles of contributors instead use the terms "public body" or "public organization". They also use the terms of administrative units to signify substructures within a public body or organization.

1.2 Foundations of the IDHEAP model

The various contributions describe the model's foundations and set out its structure and components. They are written from a practical point of view but also shed light on theoretical and empirical knowledge.

These contributions and their moulding into a model of public administration are the result of analysis and reflection by IDHEAP members. This initiative is in keeping with the traditions of the Institute which, since its founding, has monitored and supported changes in public administration. IDHEAP puts public administration at the centre of its research and its training programmes, thus placing itself "at the heart of public service".

Previously conducted synthesis endeavours have focused on institutional and political aspects (Ladner *et al.* 2013 and 2019). Today, the IDHEAP model sets itself apart by shifting the focus onto the action, management and running of public organizations. It views public administration from a broad, dynamic, contemporary perspective that encompasses multiple actors, stakeholders and areas of action.

In concrete terms, the contributions to this work set out to provide public-sector managers with solutions to help them to analyse the situation and act within their organization. They highlight the key elements to be considered, resources to be activated and the manner in which they can be used, thus adding a dynamic dimension to the model. They present available options and good practices.

These contributions are a starting point. For those who wish to explore the elements they present in greater depth, other resources are available: audio and video clips and links, lectures and training sessions given at IDHEAP, along with scientific papers and papers aimed at a general audience. These resources can be found on the IDHEAP website: www.unil.ch/idheap.

The contributions to the IDHEAP model and the model as a whole are aimed particularly at:

- those already working in the public sector who wish to add structure to their understanding of public administration or to compare their vision with that offered by the IDHEAP model;
- those embarking on training at IDHEAP or elsewhere as preparatory reading for their course on public administration, so that they can gain a systemic vision of public administration;
- political agents at the various institutional levels (Confederation, cantons and municipalities); and
- journalists and researchers in public administration, since the IDHEAP model sets out the foundations and functioning of public administration.

All the contributions that feed into the IDHEAP model have the same structure, comprising three sections. The first section deals with the importance for public administration of the theme in question. The second section examines key points of the theme in detail. The last section covers future prospects and challenges.

2 Key points of the IDHEAP model

2.1 A model that covers transformations of the state

Throughout history, in various countries, the state has been constantly shaped, and constantly transformed, by political, economic and social changes. As a consequence, public administration—the manner in which the public sector governs—has constantly been forced to adapt. The imperatives of the modern world continue, and will continue, to have direct repercussions on its organization and functioning. This is why the IDHEAP model is aimed at supporting public administration as it changes in response to the dynamics of the 21st century.

A brief historical summary provides a measure of the breadth of the changes that public administration has already undergone. Until the 19th century, public administration operated only in the limited framework of exercising the state's so-called "sovereign" prerogatives (the night-watchman state). It carried out missions requiring the use of public force, which could not therefore be delegated to third parties: public order, justice, defence of the territory.

From the late 19th century, the role assigned to the state changed profoundly in response to far-reaching transformations in the technical (scientific development and rationalization), economic (industrial revolution) and social fields (demographic transition, attitudes to migration and social inequalities). Public administration was called upon to operate in new areas. It incorporated new professions (particularly in the educational and social fields). It also brought in new techniques, leading to changes in work organization. With the advent of the "welfare state", the purpose of administration was oriented towards safeguarding social wellbeing, in addition to accomplishing sovereign functions, reflecting the evolution of social values and the emergence of the ideals of justice and equity. In 1930, the Great Depression, framed by two world wars, boosted government intervention in industrialized countries. The boundaries of public administration broadened to include the resolution of macro-economic problems such as unemployment and inflation.

The expansion of the perimeters of public administration led to serious thinking about the expediency of public administration. This process of reflection began in America. The reappearance of economic crises that had been forgotten during the three decades of strong growth between 1946 and 1975 (known in France as the "Trente Glorieuses") led to a sharp rise in public spending on social programmes and economic recovery programmes. This rise had to be financed by increased compulsory deductions. Economic instability in European countries (the United Kingdom, France, Germany) threatened the welfare-state model. Voices began calling for a scaling back of government intervention.

The credence given to neoliberal theories calling for increased use of market mechanisms and emerging globalization undermined the existing model of government. A new conception of public administration thus began to develop in the late 1980s. Its aim was to reduce the government apparatus through a reform of organization and processes based particularly on more systematic delegation of public tasks to third-party entities, including private-sector actors.

However, along with globalization have come major upsets: climate disruption, migration, successive health emergencies, financialization and international crime, to name a few. Faced with these phenomena, public administration has been obliged—to an even greater extent than in the past—to evolve. Acting at the national or even local level, or resorting to delegation, did not always met the challenges. To deal with them successfully, public administration would have to create and make use of other networks (international networks in particular), acquire new skills and bring in new professions and new technologies.

2.2 A model incorporating the interdisciplinary advances and pluralism of the science of public administration

Since its creation in 1981, IDHEAP has operated as a laboratory of ideas for public administration, with a dual objective: first, to contribute to development and change in the public sector, and second, to analyse and explain transformations in public administration. This dual objective is reflected in all the Institute's activities, from research endeavours to teaching activities and expertise provided to public communities. The Institute's founders saw it as a pluri-disciplinary university institution wholly dedicated to public administration and related topics. This gives IDHEAP a profile that remains unique in Switzerland to this day. This singular status has allowed the Institute and its members to support public administration in its evolution and in its various dimensions, both in Switzerland and abroad. Naturally, political and judicial science have had a significant influence. But the balance sought in the pluralist approach was quickly attained by strengthening skills in the areas of management, public finance and sociology. A wide variety of issues have also been addressed. As examples, we can cite social, educational and health policy; environmental, land-use and transport policy; gender and language policy; sports policy; immigration and integration policy; and information-systems, human-resources and fiscal policy. All these elements and experiences are built into the IDHEAP model.

The IDHEAP model is thus the result of a dialogue and covers many disciplines and social issues. The model is therefore fully in keeping with the development of public-administration science, its aims being both to understand and explain phenomena observed throughout the world and to conceptualize and shape public administration. This is consistent with the vision developed by Simon (1976), an American sociologist and economist who advocated public-administration science based on the observation and rigorous scientific analysis of human behaviour. He argued that facts should be kept separate from value judgments. In this way objective scientific knowledge serves to influence decisions and behaviour inside administrative organizations and society as a whole.

The science of public administration only established itself as such in the 20th century. Publication of the article "The Study of Administration" by Wilson (1887), an American academic and later politician, is seen as marking the start of the discipline. At the time, however, it did not yet have a specific theoretical foundation, and was based on contributions from other disciplines: political, legal and economic science. Subsequently it embraced organizational studies and other human and social sciences. It thus exhibits a high degree of inter-disciplinarity, leading naturally to an epistemological and methodological pluralism. It takes both descriptive and prescriptive approaches. It is supported by reasonings that may be empirical or conceptual, hypothetical-deductive or inductive, and qualitative or quantitative.

The development of public-administration science has been marked by important theories and movements, among them the theory of bureaucracy, and the New Public Administration, New Public Management and New Public Service Movements. Weber's theory of bureaucracy (1922) is still widely cited today. A German jurist, economist and sociologist, Weber held that the modern state must be characterized by rational order founded on homogeneous, impersonal application of formal rules and procedures. State power is thus delegated to public administration in order to implement public policies rationally based on the law and a codified organizational model. Weber called this conception of public administration *bureaucracy*—with no pejorative connotations, in fact quite the opposite.

In the wake of the turbulence and revolutions of the 1960s, the *New Public Administration* movement (NPA; Waldo 1968) emerged. The thinkers behind NPA considered that public administration had contributed to maintaining the social status quo, characterized by discrimination, injustice and inequality. They argued for a return to political philosophy in the discipline of public administration, which ought to focus more on promoting social equity and more democratic structures both inside and outside public bodies, rather than concentrating on the pursuit of efficacy and efficiency.

Another widely cited general theory emerged in the late 1980s: *New Public Management* (NPM). This theory was part of the neoliberal movement, which called the welfare state into question. It minimized the differences in nature between public and private management. The theoreticians of NPM, such as Hood (1991) and Osborne & Gaebler (1992), argued that services should depend on objectives predefined with expected results in mind. They also advocated greater attention to the needs of users and citizens, along with more flexible, more dynamic administration, as well as greater transparency and greater decentralization in favour of local communities or more frequent delegation in partnership with the private sector.

In the late 1990s the *New Public Service* movement emerged (NPS, Denhardt & Vinzant Denhardt 2000) in reaction to NPM, which holds that the role of public administration is to steer society based on predetermined strategic objectives. The theoreticians of NPS consider, however, that this role is not compatible with the increasing complexity of the modern world. Public administration must serve society. Public-sector managers must play the role of facilitators, allowing citizens to make their expectations known (and, when expectations are identified, must see that they are met). Public administration's first concern, then, must be to facilitate the emergence of a shared, collective understanding of what the public interest is. This, of course, requires a collaborative, democratic approach to problems in which individuals must be considered primarily as citizens rather than consumers.

These various theories and movements that have succeeded one another over time reflect developments that have taken place in specific fields, particularly the evolution of organizational theories. Until the 1930s, public administration was strongly influenced by a military style of leadership and by the classic management school, imbued with Taylorism and Fordism (hierarchy, delegation, unity of command, specialization and division of labour). Things began to change with the emergence of the school of human relations, which helped to re-centre management concerns on the individuals that made up the organization. From social psychology it borrowed notions such as professional satisfaction and motivation in seeking to understand interactions between persons working in administrative units. The school of behavioural sciences, which made its appearance in the 1960s, is an extension of the school of human relations. It is concerned more specifically with factors underlying individual choices and decisional processes within public administration (Golembiewski 1969) and, more recently, with the interface between public administration and its environment, whether this be political actors or the electorate (e.g. Moore 1995).

The scientific approach to public administration has evolved significantly, adding a descriptive and analytical focus to the essentially theoretical, normative, prescriptive approach of Weber and the theoreticians of NPM. This has led the science of public administration to bring in other methods. Empirical and comparative methods have gradually come into greater use, as they have in public policy analyses. They make it possible to examine solutions used in different organizational and cultural contexts and to evaluate the outcomes.

However, the epistemological approach to public-administration science is no longer confined to positivism. It continues to include an interpretive, constructivist dimension. In parallel, critical and pragmatic approaches have also made their entry into the literature on public administration. The strength of critical approaches lies in their deconstructivist process, which has brought to light the rationale of domination that has pervaded the discipline. Pragmatic approaches favour a solution-oriented perspective. Depending upon the approach, methods used have also evolved. One such method is "design thinking", which brings together analysis and intuition, often in a co-construction process involving end-users (Brown 2009; Lewis *et al.* 2020). A related approach is "citizen science". Research projects that use this approach rely on the contributions of scientific studies undertaken by members of the general public (Silvertown 2009). Collaboration may focus in particular on the gathering of information and data. This process is facilitated by developments in information and communication technologies. These innovative methods are not used solely to explain aspects of society and public problems: they are also aimed at changing the world, at bringing forth new conceptions and original solutions.

2.3 A systemic approach to public administration

As has already been mentioned, public administration is facing increasingly complex, interdependent phenomena and problems: under the effect of climate disturbance, extreme natural events are becoming more intense and more widespread, as are social transformations and inequalities; trade and financial (and cultural) exchanges are intensifying in a transnational perspective; technology is constantly evolving with ever-increasing speed.

These phenomena and problems constantly call on public administration to deal with unstable, uncertain, ambiguous situations. They can no longer rely on immutable ways of functioning. Public administration must adapt and work differently. Sectoral solutions that have no connection with other factors are no longer suitable. With increasing frequency, solutions must be found that include other national and international, public and private actors.

Viewing phenomena and problems in a systemic manner has become a necessity. The systemic approach was initially developed and implemented in the fields of cybernetics, biology and ecology. Subsequently, it influenced social-sciences and organizational-science methods, particularly through the work of Von Bertalanffy (1968). It is based on a number of postulates or principles. These principles are illustrated in Figure 1 and may also be translated from the point of view of public administration.

The first postulate is that any system is made up of a set of *components*. Some of these components are real or material in nature. Examples are collaborators, buildings and furniture, communication infrastructures and tangible services delivered. But an increasing number of components are intangible or immaterial in nature. Examples are legislation and other regulatory procedures, ethics, strategy, organizational structures, information, the culture of innovation or change, team spirit and intangible services.

The second postulate is that the system has a *boundary*, a limit, that separates it from its *environment*. This environment surrounds and envelops the system. It, too, is made up of real or material elements, such as the stakeholders of public administration. It also includes intangible or immaterial elements, such as societal values, expectations of government and the institutions that oversee public administration. The boundary between the system—public administration—and its environment is movable. In particular, it depends on modes of governance and the nature of relationships with external entities1.

The third postulate is that within the system, components are linked, and communicate and interact with one another. These *interactions* may take various forms: physical, informational, financial or social, for example. They alter in response to changes—societal, technological—and to changes in needs and objectives.

1 The boundary between public administration and its environment is sometimes difficult to trace. One way of doing so involves using a judicial or contractual approach. The feeling of identity or belonging is another way of tracing the boundary (the feeling of being a member of a social group, in this case a member of a public organization or administrative unit, being able to designate "others"). Lastly, functional connections and control over these connections by managers and those responsible for the organization of the administrative unit concerned provide another way of locating the boundary between the system and its environment.

The fourth and final postulate is that a system exists to serve a *purpose*. In the case of public administration, the purpose is largely imposed by the environment. It depends on societal values and the expectations of stakeholders (civil society, economic actors, etc.) It is shaped by institutions. This postulate also holds that components of the system each contribute to the common objective.

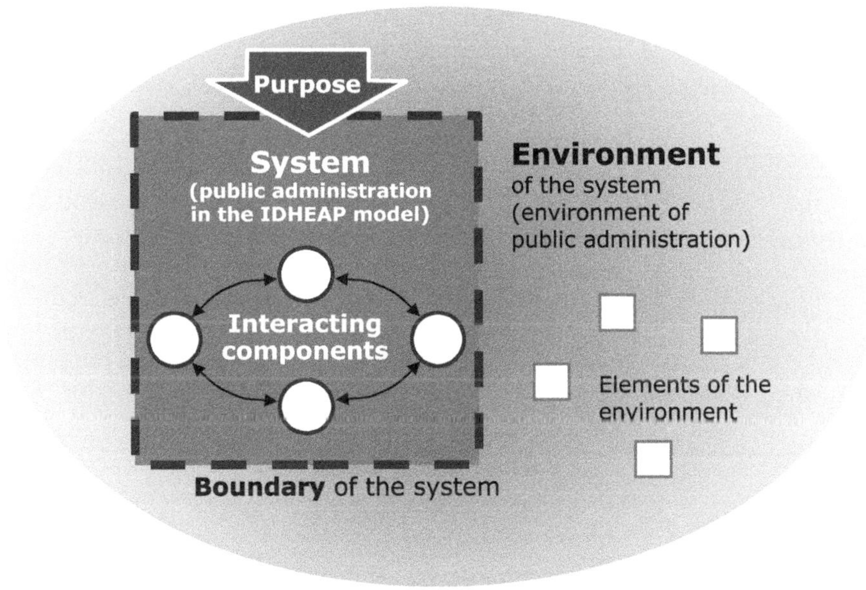

Figure 1 The principles of the systemic approach: purpose, components, interactions, boundary, environment

In view of current issues facing public administration and given that the postulates described above are part of the analysis of public administration, the systemic approach is especially effective for conceiving, organizing and steering public administration. This is why the IDHEAP model uses this approach. This being so, the changing nature of the system's environment and the effects of the environment on the system itself create a dynamic that cannot be fully grasped and demand a degree of humility. The IDHEAP model that will be described in greater detail is dependent on this dynamic. It is therefore important to remember that, as a model, it offers a representation devised at a given moment.

Nonetheless, the IDHEAP model attempts to include this dimension of change as far as possible. Moreover, it does not merely consider the various components necessary for the operation of public administration in isolation: it also seeks to focus on the links and interactions between them. A public organization or administrative unit cannot be operated in a fragmented manner, for example by considering solely the legal, financial or human-resources aspects. The IDHEAP model views operation and management from a global perspective. Public administration must strive to mobilize all components of the system. It must also interact with the elements of its environment. The systemic approach makes it easier to grasp how each component contributes to the purpose of public administration.

2.4 General architecture of the IDHEAP model

2.4.1 Components of the public administration system

Before addressing the environment of public administration, we present here the core of the IDHEAP model, that is, the public administration system and its components. In this system, represented by a cube in Figure 2, the components are divided into three dimensions: *norms and strategy; organization and processes;* and *change management*. This breakdown into three dimensions must not be seen as three successive stages in a macro-process. The three dimensions are interwoven and interdependent: they influence each other.

Figure 2 The public administration system, its three dimensions and its components

The "norms and strategy" dimension covers fundamental, global components that have long-term scope. It determines organization and processes: its components are aimed at running an organization in the short and medium term. But it is also important for managing change, for changing the organization. This aspect is often overlooked. It lies however at the basis of most actions and projects undertaken in public administration, from changing public administration itself, to developing its environment and, at a more fundamental level, to meeting society's expectations concerning government interventions. Change management is thus an essential component of public administration. Moreover, although working methods and processes for running an organization in the short and medium term naturally exist, a frequent error is the failure to adopt an organizational and operational structure capable of coping with change. Change projects are often complex. They cannot be managed successfully in dilettante fashion, without allocating the necessary resources. This is why this dimension is specifically highlighted in the IDHEAP model.

Each of these three dimensions has its own section in this book. The components of public administration mentioned under the various dimensions of the cube in Figure 2 are each the subject of a dedicated contribution. It will be seen that, regardless of the dimension under consideration, the IDHEAP model above all integrates intangible or immaterial components. This demonstrates the model's scope: administering, managing and steering public action certainly requires material components, but the essence of the public-administration system operates thanks to components—resources—that are immaterial.

2.4.2 The environment of the public-administration system

The public-administration system is surrounded—enveloped—an environment that is peculiar to it and with which it interacts. This is shown in Figure 3, representing the public-administration cube encased in its environment.

This is the context in which public administration evolves and operates. It must respond to societal needs that come from the environment. It must deal with other constraints that the environment places on it.

Figure 4 shows the various facets of the public-administration environment—four of them in the IDHEAP model. Details are provided in the contributions that follow this introduction. The *values* of liberty, democracy and responsibility largely determine society's expectations of the state and public administration. The state's *essential functions* are of three orders: promoting proper use of resources, for example environmental resources; guaranteeing equitable distribution of wealth between individuals, regions or generations; and combating major cyclical shocks and fostering sustainable growth. *Stakeholders* play a major role in expressing these values in terms of needs for state intervention through public-administration action. Stakeholders include the following institutional and societal actors: citizens, political parties and their members, businesses, trade unions, nongovernmental organizations and the media, as well as foreign countries and international organizations. *Institutions* are there to structure and guide interactions between the various facets of the environment and interactions between the environment and public administration. The characteristics of institutions vary from country to country. In Switzerland, they are the following: separation of powers, federalism, direct democracy and the militia principle.

A host of interactions play out between the different facets of the environment. These interactions are described in the various contribution to the IDHEAP model.

Figure 3 The public administration system encased in its environment

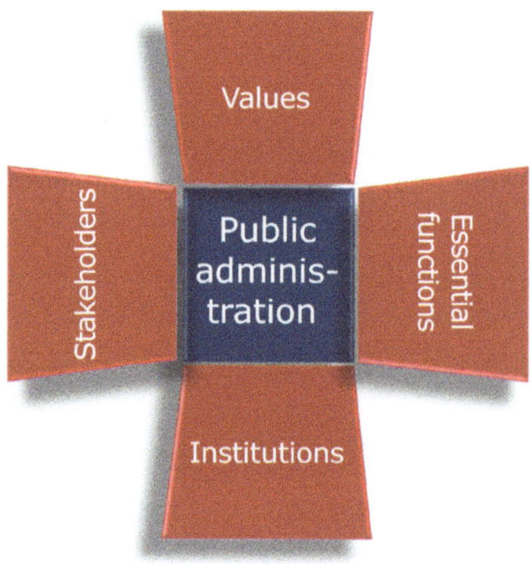

Figure 4 Public administration and the four facets of its environment

3 Future prospects and challenges

The IDHEAP model of public administration provides a representation of the manner in which public administration operates and should operate. Each contribution, whether it deals with the public-administration environment or the public-administration system itself, provides the theoretical and empirical knowledge required to manage, operate and act within the public sector.

The IDHEAP model thus opens perspectives for understanding phenomena and problems in a systemic manner. It offers administrative leaders the keys they need to analyse the situation and take action in their organization. To assist them in facing these challenges, five contributions show how it is possible to use the IDHEAP model or certain of its components to tackle issues in various areas of public policy: job-market reentry by improving governance; managing an educational institution with the issues of leadership, communication and resource mobilization that this involves; the integration of migrants and asylum-seekers by making use of digitalization and artificial intelligence; and the setting up of wind farms through mobilizing the law in the service of energy-project management and territorial governance; strategy and governance in elite sport.

Key concepts

- Administrative unit (*unité administrative, Verwaltungseinheit, unità amministrativa*). Subdivision within a public administration body, generally carrying out a specific task.
- IDHEAP model of public administration (*modèle IDHEAP d'administration publique, IDHEAP Modell der öffentliche Verwaltung, modello IDHEAP di amministrazione pubblica*). Conceived by the Swiss Graduate School of Public Administration at the University of Lausanne (or IDHEAP, the acronym of its French designation "Institut de hautes études en administration publique"), this model shows how to implement public administration using a systemic approach. Components of the system act in accordance with norms and strategies, by virtue of a structure and processes, and of change management. The system interacts with an environment made up of values, stakeholders, institutions and needs for government intervention.
- Model (*modèle, Modell, modello*). A schematic representation of an object having certain particular qualities or characteristics, given as an example to serve as a source of inspiration, or to be copied.
- New Public Administration—NPA (*nouvelle administration publique—NAP, neue öffentliche Verwaltung—NÖF, nuova amministrazione pubblica—NPA*). A movement that emerged in the late 1960s emphasizing the public sector's ethical obligations in order to restore public trust in government and public administration, which had been eroded by corruption and the pursuit of personal interest.
- New Public Management—NPM (*nouvelle gestion publique—NGP, neue Verwaltungsführung—NVF, nuova gestione pubblica—NGP*). A concept of the functioning of public administrations that appeared in the late 1970s, abandoning the classical forms of labour organization in the public sector—including Weberian bureaucracy—in favour of moving closer to private-sector management, with a clearer distinction between the task of steering, assumed by political authorities, and the task of implementation, assumed by public administration.
- New Public Service—NPS (*nouveau service public—NSP, neuer öffentlicher Dienst—NÖD, nuovo servizio pubblico—NSP*). A movement that emerged in the late 1990s in response to NPM, emphasizing the role of facilitator that public

administration ought to play. Rather than seeking to lead society in a set direction, this implies helping the population to formulate their expectations and, once they are collectively identified and stated, meeting these expectations.

- Public administration—institutional definition (*administration publique—définition organique, öffentliche Verwaltung—organische Definition, pubblica amministrazione—definizione organica*). All public powers and their implementing agencies, which are entities set up by political decision that exercise legislative, judicial or executive power over a given territorial space.
- Public administration—functional definition (*administration publique—définition fonctionnelle, öffentliche Verwaltung—funktionale Definition, pubblica amministrazione—definizione funzionale*). All activities that contribute directly or indirectly to providing various public services. Public services may be public policies, government services or—incidentally—market goods and services.
- Systemic approach (*approche systémique, systematische Ansatz, approccio sistemico*). An approach aimed at understanding an object of study—here, public administration—through its functioning mechanisms and its environment, in order to identify what would not come to light if one considered only the parties that make up the object individually.
- Weberian bureaucracy (*bureaucratie wébérienne, Bürokratie bei Weber, burocrazia da Weber*). German jurist, economist and sociologist Max Weber (1864–1920) used the term bureaucracy to designate a form of public administration whose actions are governed by law and whose agents—public servants—are recruited on the basis of their professional competence and are subordinate to their superior in the hierarchy of authority.

References

Brown, T. (2009). *Change by design: how design thinking transforms organizations and inspires innovation.* HarperCollins.

Denhardt, R. B. & Vinzant Denhardt, J. (2000). The new public service: serving rather than steering. *Public Administration Review, 60*(6), 549–559.

Golembiewski, R. T. (1969). Organization development in public agencies: perspectives on theory and practice. *Public Administration Review, 29*, 367–377.

Hood, C. (1991). A public management for all seasons? *Public Administration, 69*(1), 3–19.

Ladner, A., Soguel, N., Emery, Y., Weerts, S. & Nahrath, S. (Eds.) (2019). *Swiss public administration: Making the State work successfully.* Palgrave.

Ladner, A., Chappelet, J.-L., Emery, Y., Knoepfel, P., Mader, L., Soguel, N. & Varone, F. (Eds.) (2013). *Handbuch der öffentlichen Verwaltung in der Schweiz – Manuel d'administration*

publique suisse. NZZ-Verlag and Presses polytechniques et universitaires romandes.
Lewis, J. M., McGann, M. & Blomkamp, E. (2020). When design meets power: Design thinking, public sector innovation and the politics of policymaking. *Policy & Politics*, *48*(1), 111–130. http://dx.doi.org/10.1332/030557319X15579230420081.
Moore, M. H. (1995). *Creating public value: strategic management in government*. Harvard University Press.
Osborne, D. & Gaebler, T. (1992). *Reinventing government: How the entrepreneurial spirit is transforming the public sector*. Addison-Wesley.
Silvertown, J. (2009). A new dawn for citizen science. *Trends in Ecology & Evolution*, *24*(9): 467–471. https://doi.org/10.1016/j.tree.2009.03.017.
Simon, H. A. (1976). *Administrative behavior: A study of decision-making in administrative organization* (3rd ed.). The Free Press.
Stachowiak, H. (1973). *Allgemeine Modelltheorie*. Springer.
Von Bertalanffy, L. (1968). *General system theory: Foundations, development, applications*. George Braziller.
Waldo, D. (1968). Public administration in a time of revolutions. *Public Administration Review*, *28*, 362–368.
Weber, M. (1922). *Wirtschaft und Gesellschaft* (S. Altmann, Ed.). J.C.B. Mohr.
Wilson, W. (1887). The Study of Administration. *Political Science Quarterly*, *2*(2), 197–222.

References for further study

Marini, F. (Ed.) (1971). *Toward a new public administration: The Minnowbrook perspective* (pp. 346–367). Chandler Publishing.
Pollitt, C. & Bouckaert, G. (2004). *Public management reform: A comparative analysis*. Oxford University Press.
Schachter, H. L. (1989). *Frederick Taylor and the public administration community: A reevaluation*. State University of New York Press.

PART I
The environment of public administration

Introduction

Pirmin Bundi

1 Purpose of the "environment" dimension

Public administration can never be dissociated from external conditions, as articulated by English philosopher John Locke (1689). In the state of nature, people live their lives without realizing that they are members of a society. For Locke, the state of nature designated a kind of primordial condition of humanity—a natural and therefore perennial situation. In response to this situation, institutional and legal measures emerge to protect the freedom of individuals living in society. Institutional rules thus shape the environment of public administration. This environment—this context—is itself largely influenced by society.

Consequently, along with other important external factors such as the economy and globalization, it is the environment that dictates the guiding principles of action taken by public administration. Originally, the English term *context* was used to describe the interrelationships between the various notions influencing the debate (Riggs 1980). It is important to note that the meaning of a term or word can only be understood in the environment in which it is used. Words often have multiple meanings, and the intention of a word's user can only be interpreted by taking into account the entire context of what is being evoked. This is also true for public administration. Studies stress the importance of the national context in the creation of various structures of a public administration (Kuhlmann & Wollmann 2013). Switzerland provides an example of the Germanic administrative tradition, characterized by a particularly well-developed and exhaustive public law, governing all areas of administration. This is why it is crucial to have a legal education in such a context. This also explains the legalism that prevails in public administration. However, various significant societal aspects (essential functions, values) and institutional aspects (actors, institutions) set Switzerland apart from Germany and the Netherlands, even though these countries belong to the same tradition.

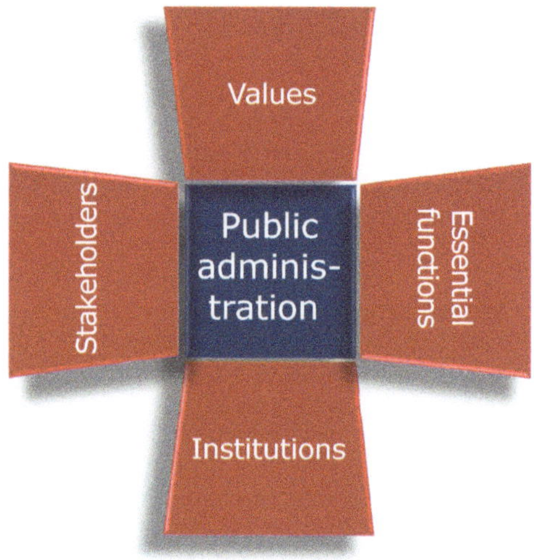

Figure I.1 The "environment" dimension in the IDHEAP model

2 Elements of the "environment" dimension

With the dimension of the environment of public administration, we will address the main ideas that hold society together (values), the main reasons that justify the actions of the state and public administration (essential functions) as well as the actors and persons concerned by public policy (stakeholders) and the structures (institutions) that define the field of action of public administration.

Although Switzerland can certainly not be considered a minimal state (Ladner 2013: 6), it can be seen as a counter-model to the classical Scandinavian welfare state in terms of expenditure. In the article on the grounds for state action (▶ 2 Essential functions), the need for a given state action is analysed from different angles: effective and efficient use and allocation of resources, equitable distribution of income and wealth and the aspiration to macroeconomic stability. The instruments that the state can implement to fulfil its missions are also presented. The principle of subsidiarity is decisive here, as is the idea that numerous tasks can be carried out by other actors (▶ 3 Stakeholders), such as semipublic or para-public, or even private, organizations. For example, in the area of digitalization, federal institutions are using cloud services from private companies to implement innovative government projects more quickly and with greater flexibility (Federal Council 2020). These providers can offer cost-effective, expandable infrastructure and platform services, since they have access to a broad range of new technologies and services that the federal administration cannot provide. To legitimize internal measures, however, it is necessary to define shared values that are regulated by law (▶ 1 Values). A distinction must be drawn between societal values (social cohesion, protection of minorities, etc.) and constitutional ones (democracy, freedom of expression, etc.). These values must first be defined and prioritized so that they can serve as a compass for public administration. In this process, Switzerland's political institutions play a hugely important role (▶ 4 Institutions), particularly those institutions guaranteeing federalism, direct democracy and the concordance system. They define the routines, norms and conventions inherent in the organizational structures of the community and political economy (Hall 1996). Together, all these elements define the context in which public administration evolves, making our country what it is.

References

Bundesrat (2020). *Cloud-Strategie der Bundesverwaltung.* Informatiksteuerungsorgan des Bundes.

Hall, P. A., & Taylor, R. C. (1996). Political science and the three new institutionalisms. *Political Studies, 44*(5), 936–957.

Kuhlmann, S., & Wollmann, H. (2013). *Verwaltung und Verwaltungsreformen in Europa: Einführung in die vergleichende Verwaltungswissenschaft* (Vol. 51). Springer-Verlag.

Locke, J. (1967). *Two treatises of government.* Cambridge University Press.

Ladner, A. (2013). Der Schweizer Staat, politisches System und Aufgabenerbringung. In A. Ladner, J.-L. Chappelet, Y. Emery, P. Knoepfel, L. Mader, N. Soguel & F. Varone (Eds.). *Handbuch der öffentlichen Verwaltung in der Schweiz* (pp. 23–45). Zürich Verlag Neue Zürcher Zeitung.

Riggs, F. W. (1980). The ecology and context of public administration: A comparative perspective. *Public Administration Review, 40*(2), 107–115.

1 Values

Sophie Weerts

1.1 The importance of values

The word "value" comes from the Latin *valere*: "to be of worth", which is in turn derived from the Greek *axios*: "that which is worthy of merit". From a philosophical perspective, the word can be understood as "an absolute conviction that a specific model of behaviour or a certain type of existence is personally or socially preferable to the opposing model of behaviour or type of existence" (Piron 2002). Writers in other disciplinary fields such as law and management have also explored the question of values, which are deemed individual, social, organizational, constitutional or public. What values have in common is that they result from a judgment between several preferences, a choice that may operate individually or may result from a deliberative process.

Values are both the source of individual or organizational action and the expression of such action. On the one hand, they have an axiological function in guiding the behaviour of individuals and organizations. On the other hand, values—which are often not explicitly stated—translate into the behaviour, decisions or discourse of these individuals and organizations. From this perspective, every action taken by public administration is driven by certain values and also reflects one or more of these values.

In a changing world, with the climate crisis, the increase in social injustices and digitalization, there is an urgent need for coordinated responses that are clearly aimed at the common good. Since values play an axiological role, they represent an invaluable resource for defining action in favour of the common good. The definition, clarification and ranking of values is a task that falls to stakeholders, providing a compass for those involved in public administration.

1.2 Key points

In order for values to constitute one of the key underpinnings of public administration, they must first be identified. This is no simple exercise. We will begin by clarifying the notion of values, highlighting its main characteristics, then pinpointing the specifics of this notion which may fluctuate, but should nonetheless be expected to play a structural and structure-building role in public administration (§ 1.2.1). We will then turn to the main values that have shaped public administration, through a brief history of the evolution of the field (§ 1.2.2). Lastly, drawing on the literature on public administration and public law, we will identify the main values of contemporary public administration (§ 1.2.3).

1.2.1 Characteristics

Values in themselves present a series of characteristics that make each a singular object. Since any thinking or discussion about values involves a process of reflection, it is useful to identify these characteristics, which will moreover illustrate the variability and indefinite character of values.

First, values are not elements that pre-exist the order of things. They are constructed by and within society. They are thus the fruit of a social and cultural environment. Changes in values are often the result of negation or confrontation. For example, it is because European society tried out political absolutism in the 17th century that Enlightenment philosophers developed a crucial reflection on the value of liberty in the 18th century. It was also because, when the second European industrial revolution in the late 19th century gave rise to a new social category—blue-collar workers—and social injustices became flagrant, people began to discuss and demand greater equality in a society where the emphasis had been on the value of freedom. Since the 2010s, the accelerating progress of artificial intelligence—a major technological and societal transformation—has highlighted the need to define a new base of shared values in the face of this technological development, with principles such as the prevention of harm to others, and explainability.

Second, values are often expressed implicitly. They are contained in a series of formal or informal elements such as law, the organizational structure of institutions, the social norms that apply in a given society, or reproduced in various individual behaviours. For example, since the Enlightenment, freedom has been considered as a basic value in modern democratic states. Whether looking at the 1789 Declaration of the Rights of Man and of the Citizen or the Federal Constitution of 1848, the value of liberty is enshrined through various provisions on specific points, without ever being elevated to the rank of a superior standard taking precedence over other values. In other words, we can say that political and social functioning is the hallmark of a particular value rather than an explicit consecration in a given place. On this point, legislation, and the weighing of interests and other arbitrations that come into play in the implementation of legislation or public policies, clearly reveal our collective priorities and thus our collective values.

Third, values are not untouchable in their content. They are sensitive to societal and environmental changes. Reforms in marriage and filiation law that have been introduced in various European countries illustrate this point. Previously, the global vision as far as representation of a family was concerned had been broadly dominated by heterosexual married couples. Law had translated this representation into a specific judicial regime concerning marriage and filiation. Fiscal and social policies were also developed by states on the basis of this initial conception. Changes in mores and social practices showed however that other conceptions of the couple and filiation were possible. This raised the question of whether or not these new representations should be considered. Taking new social practices into account required revisiting our initial representation of equality, and realizing that it was rooted in the representation of the man-woman couple. The law and public policies thus became the target of this revisited idea, which spread throughout society and, in turn, fuels other measures. The revisited conception then either gradually imposes itself or coexists with the initial representation of the value in question.

Fourth, values vary in terms of their scope and purpose. Some have a fundamental dimension. They are a matter of moral imperative and are addressed to all: individuals, institutions, public and private organizations. Among these are liberty and equality, but also democracy. Other values have an instrumental or procedural dimension, such as transparency and accountability. Yet others have an individual dimension from an organizational point of view, such as loyalty and honesty. Moreover, values may be linked to one another from the point of view of substitution or complementarity. Some may also encompass a number of sub-values. This means it is sometimes difficult to separate the value of democracy from that of equality, respect for the majority or respect for minorities.

Values are, then, multiple, fluctuating and sometimes entangled ideas, but at some point they become the object of social and political consensus (▶ 3 Stakeholders). They take root in an organization, in discourse or in documents, and can serve to guide individual and collective action.

1.2.2 A brief history of values

A short history of the field of public administration in Western countries beginning in the early 20th century highlights the evolution and the diversity of values in this specific field.

In the United States, Woodrow Wilson propounded an organizational model aimed at reducing the influence of politics and combating corruption within government departments. In Europe, Weber described an ideal type of public administration based on law and respect for hierarchy. In both cases, public officials were to become rational, neutral experts. These two visions of public administration depict a model of depoliticized organization with guiding values of neutrality, efficiency and expertise in the execution of tasks. Separation between elected officials and the administration is also seen as a guarantee that values of equal treatment for citizens will be respected.

But the Great Depression and the horrors of World War II called these initial models and their underlying values into question. In the United States of the 1940s, in a difficult economic climate, two key academic debates (Hijal-Moghrabi & Sabharwal 2018) highlighted the importance of values for public administration. Finer and Friedrich took opposing views of the question of the moral responsibility of public administration. Dwight Waldo and Herbert Simon argued about efficiency on the grounds that the latter saw it as a "value-neutral" concept. In Europe, the horrors of war were followed by a moral crisis. In her analysis of the trial of Eichmann in Jerusalem, philosopher Hannah Arendt condemned a shamelessly efficient bureaucracy in which the very idea of individual responsibility had been totally erased. As these few elements show, the role and functioning of public administration were earnestly debated on both sides of the Atlantic. But different paths were taken in response to the debate. In Europe, the prohibition of arbitrariness was strengthened, with a stronger system of judicial control, and the assertion of the values of human dignity, freedom and equality. Public administration emerged as more tightly controlled, with a stronger value of the rule of law, but the underlying values connected with the organization and operation of administration—also touching on the issue of democracy—were not raised. In the United States, only in the 1960s did a new chapter in the history of public administration begin. This was a time of strong political and social demands, with the civil rights movement and the war in Vietnam. The literature records the emergence at this time of the *New Public Administration* movement, which emphasized social equality and the margin of discretion that an administration must have at its disposal in order to avoid creating injustices. New values were put forward, including citizen participation, thus emphasizing the importance of democracy (Bryer & Cooper 2012).

The 1980s opened the door to significant changes, with the bureaucratic model being called into question. In Europe, the effects of the movement became particularly noticeable in the 1990s, with large-scale administrative reforms with New Public Management. Technical and practical values from the private sector were put forward as a new way of conceiving of the organization and functioning of public administration. This paradigm shift called for putting citizens at the core of public service, and increasing the efficiency and accountability of departments and those that work in them. The value of transparency was also stressed as a means of strengthening trust in government. This involved promoting a new mindset characterized by values such as innovation, accountability and customer orientation. But grafting the private model onto the public was not without obstacles. One of the difficulties often singled out is the fact that the New Public Management's ideological foundations are far removed from those of bureaucratic administration, characterized by the values of democracy and the rule of law (Fortier & Emery 2015). Also noted is the fact that introducing an approach based on performance measurement and management by budget implies strengthening organizational autonomy, which puts managers at risk by placing them at odds with constitutional values (Riccucci 2001).

The 2000s then ushered in a new development. Public administration no longer had the sole task of enforcing the law: it was also charged with devising and implementing public policies that had been approved by political institutions. No longer seen only in terms of the distinction between centralized organization and decentralization, it was expected to take a holistic approach. Public tasks were thus entrusted to a network of arrangements involving actors from the public, private and nonprofit sectors. Public administration of this type takes on a functional dimension and is presented as now being more strongly focused on finding solutions to public problems. In this dynamic, private organizations can also play a part in public tasks (► 8 Governance). New terms emerged in the literature to describe this new conception of public administration, such as "new public service", *publicitude normative*, "public value management", "new public government" and "new civic politics". These various proposals all share a number of aspects: an emphasis on public values, a role as guarantor of public values endorsed by the head of state, an acknowledgment of the importance of public management and service for the public, and lastly the importance of civic engagement, of taking citizens into account and of a collaborative mode of decision-making that involves them (Bryson *et al.* 2014). The proposed terms also highlight the importance of social and political consensus, which must be taken into account in orienting public management and organization.

This brief history shows that, in the field of public administration, none of the values that guide public administration has supplanted any of the others. Rather, what emerges is a broadening of the field of values, sometimes involving a readjustment of some in relation to others.

1.2.3 Identification

In an organizational context, identifying values implies reaching a consensus, which may result from a formal or informal process of deliberation. In the field of public administration, however, values are not merely the result of arbitration between individual preferences conducted in any particular organization: they are directly shaped by the political and legal environment. The literature on public administration regarding public values and public law identifies some of these key values.

Public values

Based on an analysis of the literature on public administration, Jørgensen and Bozeman (2007) identified 74 public values that they divided into seven categories. They also found that these values do not all operate at the same level and are not involved in the same relationships.

Some values play a role in the interaction between society and public administration. They enable public administration either to contribute to the public good (for example, the values of social cohesion, human dignity and sustainability), or to fulfil social expectations (by respecting the principles of majority rule, the public will or the protection of minorities). Other categories of values are concerned with the relationship between those who act on behalf of public administration and public authorities (e.g. the principle of loyalty) or within the general societal environment (the principle of transparency, or of neutrality). A third category is made up of values pertaining to organizational functioning. These are values relating to internal operation, reflecting a mechanistic conception of public administration (for example, adaptability, or punctuality). They also include values that serve to guide the conduct of those working in the field of public administration (altruism, impartiality). A final category of values is made up of imperatives that are at the core of the relationship between public administration and citizens (the principle of legality, respect for individual rights, equity, the principle of dialogue, courtesy).

For the two authors, some values were termed "prime values" and others "instrumental values". The fact remains that the values identified echoed the principles of public law. Some relate to the constitutional field (democracy, human dignity), while others fall into the category of administrative law (transparency, loyalty, impartiality). The former are classed as prime values while the latter are instrumental or procedural values. Prime values are fundamental. In liberal democracies, they correspond to what may be called constitutional values.

Constitutional values

Constitutional values are those that arise from the constitutional judicial system, in which the Constitution is naturally crucial (▶ 5 Law). They may be explicitly asserted or simply derived from the text of the Constitution or other actions and discourse by official institutions. Constitutional values have an interpretive scope, that is, they indicate the purpose to which the state in general, and public administration in particular, adhere. Given their constitutional dimension, they represent a formalized expression of values that are born out of collective deliberation on various individual preferences within political institutions. The fact that the Constitution is a legislative act that results from what is, democratically speaking, the most rigorous enactment procedure gives the values enshrined therein greater legitimacy than those that may be expressed in other legal texts, or in simple political declarations.

In Switzerland, the preamble and article 2 of the Federal Constitution identify the main values towards which political and administrative functioning must strive. Accordingly, the Swiss Confederation must undertake to promote freedom, democracy and security, sustainable development, the country's prosperity, cultural diversity, equal opportunities and sustainable conservation of natural resources, and participate in a just, peaceful international order. All these ideas reflect the values found in the doctrine of constitutionalism. Here, the values of democracy and individual liberty constitute the two great pillars out of which emerge other related values such as the rule of law, the prohibition of arbitrariness, human dignity, individual freedoms, equality of treatment, the separation of powers, transparency and respect for minorities. These aims are also broadly shared and asserted in the legal texts and political discourse of the United Nations, the Council of Europe and the European Union. Across the European continent, they are thus the subject of a broad consensus among states and international organizations, which assert their commitment to these values, testifying to their dissemination and legitimacy. These shared values of constitutionalism are born out of Western, and particularly European, history. They have been erected as a rampart against the abuse of power and against arbitrariness. They therefore act as a safeguard for those who act in the name of public interest. As a result, these values do not merely impose a duty of abstention or limitation on institutions and other organizations tasked with implementing decisions that affect individuals: they also demand an obligation to act in order to guarantee the operation of these values when translated into standards and principles. There is no point in guaranteeing freedom of education if the state fails to build schools. There is no point in guaranteeing freedom of expression if it cannot be freely exercised because of censorship measures.

The historical and spatial framework in which the doctrine of constitutionalism was forged shows that these constitutional values form a particularly strong base. Yet they are not untouchable. Often, the manner in which they evolve is incremental, even insidious, through discourse, political behaviour and legislation. The various actions taken by Polish authorities since 2015 to limit the power of the country's judiciary provide an illustration of this idea of political transformation and, incidentally, provoked a strong political and budgetary reaction from the European Union in favour of respect for its values. In Switzerland, too, values can be placed under stress. An example is the Federal Act on Police Measures to Combat Terrorism, enacted in 2021, considered by many experts as particularly problematic from the point of view of respect for the rule of law.

Constitutional values, like values in general, have a relatively abstract, or even fuzzy, aspect that makes observing them a delicate matter. For example, it is abundantly clear that international and constitutional recognition of human rights is insufficient to prevent violations of these rights. The diversity of values can also generate tensions between values. The values of liberty, equality and dignity occasionally conflict with the value of democracy, as shown by certain popular initiatives in Switzerland, such as the banning of the construction of minarets (2009), or the banning of full-face coverings (2021). Similar conflicts can arise when one administrative unit favours the protection of biodiversity while another supports economic freedom. When it comes to granting a licence to sell arms abroad, a number of administrative bodies are called on to rule on the advisability of the decision. One may consider that upholding Switzerland's economic interests justifies the sale, while another may determine that the sale is dangerous from the point of view of respecting human rights. A problem with values may also ensue from the choice of an organizational method. Private management of asylum seekers since the 2010s has shown that in Switzerland, as in other countries with no control mechanism, the principal of profitability has taken precedence, to the detriment of respect for human dignity.

Lastly, these constitutional values, erected as principles and enshrined in legal standards, are imposed on political institutions and administrative bodies and units. They are also binding on private organizations tasked with implementing political decisions or providing public services. In this context, they can be considered as providing a compass for those that execute public tasks.

1.3 Future prospects and challenges

Conflict between values is an issue of prime importance for public administration. Two examples serve to illustrate what is at stake. Climate warming is the foremost public problem, given the risks that it poses for individuals. Because of humanity's role in the development of this problem, individual behaviours and organizational methods must be changed. This means it is necessary to make decisions that entail a new balance between values. From this perspective, the value of sustainability, which implies the conservation of natural resources and protection of future generations, must gain in importance. Sustainability inevitably requires rethinking the scope of individual freedom. The digitalization of our societies is another major workstream. It is seen as a way of improving efficiency. But it is also liable to generate substantial negative effects by creating inequality between citizens as regards their ability to use new technologies, or by directing individual behaviours against individual will. In both cases, these major issues facing society disrupt the established order, or at least our conception of the values of freedom and efficiency. They require us to rethink the way in which we perceive the world. From this perspective, public administration must continue to act for the common good while integrating and supporting these changes (▶ Part IV. Change management). This can be achieved in a variety of ways, for example by fostering public debate, by helping with the formulation of a new discourse, by making the required change in its own organization or by assisting society with this change. To clarify arbitration between values, stakeholders in the field of public administration can make use of the principle of proportionality (in the strict sense), which requires that a check be performed to determine whether proposed measures are necessary, appropriate and reasonable (▶ 5 Law).

The second issue facing public administration is guaranteeing the respect of values. In this regard, it has to be said that the functional approach to public administration complicates the situation. Organizations are not always subject to the same legal rules. In this situation, it is important that they share a common conviction about the idea of the common good, which must be able to be set out in a series of key values. For administrative entities and public or private organizations performing a public task, a number of these values are already enshrined in law and must therefore be applied. For other organizations—further removed from the state on the organizational level—these values constitute moral principles to which the organization concerned will decide to subscribe and which it will reflect in its internal and external communications. From this point of view, private organizations must take care to determine their values by means of a collaborative, democratic process enabling them to justify their adoption of these values. In making their choices, such private organizations must however cleave to the values to which other actors public administration are constrained. They must also remain consistent with their undertakings. Should they fail to exhibit discipline in this regard, they will be criticized for inconsistency, inflicting significant damage to their own image and reveal themselves as fragile—as a paper tiger.

Key concepts

- Constitutionalism (*constitutionnalisme, Konstitutionalismus, costituzionalismo*): a philosophical doctrine that advocates democracy and the fulfilment of human rights.
- Constitutional values (*valeurs constitutionnelles, Verfassungswerte, valori costituzionali*): a set of ideas of fundamental importance, as affirmed in the formal sources of constitutional law.
- Individual values (*valeurs individuelles, Einzelwerte, valori individuali*): individual preferences between a number of possibilities.
- Public values (*valeurs publiques, öffentliche Werte, valori di pubblico interesse*): ideas on which there is a normative societal consensus.

References

Bryer, T. A. & Cooper, T. L. (2012). H. George Frederickson and the dialogue on citizenship in public administration. *Public Administration Review, 72*(1), 108–116. https://doi.org/10.1111/j.1540-6210.2012.02632.x (accessed 16.11.2022).

Bryson, J. M., Crosby, B. C. & Bloomberg, L. (2014). Public value governance: Moving beyond traditional public administration and the new public management. *Public Administration Review, 74*(4), 445–456. https://www.jstor.org/stable/24029426 (accessed 16.11.2022).

Fortier, I. & Emery, Y. (2015). L'éthos public en tant que processus social dynamique. *Pyramides*, 83–114.

Hijal-Moghrabi, I. & Sabharwal, M. (2018). Ethics in American public administration: A response to a changing reality. *Public Integrity, 20*, 1–19. https://doi.org/10.1080/10999922.2017.1419053 (accessed 16.11.2022).

Jørgensen, T. B. & Bozeman, B. (2007). Public values: An inventory. *Administration & Society, 39*(3), 354–381. https://doi.org/10.1177/0095399707300703 (accessed 16.11.2022).

Piron, F. (2002). Les défis éthiques de la modernisation de l'administration publique. Éthique publique, *4*(1). https://doi.org/10.4000/ethiquepublique.2479 (accessed 16.11.2022).

Riccucci, N. M. (2001). The "old" public management versus the "new" public management: Where does public administration fit in? *Public Administration Review, 61*(2), 172–175. http://www.jstor.org/stable/977450 (accessed 16.11.2022).

2 Essential functions

Laure Athias and Nils Soguel

2.1 The importance of knowing the reasons that make state intervention necessary

More government! Less government! Two cries often bandied about by people with opposing viewpoints. These hackneyed slogans are of course based on ideological biases. But they are of no use in determining whether or not the state is in phase with contemporary society. It would be worthwhile to reflect on the state's role and missions. The state cannot exist for itself. It was created to respond to the needs of society and resolve collective problems. This is its *raison d'être*, that which legitimizes it in the eyes of citizens. From this point of view, this contribution is completely in keeping with the IDHEAP model of public administration, and more particularly with the part devoted to the context and environment in which public administration is exercised. Having a clear view of the state's essential functions can tell us whether state intervention is *a priori* necessary or whether a matter can be entrusted to private actors alone.

Article 5 of the Federal Constitution asserts that the principle of subsidiarity must be observed in the allocation and performance of state tasks and that "all activities of the state are based on and limited by law." Be that as it may, the competencies constitutionally allocated to the state have widened over time. They are listed and defined in 72 of the 196 articles of the 2020 Constitution (art. 54 to 125).

This widening of competencies can be seen through the general government spending ratio indicator, which expresses state expenditure as a proportion of the country's gross domestic product (GDP). The evolution in this indicator for Switzerland during the second half of the 20th century is shown in Figure 2.1 and is compared with that of the average of member countries of the Organisation for Economic Co-operation and Development (OECD), for which we have data going back to the beginning of the 20th century. State expenditure has constantly increased as a proportion of GDP, rising from 11% in 1900 to 28% during World War II, falling

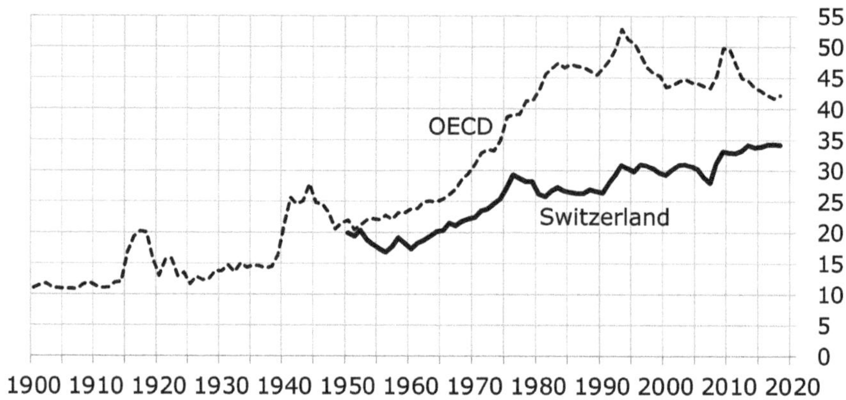

Figure 2.1 Evolution of the general government spending ratio
Source: Federal administration and the International Monetary Fund

back to 17% in Switzerland in the mid-1950s and reaching 34% at present, as against an average in OECD countries of 42%. This increase illustrates the changing role of the state. Within a century, we have moved from a night-watchman state to a welfare state, even to an enabling state. A hundred years ago, the state exercised sovereign functions: justice, police, national defence. Today, it has become—among other things—an entrepreneur tasked with making infrastructures and services available, and also a manager of income and wealth redistribution, in other words, an agent of economic and social transformation. Although the degree of state interventionism varies with the period and the complexity of the problems to be solved in an increasingly globalized world, it also varies with places and development levels. Compared in terms of the general government spending ratio, English-speaking countries tend to be more liberal (for example in 2019: United States, 38%; United Kingdom 41%) than the average of European countries (47%)[2].

That being said, the government spending ratio shows just how much state intervention is deemed necessary to improve collective wellbeing. The underlying theme, regardless of any ideological reference to "less government" or "more government", is the difficulty that the market faces in spontaneously reconciling personal interest with the common interest.

There are circumstances in which free, voluntary transactions between households and businesses—designated in abstract fashion by the notion of market—pose a problem from the collective point of view. Musgrave (1959), an American economist of German heritage, proposed a typology of reasons for which state action may prove necessary[3].

2 https://ec.europa.eu/eurostat/fr/web/government-finance-statistics (accessed 16.11.2022).

3 These reasons are founded on the goal of ensuring the population's maximum wellbeing. This economic and normative approach must not be confused with reflections in political sciences on the legitimization of the action of public administrations through the political process (Scharpf 1999).

This typology has three categories:

- Cases in which state intervention is necessary for reasons of *efficiency* in the use and allocation of resources[4]. This is because exchanges between households and businesses may affect third parties who have not given their consent, or may be carried out without full knowledge of the implications, or may be dominated and manipulated by one of the parties to the exchange.
- Cases in which intervention is necessary for reasons of equity in the *redistribution* of income and monetary and non-monetary wealth between individuals or between regions. In their transactions, households and businesses generally do not concern themselves spontaneously with questions of equity.
- Cases in which intervention is necessary for reasons of *macroeconomic stabilization*, particularly of the business cycle and growth.

This typology is widely used outside economics circles to analyse the reasons justifying state action. This contribution explores these various reasons. It also proposes instruments for intervention by the state, and by its public authorities, that is appropriate to these various cases, concluding with the major challenges for which states should prepare themselves.

2.2 Key reasons for state intervention

2.2.1 Intervention to guarantee efficiency in resource allocation

Providing an incentive to take externalities into account

The behaviour of households or businesses frequently affects third parties who have not been consulted. Cases of pollution are the best example. Pollution victims' well-being is affected without consideration by the consumers or producers at the cause of the phenomenon (i.e. they do not spontaneously take this into consideration and offer compensation). This is a typical case of a negative externality. The price paid by consumers, or the production cost borne by firms, does not reflect this external effect. In the absence of state intervention, this situation is inefficient: behaviours that generate negative externalities should be discouraged.

4 With regard to resource allocation, the question is not solely to determine what productive resources (work and capital) must be called upon to produce goods and services. This first component of the problem—how to produce—is merely a matter of efficiency. It is also a question of determining what goods and what services must be produced using the available productive resources, for the purpose of best satisfying the population's needs. This second aspect of the problem—what to produce—is added to the first in the wider search for efficiency. As for issues of equity, these are concerned with redistribution of income and of monetary and non-monetary wealth by the state. A specific category in Musgrave's typology is devoted to this problem.

In contrast, the behaviour of households or businesses can indirectly improve the welfare of third parties who have not been consulted. Anyone who gets vaccinated contributes to reducing the spread of the disease concerned and to protecting the rest of the population. This is an example of a positive externality. Individual vaccine behaviour tends to ignore this collective effect. The state should therefore act to encourage behaviours that lead to positive externalities, and preventing vaccination levels from falling below a certain threshold is efficient.

Various public intervention tools can give households and firms an incentive to take the external costs and benefits of their behaviour into account. Examples are taxes or subsidies aimed at internalizing external effects. Harmful behaviour can also be limited or prohibited by legislative measures (environmental norms, standards, quotas). Conversely, measures can force the adoption of behaviours that generate positive externalities (for example, compulsory vaccination).

Providing public goods

The market is also at fault when it allows "freeriding". A freerider is an individual (or business) who enjoys a benefit without paying the price. This type of behaviour is possible in the case of so-called public goods. Public goods have two characteristics (Stiglitz 2000: 80). On the one hand, the benefit that a person derives is not to the detriment of other users: this is an example of *non-rivalry in consumption*. On the other hand, it is not possible—technically and at reasonable cost—to prevent someone from benefiting from the good, even if that person refuses to pay the price: *exclusion is impossible*.

Broadcast radio, public security, a firework display, street lighting, national defence and a healthy environment are all examples of public goods, whether or not they are supplied by a public authority. The area served by a public good varies in size: it can be global (planet-wide), such as the fight against climate change; continental, as with missile shields; national, as with national defence; local, as with street lighting and street cleaning. A good can also lose the characteristics of a public good as a result of technological change. Until 2019, anyone with a television set could access programmes of the Swiss Broadcasting Corporation (SRG SSR) through digital terrestrial television (DTT), with no technical possibility of exclusion. Since 2019, DTT has been abandoned in favour of cable, satellite and internet broadcasting, which make it technically possible to exclude those who refuse to pay for programming.

Thus, by virtue of its characteristic of non-rivalry, a public good is provided solely in a single form, a single quality, a single quantity, from which all can benefit. But the price that people are prepared to pay to obtain this public good varies between individuals. To take national defence as an example, all the residents of a country are provided with the same service, but those who fear insecurity place a higher value upon it than those who feel less threatened. However, although the good in question is of value in the eyes of most, the property of non-exclusion means that people prefer that others pay for it. There is therefore a divergence between personal interest, which urges people to adopt "freerider" behaviour, and the common interest, which would have everyone contribute to the funding of the public good.

Consequently, without state intervention, public goods would in principle not be supplied and the situation would be inefficient. The solution is to use the state's coercive power to fund public goods through taxes, so that everyone contributes and is deprived of the opportunity to act as a freerider. Once funding is guaranteed, what remains to be determined is whether the government should supply the public good itself or whether it should hand over responsibility to a third party. This is the subject of the contribution devoted to governance (▶ 8 Governance).

Reducing information asymmetry

Another type of strategic behaviour leads to market inefficiency: taking advantage of information that has not been shared. Examples of unequal distribution of information are numerous, particularly in consumer-provider relations: the executive of a company (public or private) knows more than anybody else about the true structure of production costs and whether the prices imposed on customers are justified by the imperative of covering costs; motorists know better than their insurer whether they take risks when driving; those who contribute to public health insurance or a private plan know better than the insuring organization whether they need dental care, vision care, etc. A striking example of strategic behaviour due to information asymmetry is provided by the prominent car manufacturer who rigged its vehicles' engines to falsify the results of pollution tests.

Those who hold an information advantage are therefore tempted to cheat in order to increase their profit or other gain without the risk of sanction. But when the cheating comes to light, a major crisis of confidence may arise. Moreover, since goods of varying quality may hide behind a single price, consumers may base their willingness to pay on average expected quality. This willingness to pay may not suffice to cover the production costs of vendors of quality goods, potentially leading them to withdraw from the market[5].

Information asymmetry therefore leads to inefficient situations. However, intervention by public authorities is not always necessary in order to remedy matters. Private solutions to the problem of information asymmetry exist, such as certification, quality labels and the sharing of experiences[6]. All these seek to create confidence in the product sold. In the field of insurance, market segmentation solutions enable the insured to choose the policy (high deductible and low premium or low

5 Akerlof (1970) shows the conditions in which a laissez-faire market (one without external regulation) can be not only highly inefficient but could sometimes even disappear completely, should buyers no longer wish to make transactions.

6 Online platforms such as Tripadvisor, Airbnb and Uber typically offer the possibility of reducing information asymmetry by relying on the experience of other customers.

deductible and high premium) that suits them personally and, in doing so, reveal their level of risk.

Public authorities may also intervene by setting standards and ensuring that these standards are observed (for example, the quality of life in medico-social institutions in Switzerland is governed by cantonal-level standards), by subsidizing organizations that uphold consumers' rights, or by accrediting certain professions in order to underwrite the quality of training provided.

Regulating natural monopolies

Another source of inefficiency is present in situations in which a company has the power to dictate the nature of transactions. An extreme case is that of a monopoly that makes competition imperfect. A monopolistic company can misuse its market power to gain profits by imposing higher prices or inferior quality on consumers.

Most often in this situation, the challenge will be to ensure that a reasonable number of companies remain active on the market concerned, or to limit the monopolistic company's power to influence the market, whether in terms of price or quality. In Switzerland, the task of overseeing the proper operation of markets is assigned to the Competition Commission (COMCO).

The situation is quite different when the service to be produced gives rise to substantial economies of scale. In this case, unit production cost decreases as production increases. Consequently, a single company can produce at lower cost than several companies could. This phenomenon arises particularly when fixed costs are high (e.g. transport, water or electricity infrastructures). It then becomes more efficient—more natural—to have a single company active on the market. A natural monopoly, guaranteed and regulated by the state, must therefore be set up (see Athias and Wicht [2019] for a problematic case of the creation of a natural monopoly in the field of district heating).

This makes it important to distinguish between institutions like COMCO (who enable the proper operation of markets) from institutions set up due to defective markets stemming from a natural monopoly. In the second case, public authorities must play an essential regulating role. They must supervise the monopolistic company and oblige it to provide a price/quantity combination that is optimal for society. However, because of information asymmetry, such regulation is a complex task. In Switzerland, the task is entrusted to independent commissions. For example, the Federal Electricity Commission (ElCom) is the independent federal regulatory authority for electricity. It monitors compliance with the Federal Electricity Supply Act and the Energy Act, taking whatever measures and decisions are necessary for the purpose. It controls electricity prices, rules on disputes concerning access to the electricity network and adjudicates in cases of differences of opinion regarding cost-price remuneration for electricity from renewable energies fed into the network. It verifies the country's electricity-supply security.

2.2.2 Intervention to redistribute income and wealth

Equity in income and wealth distribution of and the need for state intervention in the matter are hotly debated issues. One thing is certain, however: in the absence of state action, the distribution of income and monetary and non-monetary wealth depends first of all on individuals' natural endowments (their physical and intellectual capabilities or the patrimony that they have amassed or inherited). Then, distribution depends on the dynamics of accumulation that vary with opportunities provided by the market (labour market or capital market, for example).

French economist Piketty (2014) described this phenomenon using historical data. He criticized the growing inequalities it creates and the threat that these inequalities pose for the stability of contemporary democratic societies. The figures show that, in Switzerland, inequalities regarding the distribution of income and wealth have not grown over the past two decades. Moreover, Switzerland currently sits at the European average for inequality in the distribution of available income[7].

Labour-market conditions in Switzerland (participation and wage-distribution rates) and the policy on training have made it possible to prevent a rise in inequalities. However, state interventions have been the primary factor in curbing the growth of inequalities. These interventions have been numerous. Among the elements that contribute to disposable income are family allowances, OASI/DI benefits, old-age allowances, employment-insurance benefits, social assistance and tax credits. Among deductions from disposable income are compulsory social-insurance contributions, income taxes (including the strongly progressive federal income tax) and health insurance premiums. Then there are financial-equalization transfers. These provide funds to jurisdictions whose resources are limited by low tax potential. Lastly, public authorities create redistribution through various public goods provided free of charge or at a modest price: education and retraining, subsidized housing and health services, public libraries and sports facilities, public transport, etc. Since these services are largely funded by income tax and most used by modest-income households, they have a progressive effect in terms of redistribution.

Human and financial efforts deployed by the state testify to a collective desire for redistribution. Only the state can introduce a social contract aimed at providing protection against global hazards that are difficult to predict: inequality of opportunity, impoverishment, mass unemployment resulting from a recession, etc.

That being said, tolerance of inequalities and means of redistributing income and wealth vary with regions and epochs. They depend on the prevailing philosophy regarding social justice, risk aversion and value judgments.

In theory, a conflict of aims arises between equality and efficiency. For example, although the prospect of wealth provides an incentive for effort, progressive income

7 See the page on "Income distribution" on the Federal Statistical Office website: https://www.bfs.admin.ch/bfs/en/home/ (accessed 17.01.2023).

tax favouring redistribution may prove inefficient, since it may discourage effort. This is the point of view advanced in particular by Friedman (1962). This American economist, a Nobel Prize winner, also emphasized the virtues of private property and economic liberalism. He did however acknowledge that society requires a minimum level of social justice in order to function. Extreme inequality discourages those of moderate means from making efforts, because it wipes out the prospects of financial and social advancement.

Be that as it may, the redistribution mechanisms in place can always be improved and work more effectively. In addition, dilemmas persist, such as the choice between universal access to social benefits and access subject to means. Lastly, a multiplicity of redistribution measures can potentially generate inconsistencies and dysfunction, leading ultimately to poor targeting and dispersal of resources.

2.2.3 Intervention to stabilize the economy

The general government spending ratio alluded to in the introduction is an indicator of the effect of public expenditure on macroeconomic issues, in particular the goals of high employment levels, strong growth, price stability or balance of (external) trade. Attaining these goals is not straightforward. Perhaps it might be, were the axioms of classical economic theory to prove true in practice, particularly with the presence of rational, perfectly informed, mobile and flexible economic agents. The reality, however, is different. Individuals are prone to errors of judgment; they are driven by reptilian-brain reflexes and herd instincts. Their capacity to adapt is limited. The same goes for companies. Imbalances, occasionally substantial, occur between supply and demand, leading to prolonged periods of unemployment and inflation. Due to their sheer numbers, the millions of consumers, producers and investors are unable to coordinate their efforts spontaneously to correct the situation. The state has a role to play in stabilizing markets, both when expenditure levels are insufficient to guarantee full employment and when they are excessive, causing inflationist tensions. A variety of instruments allow the state to take on this role, chief among them budgetary and tax policy, in the hands of public authorities, and monetary policy, in the hands of the central bank (the Swiss National Bank).

The ideas of Keynes (1936) have left their mark on the fiscal policy of public authorities. They have also found their way into the Federal Constitution, which stipulates that "[t]he Confederation, the Cantons and the communes [municipalities] shall take account of the economic situation in their revenue and expenditure policies" (art. 100, para. 4). Whereas Keynes advocated supporting global demand, by means of consumption or investment by public authorities, the Constitution does not prescribe any particular mode of intervention. This omission reflects both the political and the legal difficulties of increasing or curbing expenditure (or, in the reverse order, the tax burden) in a discretionary manner quickly enough to successfully follow Keynesian precepts. The Swiss federal structure further increases these difficulties of vertical and horizontal coordination. Automatic budget stabilizers already present in current legislation offer a spontaneous countercyclical fiscal response: expenditure, particularly social and health expenditure, increases in a recession and diminishes in an upturn; income moves in the opposite direction as the tax base contracts and expands.

In normal times, that is, except in major crises, some believe that the monetary policy, combined with the effects of automatic stabilizers, is better able to fulfil the state's mission of economic stabilization than discretionary fiscal policy.

Considering the Swiss context, however, stabilization capacities must be seen as relative. Globalization accentuates the characteristics of Switzerland's small, open economy. Consequently, macroeconomic balances are increasingly dependent on the spillover effects of other countries' fiscal and monetary policies. Expansionary fiscal measures taken abroad stimulate overall demand in Switzerland through exports. In contrast, the same measures taken by Swiss public authorities have a limited effect due to the fact that they are of some benefit to foreign actors because of the dependence on imports.

2.3 Future prospects and challenges

Here we have addressed the circumstances in which state action proves necessary. There is however a risk that such action will take on a life of its own, and that public administration will end up losing sight of its purpose, running counter to the common interest that was its initial justification. For example, even today, some states subsidize fossil fuels (gas, coal, oil), responsible for 67% of greenhouse-gas emissions. A primary challenge for public authorities is thus to be able to call into question instruments put in place in former times but that have today lost their relevance (as the result of technological progress, for example). This task can prove complex if governments are captured by private interests (e.g. election campaign funding, lobbies) to the detriment of the collective interest and if, in a democratic system, a preoccupation with being elected or re-elected takes precedence. In this way, market failures may be replaced by—or, worse, compounded by— state failures.

Another major challenge states face is the provision of public goods with an increasingly global scope: financial and economic stability, health, education, climatic sustainability, to name but a few examples. The more global the public goods to be supplied become, the greater the difficulty of ensuring the supply of an optimal quantity. For example, to combat climate change, a unilateral policy would shift production to countries facing shorter-term imperatives than climate issues. Such policies are bound to lead to simple redistribution of production and wealth, with no significant environmental benefit. To prevent this situation, supply of this type of public good must depend on worldwide agreements under the jurisdiction of supranational authorities with the power to impose penalties in case of noncompliance. Failing this, incentives to act as freeriders will persist.

This challenge brings states face to face with another: that of trust. Aghion *et al.* (2010) demonstrate a causal relation between trust and regulation. By trust is meant a belief that stems from the civicness present in a society. The higher the proportion of civic people in a society—those whose behaviour takes into account the negative externalities they create—the higher the level of trust will be. Regulation serves to constrain antisocial people and limit the negative externalities they generate. Thus regulation—which always has a cost—intervenes in the absence of civicness and social conventions. State action is hence often a substitute for social conventions. A major challenge for the state thus lies in participating in the supply of increasingly global public goods while understanding that the institutions to be put in place to supply them cannot be the same everywhere, but must be adapted to suit local social and cultural contexts.

Key concepts

- General government spending ratio (*quote-part de l'État, Staatsquote, quota d'incidenza della spesa pubblica*): a statistical indicator that expresses all public expenditure made during a year as a proportion of GDP, that is, as a proportion of the added value created in the country during the same year. It takes into consideration total expenditure—that is, current expenditure and investment expenditure—in all sectors: confederation, cantons, municipalities and social-security funds.
- Macroeconomic stabilization (*stabilisation macroéconomique, makroökonomische Stabilisierung, stabilizzazione macroeconomica*): state intervention aimed at limiting cyclical fluctuations of economic activity, particularly by maintaining high employment levels and price stability. It is also aimed at fostering growth. Various instruments exist to serve this purpose, particularly the budgetary and tax policy of public authorities, and the central bank's monetary policy.
- Market failure (*défaillance du marché, Marktversagen, fallimento del mercato*): a situation that arises when market mechanisms alone, particularly the interplay of supply and demand, are unable to guarantee a socially optimal (that is, desirable) quantity and equilibrium price. Market failure occurs when the behaviours of companies or households generate externalities, or when information asymmetry exists between the parties to an exchange, or when a natural-monopoly situation exists, or when a good takes on the characteristics of a public good. The

state is generally expected to intervene to remedy such failures, thereby fostering efficiency in the allocation of resources.

- Redistribution (*redistribution, Umverteilung, redistribuzione*): state intervention aimed at fostering a degree of equity in the distribution of income and monetary and non-monetary wealth between individuals or between regions. This transferral function is assuming growing importance. It can make use of various mechanisms to achieve equitable redistribution, such as income and other taxes, social benefits (social assistance, unemployment benefits, etc.), or financial-equalization transfers between jurisdictions.

References

Akerlof, G. A. (1970). The market for lemons: Quality uncertainty and the market mechanism. *The Quarterly Journal of Economics, 84*(3), 488–500.
Aghion, P., Algan, Y., Cahuc, P. & Shleifer, A. (2010). Regulation and distrust. *Quarterly Journal of Economics, 125*(3), 1015–1049.
Athias, L. & Wicht, P. (2019). Distinct heating networks, legal norms, and market structure: what role for public authorities ? *Revue d'économie industrielle, 166*, 39–63.
Friedman, M. (1962). *Capitalism and freedom.* University of Chicago Press.
Keynes, J. M. (1936). *The general theory of employment, interest, and money.* Houghton Mifflin Harcourt.
Musgrave, R. (1959). *The theory of public finance.* McGraw-Hill.
Nelson, P. (1970). Information and consumer behavior. *Journal of Political Economy, 78*, 311–329.
Piketty, T. (2014). *Capital in the Twenty-First Century.* Harvard University Press/Belknap.
Scharpf, F. (1999). *Governing in Europe: Effective and democratic?* Oxford University Press.
Stiglitz, J. E. (2000). *Economics of the public sector.* WW Norton & Company.

References for further study

Barr, N. (2020). *Economics of the Welfare State.* Oxford University Press.
Makin, A. J. (2018). *The limits of fiscal policy.* Palgrave Macmillan.
Mueller, D. C. (2003). *Public choice III.* Cambridge University Press.

3 Stakeholders

Pirmin Bundi

3.1 The importance of stakeholders for public administration

The political decision-making process is made up of a chain of activities resulting from repeated interactions between various public and private actors. Public administration must therefore deal with a large number of actors, all of whom are important for its daily work. The list ranges from political actors (government, parliament, courts, political parties, cantons and municipalities) to members of the public, and also includes private organizations in the form of interest groups and trade unions, media companies and social movements.

Any individual or social group can be considered as a stakeholder, as can any organization with an interest (a "stake") in the decisions and outcomes of public administration (Manuel-Navarrete & Modvar 2007: 921). Stakeholders then, are directly or indirectly affected by the attainment of the goals of public interventions. They also attempt to influence these interventions. In a neo-corporatist country like Switzerland, which has a long tradition of direct democracy, stakeholders are closely involved in decisions of the state. This approach is based on the assumption that involvement of the most relevant actors makes it possible not only to find the best solutions to a given societal problem, but also to improve public acceptance of government interventions and hence their implementation.

Accordingly, stakeholders are involved to varying degrees in the genesis, formulation and solution of political problems. On the political front, stakeholders in public administration can be differentiated on the basis of their organizational profile. On the one hand, they are composed of institutional actors invested with public authority who actively shape the political decision-making process. And on the other hand, they are composed of actors belonging to the socio-economic and cultural spheres of society that are directly or indirectly affected by public intervention. The latter can be divided into two groups: 1) policy addressees—those who form the direct target group—since it is their behaviour which, from a political point of view, is defined as the primary cause of the problem; 2) the beneficiaries of the policy who, in contrast, benefit from the change in the first group's behaviour, since they bear the negative effects of the problem, and since the public measure is aimed at improving their situation. There are also other stakeholders who, while not being directly affected by an intervention, have some interest in it. When planning public policy, it is always wise to involve all actors concerned. For this reason, public organizations, as the authority implementing a policy, must often deal with the conflicting interests of institutional and societal actors. Here, the manner in which the government conceives and establishes public policies plays an essential role.

The way that public measures are organized and implemented has changed fundamentally over the past 50 years (▶ 8 Governance). In the 1960s, political decision-makers strongly believed that the administration could plan the deployment of public interventions in top-down fashion. But as Pressman and Wildavsky (1984) have shown, this approach did not work, because the administrative units involved did not always implement measures in the way imagined by political decision-makers. Public administration is influenced by a complex web of individual and collective actors advocating for divergent interests and exerting ever-increasing political pressure As a result, in the literature it is often asserted that the mode of governing in modern democracies has moved from "*government*" to "*governance*" (Mayntz 2006). Contrary to the static, *top-down* approach ("*government*"), *governance* is founded on the idea that collective decisions are taken in a non-hierarchical manner, in which public and private actors are independent. The term "*cooperative governance*" is often heard, whereby the state does not take a sovereign position, but tries to "steer" political networks, indirectly and with varying degrees of success (Rhodes 1997: 53).

This chapter looks first at the paradigm shift in the mode of governing, which has brought about a change in the understanding of the role of stakeholders in public administration. We then turn to the various types of actors that participate in or are affected by public policy, before setting out the various approaches aimed at bringing these actors into the design and implementation of the policy. The final section deals with future prospects and challenges regarding the involvement of the various institutional and societal actors.

3.2 Key points regarding the stakeholders of public administration

3.2.1 Changes in the understanding of the role of stakeholders

Since the 1970s, we have seen modern democracies move from a hierarchical mode of government to a more collaborative approach, or "governance". This shift has had a major impact on public administration, leading to changes in the way certain policies are implemented. The shift began in the administrations of Western European countries, before spreading to the non-hierarchical system of the European Union, the organization of which resembles a network of various actors (Commission, Council, Parliament, member states and societal stakeholders). Mayntz (2006: 19) sees this paradigm shift in the mode of governing as resulting from the failure of desired political reforms after the end of World War II. Although the economy rebounded strongly during the first two postwar decades, growth collapsed in the early 1970s. Unable to deal with this situation on their own, policymakers began to look for new ways to manage the economy.

Deregulation and privatization were soon presented as possible solutions to the problem. It was argued that the state alone was unable to guarantee long-term growth and that it was therefore necessary to give private actors maximum freedom. Market principles became the cornerstone of the political ideology known as neoliberalism that emerged in the 1980s. With the collapse of the Soviet Union and its satellite states, support for this ideology was further strengthened, leading to a new wave of privatization in many areas. In Switzerland, the telecommunications market was deregulated in the 1990s, with the former PTT (post, telephones and telegraphs) giving rise to new autonomous entities in 1997: Swisscom and Swiss Post. This conception of the economy persisted until the global financial crisis of 2007 and the ensuing euro and sovereign debt crises. Since that time, state actors have once again strengthened their grip, particularly through "independent regulatory authorities".

In spite of recent trends, civil-society stakeholders have continued to exercise their relatively substantial weight in the implementation of political interventions. Today, efforts are being made to strengthen collaboration between institutional and societal actors. Private actors must be involved not only in the formulation of political measures, but also in their deployment. Stakeholders' know-how, particularly in complex fields, must contribute to developing more efficient, more effective solutions. Table 3.1 shows the modes of government just mentioned, which differ according to their levels, policy areas and dissemination.

	Public sector	Privatization	Governance
Type of service	Production and distribution by the public sector	Production and marketing in the private sector	Distribution under an agreement between the public sector and private actors
Actors	Institutional	Societal	Institutional and societal
Decision-making process	Vertical, top-down	Horizontal (societal actors only)	Horizontal (institutional and societal actors)
Relationships	Dependence	Independence	Interdependence
Code of conduct	Regulations, directives and procedures	Price structure, supply and demand	Social exchanges, reciprocity
Negotiation style	Rules-based, procedural	Competition, private interest, emphasis on the short-term	Interest-based, emphasis on the long-term, win-win

Table 3.1 Modes of government
Source: Keast (2016: 443)

3.2.2 Types of stakeholders

In designing and implementing public policy, public administration must in most cases take into account a large number of organizations and individuals. Here, we are drawing a distinction between institutional and societal actors (Bussmann *et al.* 1997: 64). *Institutional actors* are bodies whose involvement in a public intervention is generally formally defined, particularly as regards the period of involvement and the resources to be committed. They include the various administrative units concerned, but also other political bodies such as the government, the parliament or the courts. These authorities intervene at all levels of government (Confederation, cantons and municipalities) and are important stakeholders at every level of public administration. *Societal actors*, for their part, include all individual actors (citizens) and collective ones (interest groups) in society, whose contribution to a policy is most often informal and not obligatory. The best example is provided by the federal-level consultation procedure which, although enshrined in the Constitution, does not provide for compulsory participation of societal actors in all political business, merely inviting them to express their views on "important legislation or other projects of substantial impact" (art. 147). Table 3.2 gives an overview of the various groups of stakeholders.

Societal actors include not only the general public and economic-interest groups, but also associations, social movements and the media. Political parties also fall into this group, since in principle they represent the interests of their electors, whereas members of parliament are institutional actors, since their mandate gives them a role in the political decision-making process. Both institutional and societal actors are termed "stakeholders" because they hold a "stake" (an interest) in the

Institutional actors	Bodies whose involvement in public policy is generally formalized
Societal actors	All individual (citizens) and collective (interest groups) actors in society, whose contribution to a policy is most often informal and not obligatory
Policy addressees	A group of actors whose behaviour is considered relevant to a public policy aimed at resolving a particular problem. The behaviour of addressees must be modified to resolve a societal problem
Beneficiaries of a policy	A group of actors directly or indirectly, positively or negatively affected by an attempt to resolve a problem of any nature through public policy
Third-party groups	All persons and organizations that have an interest in a public policy and whose individual and/or collective situation undergoes lasting change (positive or negative). These groups are not directly affected by the policy

Table 3.2 Types of stakeholder groups

government measure concerned. Stakeholders often use their own resources (networks, competencies, personnel, etc.) to influence one or more decision-making processes involved in public intervention.

When designing and implementing a policy, two different types of groups of social actors are distinguished: policy addressees and beneficiaries of a policy. *Policy addressees* designates the group of stakeholders whose behaviour is considered as a lever for action relevant to the resolution of a given societal problem. They represent the direct target of a public intervention aimed at modifying their behaviour through suitable measures (information, financial incentives, obligations and prohibitions). *Beneficiaries of a policy*, on the other hand, are societal actors who are affected, directly or indirectly, positively or negatively, by the public intervention implemented to resolve the societal problem in question. There are also *third-party groups* who are not directly affected by a public policy, but whose situation undergoes lasting change (positive or negative) and who thus also have an interest in the policy.

A concrete case is useful to illustrate the various groups of stakeholders: for example the communication strategy regarding the prevention of seasonal influenza, which has been implemented every year since 2001 by the Federal Office of Public Health (FOPH) (Frey *et al.* 2012). The societal problem here is the spread of the seasonal influenza virus in Switzerland. In response, the Confederation mounts a communication campaign with information instruments such as posters and brochures (direct influence on policy addressees), and cooperation with physicians (indirect influence through intermediaries). The aim of the policy is not only to improve people's knowledge about influenza, but also to strengthen the extent of vaccination acceptance. Various institutional actors are involved in the development of this measure, with the FOPH remaining the principal decider regarding the campaign. The direct addressees of the policy are the general public, at-risk groups, medical and healthcare personnel, contact persons and physicians, to whom the campaign has to be addressed. Physicians, cantons, the media and employer organizations act as intermediaries, distributing the campaign message to policy addressees. At-risk groups and, to a lesser extent, the general public benefit directly and positively from these measures. Indirect benefits accrue to healthcare services, particularly hospitals, who have fewer sick people to deal with and are therefore less subject to overloading, and to vaccine manufacturers and organizations in charge of vaccination (physicians and pharmacies). Negative impacts fall to pharmaceutical companies that produce and market medications to treat influenza symptoms.

3.2.3 Stakeholder involvement

Public authorities must inevitably deal with a variety of actors. The question then becomes how to take these stakeholders into account in the decision-making process. Other than formal involvement, such as in the consultation procedure mentioned above and the instruments of direct democracy (▶ 4 Institutions), there are various ways of involving stakeholders and implementing the corresponding models. The following subsection gives an overview of three different approaches (see Table 3.3).

From a democratic and societal point of view, involving stakeholders and taking their interests into account in public policy has proved to be more effective than traditional management approaches, since the latter are often aimed merely at improving processes and their efficiency (Manuel-Navarrete & Modvar 2007: 918). In this context, stakeholder involvement must be translated into a better understanding of the needs of the affected groups in order to define the limits and strengthen the effectiveness of public interventions. This requires carrying out an analysis of stakeholders, for the purpose of identifying and characterizing the most important actors for public administration. Stakeholders must then be divided into primary and secondary groups. Although the main stakeholders are of fundamental importance in the organization and deployment of measures (departments, implementing partners, etc.), secondary stakeholders are those affected by the public intervention in one way or another (addressees and beneficiaries of a policy), but who do not participate directly in the implementation of measures. These actors may be of great strategic importance for the effectiveness and impact of public interventions, which is why they are often consulted. In what follows, we present various approaches to bringing stakeholders into the design and implementation of public interventions.

Participatory governance

Participatory governance is an approach to governing that emphasizes demographic engagement, particularly deliberative practices (Fischer 2012: 457). In recent decades this approach has established itself in political organizations. At the international level, this development is a response to criticism of the democratic deficit of certain governments and certain organizations. In Switzerland, on the other hand, this approach has long been neglected because of the deep institutional roots of the instruments of direct democracy. This framework empowers citizens and other non-state actors to influence and shape decision-making processes. However, all too often these actors have no access to relevant information, which is why participatory governance practices attempt to reduce these "democratic deficits" by fostering the provision of information to citizens, and making them aware of their rights, participation and interests. The aim is not to involve every citizen in every decision, but to guarantee fair representation of various interests and groups in society, particularly disadvantaged or traditionally excluded groups, in decisions and processes that have direct consequences on their lives. The potential for participatory governance practices is unquestionably most important at the local level, where the population enjoys easy access to authorities and where the effect of government measures is most directly felt. This is why the number of participatory projects has increased at the local level since the early 1990s. As an example, the City of Sion and the University of Geneva are currently working together on the "demoscan" project, in which a citizen chosen at random is asked to look critically at the arguments being put forward regarding a federal referendum and to make recommendations. The persons concerned therefore not only must learn about a complex subject by being brought into the opinion-forming process, but also must understand it and formulate their own opinion.

Collaborative governance

Collaborative governance is a mode of cooperative government in which authorities integrate stakeholders directly into the collective decision-making process. This approach developed in response to the failure of top-down deployment and to the substantial costs of regulation and its politicization. It is seen as a response both to the antagonism created by the plurality of interest groups and to management-style approaches (Ansell & Gash 2008). In principle, the increase in collaboration stems from the broadening of knowledge and institutional capabilities. Growing specialization, the sharing of knowledge, increasing complexity and the interdependence of institutional infrastructures are stimulating the need for collaboration. Four elements are necessary to guarantee the success of these collaborative governance regimes and attain the desired results (Emerson *et al.* 2012: 14-16). First, procedural and institutional arrangements provide a basic structure, enabling repeated interactions with stakeholders during cooperation. As collaborative networks grow larger and more complex, structures and processes must be increasingly explicit in order for the arrangement to work. Second, collaboration of this type requires assertive leadership (▶ 9 Leadership). Leadership can be provided by a person from outside or from the collaborative governance structures, or can be set up in the specific framework of a collaboration. Moreover, these networks require different leadership techniques during the various phases of a collaboration. Third, specific knowledge of proximity politics is essential oiling the gears of collaboration. This requires the aggregation, categorization and reorganization of information and the generation of new knowledge. Analysing information as a group can turn individual knowledge into social capital. Fourth, pooling of resources is the culmination of joint action. Collaborations can benefit from the sharing and common use of limited resources—not only financial, but also temporal, technical and logistical resources. An example of such a structure is provided by the EduNum digital education project in Vaud canton, through which the cantonal authorities are implementing a digitalization programme in state schools with the help of experts from the Swiss Federal Institute of Technology in Lausanne (EPFL) (Cahlikova & Bundi 2020).

Regulatory governance

Regulatory governance is a mode of government in which societal actors play an increasingly active role in the definition, monitoring and implementation of regulatory standards and partnerships with, or in parallel with, institutional bodies (Yasuda 2016: 428–429). Of course, there is still the traditional mode of monitoring by the state, as it remains the most effective way to bring about a change in the behaviour of firms subject to regulation, even though it is extremely costly. This mode has proved to be considerably more effective than market-based mechanisms, particularly when the costs of monitoring are too high for private actors. Another argument is that classical control instruments should sometimes be preferred over a decentralized monitoring system. This is because a decentralized system is often dependent on automatic alert systems, such as fire alarms, whose success depends on the reaction capability of monitoring units and the reliability of the companies to whom mandates are given. In contrast, regulatory governance involves operating more traditional regulatory approaches, in collaboration with non-state actors. Agreements between institutional and societal actors are thus not merely ad-hoc commitments: increasingly, they are given a legal foundation, thereby creating a solid basis for collaboration. The old dichotomies between regulators and regulated fields are attenuated by this approach, because the regulator brings together companies and NGOs in order to attain the goals of regulation. The classical state-centred form of regulation is thus transformed into a process of regulation in which a broader range of different actors participate. This also calls for cooperative regulatory efforts between the state and industry, in which the state sets the overall standards for production quality and calls on industry to self-regulate. Companies develop internal control systems, which guarantee quality of production, with the involved actors themselves defining, monitoring and certifying control parameters. These risk-management plans are then submitted for approval to the state supervisory authorities, and the authorities monitor the companies' compliance with these regulations in accordance with the plans they have established. By involving government, business and community groups in the regulatory process, incentives are better aligned and the cost of government oversight is reduced. An example of this approach is provided by the Financial Market Supervisory Authority (FINMA), which is not funded and managed by the Confederation, but by contributions and taxes paid by the entities subject to surveillance.

Approach	Target group	Goal	Organization	Administrative role
Participatory governance	General public	Democratization of political decisions	Spontaneous, at irregular intervals	Gatekeeper
Collaborative governance	Implementation partners	Improvement of implementation	Institutional, at regular intervals during implementation of the policy	*Primus inter pares*
Regulatory governance	Policy addressees	Monitoring of compliance with the policy	Periodic, incremental legal foundation	Guarantee of quality

Table 3.3 Overview of governance approches

3.3 Future prospects and challenges

The importance and role of stakeholders for public administration have changed considerably over the years. The multiplication of actors and types of participation has made it more difficult for the administration to identify and take them into account in a timely manner. There is also the question of the impact of technological progress on the integration of stakeholders. In addition, there is always uncertainty surrounding ways of guaranteeing the involvement of stakeholders when areas of policy are complex. Some policy fields are dominated by a small group of experts from public bodies and scientific circles, and as a result other stakeholders may find themselves excluded from the decision-making process. What options does public administration have in such cases?

New technologies can be a great boon for the administration. Meetings between institutional and societal actors no longer need to be conducted in person, but can be held online, which simplifies matters. Moreover, those who share similar interests can organize themselves more easily through using the internet and are no longer dependent on sectoral associations. Even our federal government can make use of new social media to instigate direct exchanges with the population. Organization and exchanges are simplified, although this does not mean that stakeholders will be automatically involved.

Often, administrative units continue to rely on traditional means of participation and have not yet taken advantage of the new media available to them. This may very well work at the organizational level, for example as regards the regulation of a given field, but classical means are unlikely to foster "democratic innovations". This is not always the fault of public administration, which often lacks the means and the will to adopt ad-hoc instruments. However, it would be preferable to invest more in digitalization projects and insist on their implementation—not only for internal collaboration, but also for cooperation with outside actors (▶ 14 Digital transformation).

Another problem is the specialization of numerous political fields. Even today, members of public bodies often specialize in a specific field and can hardly be considered as generalists. This leads to a multiplicity of exchanges between specialists, with the attendant risk of losing sight of the big picture and hindering the attainment of the main goals. Here we are not talking about technocracy, but about the predominance of expert opinion. Public servants must be made aware of this phenomenon. This problem can be mitigated relatively easily by consulting as many stakeholders as possible when implementing a policy, for example by using digital tools. The success of a policy depends not only on the details of its deployment, but also on the degree of acceptance by political and societal actors. Scientific evidence is one basis for decision, but certainly not the only one. As Alain Berset explained with regard to management of the Covid-19 health crisis: "It is not the job of the scientific task force to conduct policy. The Federal Council incorporates scientific conclusions into the policy. We make the decisions."

Key concepts

- Beneficiaries of public policy (*bénéficiaires de la politique publique, Politikbegünstigte, beneficiari della politica pubblica*): a group of actors affected, directly or indirectly, positively or negatively, by measures taken in the framework of a public policy aimed at resolving a particular problem.
- Governance (*gouvernance, Governance, governance*): designates a situation in which public intervention is implemented in a non-hierarchical manner, with public and private actors independent of each other.
- Policy addressees (*destinataires de la politique publique, Politikadressaten, destinatari della politica pubblica*): a group of actors whose behaviour is considered as a lever for action for a public policy aimed at resolving a particular problem.
- Public policy (*politique publique, öffentliche Politik, politica pubblica*): a set of considered, consistent, targeted measures taken by various actors, public and sometimes private, to resolve a problem that has been politically defined as a collective problem.

References

Ansell, C. & Gash, A. (2008). Collaborative governance in theory and practice. *Journal of Public Administration Research and Theory, 18*(4), 543–571.

Bussmann, W., Klöti, U. & Knoepfel, P. (1997). *Einführung in die Politikevaluation.* Helbing und Lichtenhahn.

Cahlikova, T. & Bundi, P. (2020). Managing the Rise of the Digital State: Implementation of Digital Education by Local Government. *Jahrbuch der Schweizerischen Verwaltungswissenschaften, 11*(1), 145–157.

Emerson, K., Nabatchi, T. & Balogh, S. (2012). An integrative framework for collaborative governance. *Journal of Public Administration Research and Theory, 22*(1), 1–29.

Fischer, F. (2012). Participatory governance: From theory to practice. In D. Levi-Faur (Ed.). *The Oxford Handbook of Governance* (pp. 457–471). Oxford University Press.

Frey, K., Fontana, M. C., Itin, A., van der Heiden, N., Debrunner, A., Blaser, N., Häner, F., Schubiger, M., Stadter, C., Bonfadelli, H., Widmer, T., Kübler, D. (2012). *Evaluation der Kommunikations-strategie zur Prävention der saisonalen Grippe: Schlussbericht.* Institut für Politikwissenschaft, Forschungsbereich Policy-Analyse & Evaluation.

Keast, R. (2016). Network governance. In C. Ansell& J. Torfing (Eds.). *Handbook on Theories of Governance* (pp. 442–453). Edward Elgar.

Manuel-Navarrete, D. & Modvar, C. (2007). In M. Bevir (Ed). *Encyclopedia of Governance* (pp. 917–921). Sage.

Mayntz, R. (2006). From government to governance: Political steering in modern societies. In D. Scheer & F. Rubik (Eds.), *Governance of integrated product policy* (pp. 18–25). Greenleaf Publishing.

Pressman, J. L. & Wildavsky, A. (1984). *Implementation: How great expectations in Washington are dashed in Oakland.* University of California Press.

Rhodes, R. A. W. (1997). *Understanding governance: Policy networks, governance, reflexivity and accountability.* Open University Press.

Yasuda, J. (2016). Regulatory governance. In C. Ansell& J. Torfing (Eds.). *Handbook on theories of governance* (pp. 428–441). Edward Elgar Publishing.

References for further study

Ansell, C. & Torfing, J. (2016). *Handbook on theories of governance.* Edward Elgar Publishing.

Levi-Faur, D. (2012). *The Oxford Handbook of Governance.* Oxford University Press.

Linder, W. & Mueller, S. (2017). *Schweizerische Demokratie. Institutionen, Prozesse, Perspektiven.* Haupt.

4 Institutions

Andreas Ladner

4.1 The importance of political institutions for public administration

What are political institutions? For a definition of the concept of political institutions, we can refer to sociology and social sciences, where institutions are defined as "humanly devised constraints that shape human interaction" (North 1990: 3). Their basic characteristics are that they are created by humans, bring a degree of order to human relationships, open up or limit possibilities for action and are intended to last. The need for political institutions arises when the satisfaction of social needs, based on the production and distribution of goods, leads to divergences of interest that cannot be resolved simply by the natural order of things (Czada 2002: 354).

An institution is deemed to be political when its function is to authoritatively settle disputes using standards established for the purpose, by deploying an apparatus staffed with appropriate personnel to ensure that those standards are respected. The standards referred to include constitutional norms, laws and regulations, and also the organizational structure of government and administration (Czada 2002: 354).

In this chapter we therefore, on the one hand, identify the purpose of *institutions*, that is, the binding resolution of conflicts on the basis of standards formulated for the purpose, using appropriate personnel to ensure implementation. On the other hand, we consider the potential scope of the concept of institutions, ranging from simple procedures to the Constitution and the organization of the state. Lastly, we link public administration itself with the term "institutions".

Institutions make an essential contribution to legitimization of the system. They stand above political decisions. As long as institutions are accepted, political decisions will be as well, even if a person might have decided differently on an individual basis. In Switzerland, institutions play an important role. Their acceptance is sometimes seen as a fundamental element ensuring the country's cohesion (institutional patriotism).

Although they are designed to last, institutions are capable of changing over time and of adapting to new realities (*institutional change*). This process may take the form of incremental changes, but may also be the result of large-scale institutional reforms.

Common theoretical approaches to institutions can be distinguished by how they assess the possibilities for institutional change. New institutionalist theories are frequently advanced (March & Olsen 1984). They variously attempt to explain a country's political institutions by its history (*historical institutionalism*), its structure or its predominant cultural values (*sociological institutionalism*), or by balancing costs and benefits (*rational-choice institutionalism*) and the influence of certain actors and parties (*actor-centred institutionalism*). A number of approaches afford relatively limited room for manoeuvre (path dependency), while others confine the possibilities for change to certain situations (windows of opportunity).

In the model proposed here, institutions represent the rules of the game with which public administration must comply. They define the tasks of the administration, dictate its modus operandi, set the boundaries of its field of activity and—a point that is often overlooked—protect areas of and possibilities for freedom. From a political perspective, however, the administration is often also an integral part of institutions by virtue of its affiliation with the executive, its relationship with parliament and citizens and by virtue of its nature as a cornerstone of the state. Its activities, over the long term, are aimed at conflict management and are a guarantee of predictability.

In short, administrations are in general seen (especially in Switzerland) as not part of the political system. They are seen as "agents of execution" in the service of politics, and are almost absent from political science textbooks. But this view of matters is highly reductionist and outdated. Today, administrative bodies are important political actors, and this aspect is also taken into account in the IDHEAP model. It is impossible to understand government action or the role and operation of the administration without knowledge of the interactions between various institutions, with their interdependence and mutual influence. Consequently, we must also put into perspective the impact of the various elements of the political system on public administration. For this purpose, we first present the main pillars of the institutional framework (federalism, direct democracy and concordance) and the logic behind them. We then look at the way the administration shapes the world of politics and institutions.

4.2 Key elements of the Swiss political system

From a political viewpoint, there is substantial unanimity about the institutions regarded as fundamental. These are, in order of appearance, federalism, direct democracy and concordance. These three keystones of the institutional framework all exercise a restraining effect on power in that they represent a form of power sharing. They are thus an expression of our country's predominant political culture, which is geared towards reconciliation and compromise, and is averse to the idea of a dominant, centralized government at the head of the country. Sometimes, the militia system and neutrality are also regarded as key institutional characteristics of the Swiss political system.

Understanding the importance of the functions and functioning of institutions calls for a basic knowledge of their validity and origin[8]. The very nature of the Swiss state is determined by the fact that it is built from the bottom up. Unlike other countries with a history of monarchy, Switzerland has never had a centralized state power, and has been driven by the desire to build a nation-state around a coalition of partners with more or less equal rights. After the failure of the centralizing attempts of the Helvetic Republic (1798–1802), adoption of the Federal Constitution in 1848 marked the birth of the nation-state. The federation of states became a federal state to which the cantons had to surrender part of their sovereignty.

The objectives of creating the federal state were that it should present itself to other states as a lasting unified entity with the capacity to act, defend the interests of Switzerland, guarantee its external security and preserve its independence and neutrality. In this perspective, internal security was associated with a guarantee to maintain peace and order together with "promotion of the common good", openly proclaimed, and with the broad authority granted to the Confederation to carry out "public works" (see Maissen 2010: 202). The first step—and here there are obvious analogies with the development of the European Union—was the laying of the foundations of a unified Swiss economic space, with the abolition of customs duties between cantons and the introduction of a single national currency. The welfare state and the emergence of a sense of nationality came later.

The foundation of the current federal state was enshrined by the constitutional referendum held shortly after the end of the Sonderbund War in 1847. Certain cantons were very reluctant to accept the centralization of powers, and substantial prerogatives remained the preserve of the cantons, particularly most jurisprudence and tax law, police, transport, schools and church sovereignty (Maissen 2010: 200). The aim was, moreover, to guarantee that the cantons would have political influence worthy of the name at the national level. From an institutional point of view, this guarantee was provided by the upper chamber, the Council of States (endowed with the same powers as the National Council), to which every canton could elect two representatives. This meant that sparsely populated cantons, among them those defeated in the Sonderbund War, were overrepresented.

Despite concessions in the draft constitution offered to the losers of the Sonderbund War, who wanted greater cantonal autonomy, it proved impossible to secure their support. The Constitution was roundly rejected by the Catholic

8 See also Ladner (2013) and Ladner (2019a et b).

cantons (Uri, Schwyz, Obwald and Nidwald, Zoug, Valais, Tessin and Appenzell Rhodes-Intérieures). In order to obtain the hoped-for clear majority of cantons in favour of the Constitution, the Catholic canton of Fribourg fell in with the decision of the liberal government of the time, while in the canton of Lucerne (also Catholic) abstentions were counted as votes in favour. That is how the Federal Diet was able to validate the new constitution on 12 September 1848.

Switzerland thus became a nation-state organized as a democracy quite early on. The price of unification, however, was strong federalism and a weak centre. The residual competence remained, as it still does today, in the hands of the cantons. This meant that any extension of the Confederation's prerogatives and the adoption of new mandates would require the assent of the electoral body and the cantons. Conservative Catholic opponents of the federal state thus enjoyed a degree of protection, meaning that they would have to be reckoned with on matters including future development of the state.

4.2.1 Federalism

A federalist state structure was thus a prerequisite for the founding of the nation-state in 1848. Each of the 26 cantons (or states) has its own parliament, its own government, its own courts and its own constitution (which cannot, however, contradict the federal Constitution). The cantons implement directives from the Confederation (federalism of execution), but organize activities based on their own needs. For example, they have great latitude of action in the areas of education, healthcare, culture and policing. The cantons employ about half of the country's public servants. Moreover, every canton finances itself by levying income and wealth taxes.

The cantons are also involved in decision-making at the national level. The authority provided for this purpose is primarily the Council of States (the upper chamber of parliament), in which every canton is represented with two seats.

In addition, the cantons enjoy a special status in the framework of direct democracy. The crucial point is that, in principle, any extension of the powers of the Confederation must be approved by a majority of the cantons. The influence of the cantons is also keenly felt during the preparation phase of new legislative proposals, when their representatives are consulted as experts (▶ 3 Stakeholders). Lastly, they play an important role when it falls to them to implement policies that are defined at the national level, where they can enjoy a degree of autonomy.

A special place is moreover held by contractual agreements of various kinds between cantons (concordats), by the Conference of Cantonal Governments, and by numerous technical conferences at which administrative managers are represented. These agreements are aimed at coordinating political solutions. They are also intended to obviate transferring tasks upwards to a higher institutional level and to prevent the cantons from losing influence to the Confederation.

A particularly attractive aspect of Swiss federalism is its willingness to accept different solutions and its explicit tendency towards competition. In contrast with German federalism, the Federal Constitution carries no obligation to ensure the same living conditions throughout the country. Swiss federalism operates on the principle of a minimum staffing level that should be achieved in all cantons with the help of financial-equalization transfers. Since the cantons and the municipalities are responsible for their own resources, and since these resources depend on the financial capacity of taxpayers, tax competition leads to substantial gaps in tax levels.

These principles are rooted in the wide-ranging reform of federalism that came into force in early 2008. This reform redefined the rules of equalization transfers between cantons that are economically strong and those that are structurally weak. It also disentangled a number of tasks and reorganized collaboration between the cantons and between the cantons and the Confederation. Growing centralization remains on the agenda, however: increasing numbers of tasks require uniform regulation—also due in part to international demands towards Switzerland. The cantons, meanwhile, with education, healthcare and their share of social spending, find themselves engaged in areas that have greatly expanded in recent years. Another problem is the expansion of inter-cantonal cooperation which tends to take decision-making power away from citizens and put it in the hands of the government and administration.

Federalism, to which can be added the strong autonomy of mostly very small municipalities, explains the relatively small size of the administrations of various public bodies. The result is that, in many policy areas, concrete expertise is found at the lower levels of administration.

4.2.2 Direct democracy

Next to federalism, direct democracy constitutes the second great pillar of the institutional framework. Its governing principle is that any amendment to the Constitution, and any move to join collective security organizations or supranational communities, must be subject to a vote (mandatory referendum) and receive the approval of both a majority of voters and a majority of cantons (double majority). Citizens can moreover request a constitutional amendment by means of a popular initiative. In order to take effect, a popular initiative must collect 100,000 valid signatures within a period of 18 months. It must then be approved by a majority of the people and the cantons. Lastly, citizens can resort to a referendum to oppose a new law and certain state treaties (facultative referendum). This requires gathering the signatures of 50,000 persons entitled to vote within 100 days. If the referendum does not secure a majority at the ballot box (simple majority), the pre-existing law applies. A canton may also launch an initiative individually, and eight cantons working together can trigger a referendum.

The roots of direct democracy go back to the 1830s, when citizens were granted the right of veto in the cantons of Saint-Gall and Bâle-Campagne (Kriesi & Trechsel 2008: 4). At the federal level, the Constitution of 1848 provided for a mandatory referendum requiring popular and cantonal approval of constitutional amendments, as well as a limited and relatively complex version of the initiative to call for a complete revision of the Constitution. Facultative legislative referendums were introduced in the 1874 revision of the Federal Constitution, and in 1891 the initiative for a partial revision of the Constitution was introduced. More recently, a major change took place with the extension of direct democracy to foreign-policy matters. This change should be seen in the context of the increased role of supranational alliances and international treaties.

The principle of the referendum has without a doubt acted as a brake on the multiplication of state tasks. Particularly at the beginnings of the federal state, a series of modernization and centralization projects were blocked by the opposition of conservative Catholic cantons. But independently of this, the growth of the state (and, even more so, that of the welfare state) has been relatively slow and modest in extent (Linder & Mueller 2017: 319).

Moreover, the referendum principle also requires involving the principal political forces in governmental responsibility, thereby making a substantial contribution to the third pillar of the institutional framework, concordance. Referendums give interest groups, political parties and other organized groups the possibility of blocking undesired constitutional and legislative changes. To prevent such reversals, the major political parties in government are involved in the preparation of a project and are required to give it at least moral support. Generally, projects will attempt to respond to the legitimate arguments of opponents, thereby reducing the temptation to trigger a referendum. Evidence of this can be seen in the consultation procedures that accompany the legislative process, which have been greatly expanded recently. Popular initiatives, for their part, give groups less strongly represented in the political system a tool with which to put forward their requests and influence politics.

But forcing politics to be more responsive to the "will of the people" is not the only effect of direct democracy: public administration, too, must give greater consideration to the wishes of citizens. Every project has to convince a majority of voters, and decisions made at the ballot box will also have an impact on action by the administration. While it might be going too far to suggest that public administration, by virtue of the principle of direct democracy, is acutely aware of the attitude of citizens, the fact remains that a verdict of the people has a value distinct from that of government directives.

4.2.3 The concordance system

The "concordance system" (the third pillar of the institutional framework) refers to the participation of the main parties in government (with varying degrees of willingness) and the idea of governing jointly amid changing majorities. At each of the three levels of government, all the major parties are generally represented in the executive branch.

The national government, the Federal Council, has seven members—seven ministers—of equal rank from the country's various regions and currently belonging to the four main political formations. The Federal Council makes decisions in a collegial manner: its members seek consensus so that their policy can gain a majority. In relation to the world outside the Council, each member upholds the collegial position, even if it does not coincide with his or her personal position or the line of his or her party (principle of collegiality). In contrast to foreign systems, in Switzerland there is no strict separation between the government and the opposition. Policies for the coming term are not decided by a single party or coalition of parties, but by the various representatives of different parties who form different majorities depending on the project. Governments at lower political levels operate in a very similar way. Changing majorities are a feature of parliaments and commissions, where the main task is to gather enough support from different partners to carry a project through.

4.2.4 Interactions between institutions and public administration

The concordance system also has a number of indirect effects on administrative activity. Although departments (i.e. ministries) are headed by representatives of political parties, a department's political orientation is ultimately more heterogeneous than in a system where executive positions are held by members of the parties in power. In Switzerland, administrative heads do not necessarily come from the same party as department heads (ministers). This does not prevent employees from very quickly realizing what proposals they can use to win over their political superiors, but there is nevertheless space for different points of view and different arguments. Putting forward projects is definitely not merely a matter of rallying votes from members of one's own party: the other members of the government need to be convinced, and the interest of other parties must be aroused in order to secure a majority in Parliament or among the population.

But in addition to the somewhat moderating effects of direct democracy on administrative activity, there are some very direct implications. Political processes need a great deal of time before all obstacles are overcome. The greatest difficulty lies in presenting projects likely to obtain a majority; they are filled with compromises and concessions (sometimes costly ones) granted to various stakeholders.

Federalism, and the autonomy of the municipalities, combined with respect of the principle of subsidiarity, have much more significant and direct effects. The result is a strong horizontal and vertical segmentation, which makes it possible to take better account of social and cultural differences and to create much more homogeneous subunits—public authorities. The first consequence is, however, fragmentation of a state whose size is already reduced, and the second is considerable diversity. Numerous tasks must be carried out using alliances aimed at collaboration between different levels. It is therefore unsurprising that on many occasions and in many fields it has been virtually impossible to set up professional administrative structures. In this situation, extensive use has had to be made of the militia system and cooperation with the private sector in order to provide the public goods required.

4.3 Future prospects and challenges

Despite the criticism levelled at them over the past few decades, institutions have been surprisingly successful and have sometimes even shown the ability to adapt and reform themselves (RPT, new management model for the federal administration, merger of municipalities). They have made a significant contribution to the success of the Swiss model of society and government. Nevertheless, developments and changes are emerging that require thinking outside the box and which place new demands on public administration and its personnel. These include digitalization, the multiplication of governance structures and the administration's involvement in politics and democracy.

a) For almost a quarter of a century, people have been asking what opportunities digitalization offers to democracy, politics and political institutions. Despite some progress in highly circumscribed fields (information delivery, transparency, commercial databases), the success of major projects such as electronic voting has been less impressive for the time being. One may suppose that in the future, digitalization will transform political participation and reshape the formulation of demands and involvement in decision-making processes. This includes the transfer of information and collaborative decision making.

b) Governance systems are non-hierarchical political networks, often involving multiple levels of government and public and private actors, whose decisions are based on compromise and the search for consensus. Networks of this type can be found in the international political arena, but also in certain areas of policy (social policy, health policy, cultural policy). Successful development in such networks requires a broad knowledge base to understand the background of the demands of different actors at different levels and to contribute to solutions that can definitively overcome the various "veto points". In the context of such networks, administrative activity is complex. Competences and responsibilities are not clearly defined. How is a political mandate to be accomplished on a consensus basis, and is there not a risk that the administration will be monopolized by a community of interests?

c) The increasing complexity of politics entails a specialization and an added professionalization of administrative activity. Ultimately, this leads to a disconnect between the administration and the world of politics and the aspirations of citizens. The technocratization of political solutions and the growing influence of international bodies and organizations are having similar effects. An advantage of the way that institutions are organized in Switzerland has long been their accessibility and their proximity to the people, expressed particularly through the militia principle. For politicians, it is becoming increasingly difficult to navigate through complex files: this is particularly evident at the municipal level, where local politics is facing growing recruitment difficulties. The resulting danger is that the administration could become increasingly autonomous and pursue its own political agenda thanks to its superiority in terms of knowledge. This gives rise to two clear requirements for administrative staff: on the one hand, a very high level of technical expertise is expected of them, and on the other hand, a precise understanding of roles backed up by the necessary integrity as regards its tasks and competences. The administration is responsible for the implementation of policy programmes and provides the basis for policy decisions. It is capable of clearly identifying the political implications of decisions, but does not itself engage in politics.

Key concepts

- Governance structures (*structures de gouvernance, Gouvernanzstrukturen, strutture di governance*): political programmes are increasingly organized in hierarchical, reticular, multilevel structures. This results in an intertwining of public and private actors, and decisions, which are subject to negotiation, are often based on compromise.
- Institutional change (*changement institutionnel, institutionneller Wandel, cambiamento istituzional*): institutional change occurs when the configuration of institutions shifts under the effect of determining factors. This change may take place slowly and gradually, but can also result from institutional reforms. Institutions are often endowed with a historical legacy (*path dependency*) which allows fundamental change only in certain situations (*windows of opportunity*).
- New institutionalism (*néo-institutionnalisme, Neo-Institutionalismus, neoistituzionalismo*): new institutionalism, an important theoretical current in social sciences, postulates that institutions harbour the potential for, and restrictions on, action. It takes various forms, such as sociological institutionalism, historical institutionalism, actor-centred institutionalism, and rational-choice institutionalism. According to the theory of new institutionalism, institutions may be understood as dependent or independent variables.
- Political institutions (*institutions politiques, politische Institutionen, istituzioni politiche*): political institutions include political constitutions, the entire system

guaranteed by the state to ensure the rule of law, legislation and regulations, and the organizational structure of government. Institutions are human creations that put order into political processes, are designed to last, and open or limit possibilities for action. The key institutions of the Swiss political system are federalism, direct democracy and concordance.

- Power sharing (*partage du pouvoir, Machtteilung, condivisione del potere*): the concept of power-sharing is a characteristic feature of the Swiss institutional framework. In contrast to majoritarian democracies, such as the United Kingdom, power is not concentrated in the hands of a single party, but divided between a number of major political formations. Federalism and direct democracy also act to prevent certain actors from becoming too powerful.

References

Czada, R. (2002). Institutionen/Institutionentheoretische Ansätze, In Nohlen, Dieter & Rainer-Olaf Schultze (Eds.). *Lexikon der Politikwissenschaft. Theorien, Methoden, Begriffe* (pp. 354–360. C. H. Beck.

Kriesi, H. & Trechsel, A. (2008). *The Politics of Switzerland. Continuity and Change in a Consensus Democracy*, Cambridge University Press.

Ladner, A. (2013). Der Schweizer Staat, politisches System und Aufgabenerbringung, In A. Ladner, J.--L. Chappelet, Y. Emery, P. Knoepfel, L. Mader, N. Soguel & F. Varone (Eds.) (2013). *Handbuch der öffentlichen Verwaltung in der Schweiz* (pp. 23–46). NZZ libro.

Ladner, A. (2019). The Characteristics of Public Administration in Switzerland. In A. Ladner, N. Soguel, Y. Emery, S. Weerts & S. Nahrath (Eds.) (2019). *Swiss Public Administration. Making State Work Successfully* (pp. 43–66). Palgrave.

Ladner, A. (2019). The Organization and Provision of Public Services. In A. Ladner, N. Soguel, Y. Emery, S. Weerts & S. Nahrath (Eds.) (2019). *Swiss Public Administration. Making State Work Successfully* (pp. 21–42). Palgrave.

Ladner, A. (2019). Society, Government, and the Political System. In A. Ladner, N. Soguel, Y. Emery, S. Weerts & S. Nahrath (Eds.) (2019). *Swiss Public Administration. Making State Work Successfully* (pp. 3–20). Palgrave.

Linder, W. & Muller, S. (2017). *Schweizerische Demokratie. Institutionen, Prozesse, Perspektiven*, Haupt, 4. Auflage.

Maissen, T. (2010). *Die Geschichte der Schweiz.* hier + jetzt.

March, J. G. & Olsen, J. P. (1984). The New Institutionalism: Organizational Factors in the Political Life" *American Political Science Review, 78*(3): 734–49.

References for further study

Knoepfel, P., Papadopoulos, Y., Sciarini, P., Vatter, A. & Häusermann, S. (Eds.) (2014). *Handbuch der Schweizer Politik.* Verlag Neue Zürcher Zeitung.

Lijphart, A. (2012). *Patterns of Democracy.* Yale University Press.

North, D. C. (1990). *Institutions, Institutional Change and Economic Performance.* Cambridge University Press.

Vatter, A. (2020). *Das politische System der Schweiz,* 4. vollständig überarbeitete und aktualisierte Auflage. Nomos.

PART II
Norms and strategy

Introduction

Sophie Weerts

1 Purpose of the “norms and strategy” dimension

Public administration is not an activity left to the free choice of those engaged in it. It is carried out within a framework and follows a direction that is instilled in it. This idea of framework and orientation is reflected in the designation “norms and strategy”, which covers all the components considered fundamental to the system, that serve as a basis for the system itself. The “norms and strategy” dimension thus encompasses the components that lend public administration a function that is not merely ontological, but also axiological. The term “norms” refers to the system’s constituent elements: the rules, principles and criteria that enable decisions to be made (ontological dimension). The term “strategy” evokes the idea of movement, of orientation, and thus reflects the axiological aspects of the system.

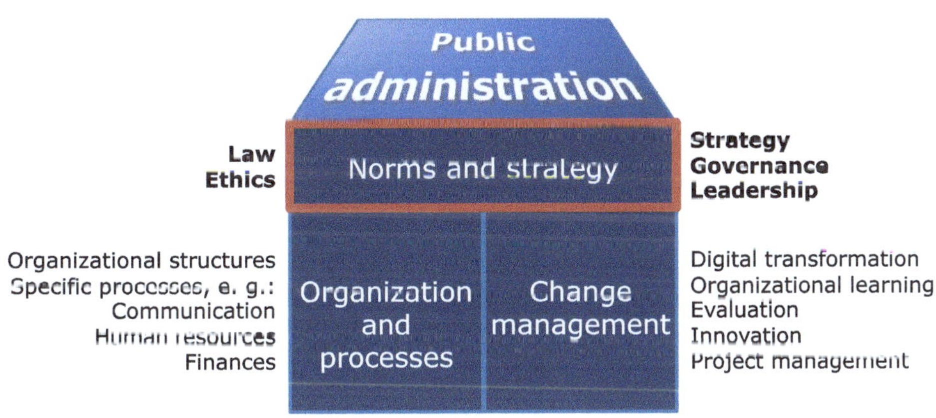

Figure II.1 The “norms and strategy” dimension in the IDHEAP model

2 Components of the "norms and strategy" dimension

Concretely, there are five components that act as the foundation of public administration: law, ethics, strategy, governance and leadership. Each of these components serves to define and guide not only the organization and processes of public administration, but also the management of change, which public administration must face in its dialogue with the environment in which it is deployed. In short, people involved in the field of public administration must not ignore these fundamental components.

Law (▶ 5 Law) obliges public administration to act in accordance with legally binding rules. This means that organizations active in the field of public administration are liable to sanctions if they fail to observe these rules. Law also brings a palette of instruments that enable organizations to modulate the scope of their action (such as legislation, administrative decisions and contracts and other conventions of public law). These instruments provided by law are used to participate in carrying out public tasks. Ethics (normative ethics) also implies the idea of rules and principles. Its constraining dimension for public administration involves the field of morality, of public expectations, and thus requires the adoption of a certain form of behaviour. Ethics (▶ 6 Ethics) can also be understood as a reflective process (applied ethics), serving to resolve dilemmas with which those involved in public administration may be confronted. Strategic management (▶ 7 Strategy) constitutes another mode of operation, one that enables public organizations to set themselves objectives in order to respond to public problems encountered. It can be recorded in a document, deemed a strategy, that will very concretely set out the values that serve as the foundation for the action of those engaged in public management. Strategy also and above all allows the setting of goals, objectives to be attained. In this way it helps to guide the decisions and actions of organizations involved in public administration. It has itself an organizational dimension. Governance (▶ 8 Governance) is another component that must be seen as a stabilizing force for public administration and as lying close to the "organization and processes" dimension. The question of governance is primarily that of a choice of a particular mode of governance which then takes root in organizational logistics. Moreover, the mode of governance enables the various actors to better identify their role and the purpose of their actions. Leadership (▶ 9 Leadership), lastly, is the component that calls on the human dimension of management, on all those immaterial elements—emotions, energies—that are required to guarantee the entire organization's commitment to achieving its objectives. Leadership has a strong axiological vocation, and the figurehead of the leader also acts as a reference point for collaborators.

That being said, although all the components that make up this dimension convey a strong sense of stability, it must be kept in mind that these components are not exempt from adjustment in the long-term, highlighting their connection with the question of change. Schematically, these five components can be grouped into three strata. The first stratum consists of law and ethics. These are the most fundamental components. Both law and ethics (the values at its base) represent the greatest stability and autonomy. Their evolution is directly connected to their external environment (the law for political actors, and values for the whole of society). They are not greatly influenced by public organizations or public administration in itself. Strategy and governance form the second stratum. The definition of these two components depends both on the external environment and on the particular needs of public administration. They are also very closely linked to the choice of values and to the legal framework. Leadership represents the third and final stratum, the most operational of the three in that it is based more on individuals than on the organization itself. As a result, this component is the most likely to undergo change. Individual action must however continue to observe the legal and ethical guidelines that are the foundation of public administration.

5 Law

Sophie Weerts

5.1 The importance of law for public administration

To begin with, it must be noted that the French word *droit* has multiple meanings. First and foremost, it is understood as the set of rules which, in any given society, govern relationships between individuals ("laws" or "the law"). In the French language, jurists refer to these rules as "objective law" (*droit objectif*, whose purpose is to ensure peaceful coexistence. In this conception, law is indissociable from life in society: *ubi societas, ibi jus*. In other words, wherever there is a society, there is law. But the word *droit* also means a "right": a prerogative recognized by objective law that individuals can assert before a judge. In French, rights are termed "subjective law" (*droit subjectif*). A third meaning of the word covers all the rules that have been posited by authorities empowered to produce law and that apply to individuals and organizations. This is known as *droit positif*, or "positive law", and is synonymous with the legal system itself, the legal order. As regards public administration, these three meanings remind us that public administration is framed a by system of rules (Swiss law), some of which define procedures and obligations that must be followed (positive law) while others grant rights (subjective law) to persons who have a connection with organizations carrying out public tasks.

Public administration has a special relationship with the law. Unlike individuals, administrative organizations or units have no individual rights, and do not benefit from individual freedom, but have power. This power is limited. It derives from positive law. Thus, an administrative organization or unit exists because it has been instituted by law and because its operation is defined by law. Intimately related to the state, which is also one of the main authorities that produce law, administrative organizations and units are subject to specific obligations. In this regard, paragraph 1 of article 5 of the Federal Constitution is emblematic. It states that all activities of the state are based on and limited by law. It expresses the *principle of legality* and the philosophy of the *rule of law*, the idea that the state is governed by law and not by divine will or the free will of a leader. This means that every public action must be based on the law and must also comply with the law. This idea of compliance with the law implies therefore that every public action has as its foundation a current *legal rule*. A public action must also respect other constitutional principles, namely the public interest, the principle of proportionality, the principle of equality of treatment between persons, the principle of good faith and the prohibition of arbitrariness (Tanquerel 2018). Again, this is a matter of complying with all the legal rules that apply to public and private units and organizations charged with a public task. Thus, when a community intends to develop a new infrastructure, it must be legally empowered to act in the field for which the infrastructure will be developed. Other rules must also be respected in the completion of such a project, for example ensuring that the goal is in the public interest, respecting the principle of proportionality between the means used and the end sought or respecting the Federal Act on Public Procurement.

But the law's importance for public administration is not limited to this function of foundation and supervision. The law also provides public administration with instruments to carry out measures. Given a political history in which efforts have been made to limit the arbitrariness of power, one can even say that legal instruments such as laws, ordinances, administrative decisions and contracts are the primary instruments of public administration. These legal instruments are different from material acts[9], which represent a non-legal category. Nevertheless, it must be said that the range of instruments for public action is not limited to classic legal instruments. Tax incentives, awareness campaigns, authorization to use a label and publication of a strategy are all seen as tools at the disposal of public administration. However, these instruments are not developed outside the legal framework, since that would challenge the philosophy of the rule of law. All these instruments then, whatever the nature, remain subject to the principle of legality.

Finally, the law represents a challenge for public administration. It is a living thing. It is not cast in stone, is not immutable. Indeed, the law emerges as society's needs evolve, and sometimes even backtracks when it no longer meets an existing need. Public administration, for its part, also evolves and changes (▶ 15 Organizational learning). These changes must be made in compliance with the law. Moreover, sometimes, the changes are triggered by the evolution of the law. The law and public administration are thus bound by a dialectical relationship. The former may require adaptations in the latter, which may in turn echo a need for change that impacts the law. Since they are required to observe the law, organizations charged with public tasks must keep a watch on changes in the law. They reflect needs for change, but can also propose changes themselves.

9 See the definition in Section 5.2.

Foundation, framework, instrument and challenge: these, then, are the various facets through which the theme of law can be seen from the public-administration viewpoint. This contribution presents some fundamental notions and instruments that are key for public administration from a legal standpoint. It then turns to issues and challenges that changes in public management pose for the field of law.

5.2 Key points of law

5.2.1 Key notions in law

Since public administration is obliged to comply with the law, it is important to determine what the law is and to understand its internal logic, so that we can grasp what it implies for public administration. For this purpose, three questions must be addressed: the sources of law, the hierarchy of norms and the distinction between norms of general, abstract scope and norms of individual, concrete scope.

Sources of law

Law is not a synonym for legislation. In ordinary speech, we do not say that people study laws, but law. This means there is a difference between the idea of "a law" and "(the) law". The fact that the expression "sources of law", used by jurists, is in the plural shows that law does not have a single origin. The term designates all the authorities that produce norms or a discourse on law. In Swiss law, the Civil Code lists these sources (art. 1, C. civ.). They are legislation, customary law, case law and established doctrine. These are, then, the different sources that must be mobilized when an organization wishes to verify whether it has the power to act, and to confirm its margin of discretion. Since recourse to customary law has become marginal, the notions of legislation, case law and established doctrine must be presented.

Legislation covers all the norms adopted by the state, either in the form of legislation and ordinances enacted unilaterally, or in the form of bilateral or multilateral agreements (international treaties, concordats, inter-cantonal agreements). It is the most important source of law. Looking at federal law alone, it can be said that the essence of the law is contained in the Constitution, laws and ordinances. In order to have mandatory force, these documents must be divulged at the end of a formalized procedure, which includes the requirement of publication in an official journal. Thus, in federal law, all these texts are published in the Official Compilation of Federal Legislation and also in the Systematic Compilation. The multiple authors of these texts must be empowered to legislate, that is, to set general, abstract norms. The Federal Assembly is the most important legislative body—after the people—by reason of its political legitimacy and its great legislative power. The Federal

Assembly can impose the greatest restrictions on human rights provided that the requirements of public interest and proportionality are respected. Depending on the type of measure, cantons and/or the people are or can be included in its law-making. It is involved in the adoption of the Constitution, but its most important instrument for legislating is certainly laws. It can also issue ordinances—in cases provided by the Federal Constitution or by law—or federal decrees, such as for a credit decision, a major planning decision or approval of an international treaty (a federal decree can then be submitted to a legislative referendum). The Federal Council also has legislative power. Its instrument is the ordinance. A so-called executive ordinance enforces and implements the rules contained in legislation (art. 182 Cst.). A substitute (or independent) ordinance (art. 184 al. 3, and 185 Cst.) is one that the Federal Council issues when the power to do so is expressly conferred by the Constitution or by law. In addition, an administrative unit may also be given legislative authority. At the federal level, article 48 of the Government and Administration Organisation Act (GAOA) provides that, depending on the scope of the norm envisaged, the Federal Council may delegate responsibility for enacting legal rules to departments. Such legislative power may even be delegated to an office, provided that this is expressly authorized by law (art. 48 al. 2, GAOA). Note also that legislative texts adopted by authorities outside the Confederation may also have normative content.

That being said, legislation is not limited to norms issued unilaterally. It also contains norms produced in a bilateral or multilateral framework. This is the case for international public law. States develop legal relationships with other states and international organizations on the international scene. These relationships are sometimes take the form of treaties or conventions. These texts are of a legal nature. This means that each party is legally responsible for and must fulfil its commitments. In the case of Switzerland, as soon as such an international instrument has been ratified by competent authorities, it becomes an integral part of Swiss law. In this regard, the Swiss legal system is said to be monistic. It is binding on all state authorities, including administrative units. More specifically, the legal rules contained in international agreements may be directly or not directly enforceable. In the first case, each administrative unit, and also each judge, must apply the international legal rule in every case that comes before it. In the second case, the international norm has to be transposed by internal authorities so that it can be enforced. In such cases, the competent administrative unit in the field governed by the international agreement must draw up the legal texts that will enable the legislator to make Switzerland's international commitments enforceable. Inter-cantonal law includes yet another type of legal text adopted in a bilateral or multilateral framework that belongs to the field of legislation. It does not necessarily belong to federal law, unless the Confederation can play a part by virtue of its competences (art. 48 al. 2, Cst.). Inter-cantonal agreements represent an alternative to the development of federal law, which in every case requires a specific constitutional basis legitimizing intervention of the Confederation.

The second source of law is case law. This is made up of all decisions rendered by the various jurisdictions regarding a given legal problem. The importance granted to case law among sources of law shows that the mission of judges is not solely to render justice, but also to participate in the development of the law. The magistrate's role as judge is to clarify and specify the content of a general, abstract norm laid down in an article of a law or ordinance, and even to formulate this content where there are gaps, or to develop it when cases arise that could not have been anticipated by the legislator. Concretely, they must enforce the general norm that allows the case before them to be resolved. This process of enforcement necessarily involves interpretation, for example to identify the contours and content of a norm laid down in an article of a law. Bear in mind here that not all judicial decisions or decrees have the same explanatory and constitutive scope for the development of the law. Given the Federal Supreme Court's functions of supreme judicial authority and guarantor of case-law unity, its decisions have a crucial interpretive scope in comparison with those rendered by cantonal and other federal jurisdictions. In this regard, federal case law constitutes a source that is added to legislation. It enables any litigant—and also any administrative unit or organization—to know the scope and content attributed to a legal norm.

Lastly, the third source of law is established doctrine. This covers all documents published on a given legal question. These texts differ from the two other sources in that they have neither coercive value nor a legitimate interpretive function. They therefore constitute a subsidiary resource which can shine light on knowledge of the law. This source is however not devoid of interest. It is characterized by both descriptive and normative discourse. Doctrine thus generally serves to monitor and synthesize the law, which is becoming increasingly multifaceted. From this perspective, it sometimes also serves to systematize the law, providing a better understanding of legislative and judicial developments. It moreover quite often adopts a normative stance, underlining the inconsistencies between legislators and judges, the two key actors of law. All these developments, then, can provide inspiration for a legislator who wishes to respond to a new or recurrent public problem as well as a judge who wishes to modify a point in his or her interpretation. Doctrine often provides an overall picture of the state of a legal question, and also represents a useful tool for public administration.

The hierarchy of norms

The above presentation of legislation and case law has shown that the law is produced by a large number of actors. However, it is not merely an amalgam of legal norms that are progressively adopted, published and interpreted by various competent authorities. The law is an organized, structured whole. There are thus, within the law, relationships of unity and coherence that are contained in what is known as the principle of the hierarchy of norms. This idea of coherence is not a simple aesthetic requirement: it is the expression of a certain political and legal conception of the state. More specifically, it is related to the organization of the various institutions that participate in the creation and development of the law. In this way, a legal norm adopted by a democratically elected assembly (for example, a law enacted by the Federal Assembly) takes precedence over one adopted by an authority designated by the former (ordinance of the Federal Council). The same applies to jurisdictions where the Federal Court is raised to the rank of Supreme Court in relation to other federal and cantonal jurisdictions. The federal structure of the state also has an impact on the hierarchical organization of Swiss law. Federal norms take precedence over cantonal norms, just as the latter take precedence over communal norms. This principle of hierarchy has a societal vocation: it contributes to legal certainty, by limiting the contradictions between norms. By establishing rules of the primacy of one norm over another, it reduces the risk of uncertainty in determining the behaviour to be adopted.

The hierarchy principle also applies to the relationship between internal law and international law. Article 5, paragraph 4 of Constitution obliges the Confederation and the cantons to respect international law. Article 199 of the Constitution stipulates that the Federal Supreme Court also has an obligation to enforce federal law and international law. Based on these provisions, Federal Supreme Court case law asserts the principle of the primacy of international law over internal law. However, the development of international law and internal law may create situations that are complex to unravel. Faced with potentially conflicting situations, it is up to the judge to settle conflicts between legal norms by calling on his or her power of interpretation, which in turn is based on several techniques. In this respect, the Federal Supreme Court brings in two additional elements. The first exception is that if the Federal Assembly knowingly adopts a law that contradicts an Swiss international commitment, that law takes precedence over the rule of international law. The second exception, which in fact constitutes a counter-exception to the preceding one, is that norms that guarantee human rights—such as the European Convention on Human Rights—always take precedence over federal laws that contradict them. These two exceptions formulated by the Federal Supreme Court serve as a reminder of the importance for institutions of these two key elements, namely respect for the democratic will and respect for human rights.

The distinction between norms of general scope and norms of individual scope

A final point to be made in this section on key elements for understanding the idea of the law as it relates to public administration is the distinction between norms of general scope and norms of individual scope. This distinction illustrates the difference between the legislative function and executive function, in which entities charged with public tasks participate.

A norm is said to be of general, abstract scope when it addresses a circle of targets that is not precisely defined and when it is written in general, abstract terms. A general norm is intended to last, since it will be applied repeatedly, that is, whenever situations that match its abstract hypothesis appear. It must, therefore, be able to regulate an indeterminate number of concrete situations. This manner of regulating societal relationships through norms of general scope has the advantage of providing a guarantee against arbitrariness to members of the society . This gives members of the society "legal certainty". This is because the principle of stability of a general rule enables addressees to consider their actions and the consequences thereof. Concretely, these are the types of norms enshrined in the articles of the Constitution, a law or an ordinance. Since these legal texts of different levels are entwined with each other, a constitutional norm will have the dimension of a principle that will progressively be specified by laws and ordinances. Administrative units participate in formulating a general norm as part of legislative procedure: they have a dominant role in the preparation of a legislative project. At times they may initiate a project, finding that the law needs to be supplemented.

Norms of individual, concrete scope, on the other hand, are aimed at a determined or determinable number of addressees. They are designed to resolve a state of affairs that is defined in time and space. They are the result of the application of a general norm in a concrete case by a competent body. This type of norm can be issued by an administrative unit, and also by a judge— for example, when a judge has to rule on the custody of children during divorce proceedings.

In Swiss positive law, the distinction between norms of general scope and norms of individual scope refers to the distinction between "legal rule" and "decision" (Table 5.1). Indeed, the qualities of a norm of general scope are expressly laid down in the Federal Act on the Federal Assembly (art. 22 para. 4, Lparl.). A legal rule must follow a specific adoption procedure, namely the legislative procedure. A decision on the other hand covers the various measures taken by authorities that attribute, declare or modify rights or obligations, or reject requests intended to assert these rights and obligations. All such decisions thus contain norms—or in other words, obligations— that have individual, concrete scope. As with a legal rule, formal requirements are also imposed on a body that renders a decision. It must comply with the administrative procedure and procedural guarantees for individuals concerned by the decision. However, an intermediate category of decisions has also emerged. These are decisions of general scope that have the characteristics of an individual decision (they concern a determined situation), but whose scope extends to an indeterminate number of persons. An example is the banning of a demonstration (Tanquerel 2018).

This distinction is a key element in understanding public action. It involves distinct formalities that must be fulfilled by a body that intends to make a legal act, which will take the shape either of a legal rule or a decision. When the body has a doubt regarding the legal form it should choose, it must examine whether a legal act, in order to produce its effects, needs to be made concrete by individual acts. If this is the case, the scope of the legal act to be adopted is still undetermined, which is a characteristic of a legal rule. The distinction also helps us to understand differences on the procedural level (competence, judicial remedy, publication and notification of the legal act).

Let us point out that between these two types of norms lie rules whose scope is less clear. These are decisions of general scope. They have a circle of addressees who, as in the case of legal rules, is undetermined and indeterminable. However, like (simple) decisions, they settle a state of affairs that is circumscribed in time and space.

	Legal rule	Decision of general scope	Decision
Addressee	general	general	individual
Situation	abstract	concrete	concrete

Table 5.1 Legal norms

5.2.2 Instruments of public action

The importance of the law for public administration lies not only in the fact that it is the basis and a framework for public action, but also in the fact that it offers a variety of instruments for action. In other words, it is a means available for the completion of public tasks. The elements discussed above have identified various types of instruments for conducting public action: laws, ordinances, decisions. However, not all the rules contained in these legal instruments are necessarily orders or commands. They may for example set objectives, or provide for coordination between stakeholders. Moreover, an administrative body has more than legal instruments at its disposal. As an authority charged with accomplishing public tasks, it must sometimes also take very concrete action. Actions of this type are known as material acts. This category of acts includes, for example, road construction, maintenance of parks, concrete execution of bank transfers, preventive health campaigns, etc. Lastly, in recent decades, in the face of global issues and under the influence of international organizations, other terms have been seen to emerge in the functioning of states and their respective administrative bodies, terms that appear to complement the simple, effective initial distinction between legal acts and material acts[10]. Examples are the recommendations, guidelines, strategies, action plans, partnerships and toolboxes that we see being communicated and sometimes even published

10 This development is also being seen in international organizations.

in official channels. Sometimes, private actors develop their own regulatory instruments (Black 2001). All these documents—produced by public or private actors and sometimes resulting from coordination between the two—are aimed at guiding and directing the behaviour of various stakeholders. These developments outside classical legal acts generally fall under what is called "soft law". This term conveys the idea of incentive norms, which encourage rather than compel a change in behaviour. The success of instruments of this type lies, first, in the absence of formalism with which they are developed and adopted—in contrast with legal formalism—and, second, the fact that they represent a calling into question of legal rules for obtaining the desired change or behaviour.

5.3 Future prospects and challenges

Public administration is no longer the sole prerogative of agents of the state, but can be entrusted to other organizations. It forms part of a multilevel governance approach, involving a host of stakeholders, whether these be other infra-state or state public authorities, international organizations, businesses or nonprofit organizations. Means of action have also multiplied, with codes of conduct, labels, etc. Governance is thus supported by an expansion of the instruments of public action. Legislation is no longer sufficient, and so the focus is on regulation (Morgan & Yeung 2007). These changes have not called into question the hierarchical conception of law, or the philosophy of the rule of law. But they have led to the emergence of certain dynamics that have had an impact on law, and more specifically on legislation. These dynamics may be related both to New Public Management and to the analysis of public policies. They allow us to assert that the law can no longer be considered as a separate domain, standing above other political, social and economic issues, but that it must also preserve its purpose, which is to guarantee the rule of law. Two challenges serve to illustrate these dynamics: first, the relationship between legislation and strategy and, second, the legislative process.

5.3.1 Coordinating legislation and strategy

As we have stated, public administration must be exercised in compliance with the principle of legality. Legislation determines what can be done, by whom, with what means, and how. Laws—understood in the wider sense as all legislative acts—create a framework that defines rights, obligations and procedures that must be respected and executed. On the one hand, public administration does not operate in a vacuum, executing its mission in an environment devoid of other factors. It has to deal with limited public resources, political commitments on the international or national level and economic, social and ecological environments. In short, its implementation must be carefully thought out and coordinated in view of all these constraints. To this end, political—or administrative—planning is seen as a means of facing up to all these constraints. This involves organizing and coordinating the various actors and setting fixed schedules.

From the point of view of public administration, infrastructure development and the management of financial or food resources demands programming. This activity implicitly derives from administrative management. However, planning also has a legislative dimension in parliamentary regimes, where the government is obliged to earn the confidence of parliament. It takes the form of speeches or programmes of legislation. Since parliament has the material competence to legislate, it also has the power to organize its legislative work. New Public Management has given the issue of planning a new impetus with goal-oriented governance, expressed in the form of a strategy and broadly developed and steered by the executive.

The drafting of strategies falls within the framework of public administration. Formulation is the responsibility of administrative units, depending on the field in question. Strategies provide a roadmap towards a specific objective. They determine principles for action which must then be implemented for each priority goal and the measures to be taken to achieve it. Planning therefore makes it possible to identify needs and means. Among these, it may be necessary to propose draft legislation to parliament, to write administrative-law contracts, or launch an information campaign. In doing so, the prospective law forms part of a policy set. It constitutes one among several elements in the realization of a public policy. The situation reminds us that every law is the product of a formalized political choice, to which the political system attributes a specific normative value, that of being able to be enforced by law.

Goal-oriented governance and the drafting of strategies do not however lead to inverting the pyramid. Political action, however strategic it might be, must be thought out and applied within the framework of the law. For example, the Confederation adopted a strategy on free access to public data for the 2014–2018 period. This strategy was based on article 180, paragraph 2 of the Constitution and article 10 of the GAOA. It therefore has a clear legal foundation. From the point of view of implementation, this strategy involved taking a whole series of measures, including making current law compliant. In other words, it demanded legislative changes. Strategy is thus a tool of public administration. Sometimes, it announces a political programme, which may raise questions in a democratic system where the legislative chambers are the dedicated place for public deliberation. In doing so, it calls for an effort to balance managerial rationale and legal rationale.

5.3.2 The "Better Regulation" approach

In the field of public administration, the law is a recurrent target of criticism. Among the charges are that it is inefficient, incomprehensible, or outdated, or that it holds back innovation (Ayres & Braithwaite 1992; Baldwin 1990). To answer these criticisms, a movement in favour of better legislation has emerged. As always, such a movement results from a combination of factors: scientific studies in the fields of law, economics and political sciences, a political context and, lastly, the issue being put on the institutional agenda. Today, it is known as "better regulation" and has even been elevated to a regulatory policy promoted by the OECD and the European Union (European Parliament, The Council of the European Union & The European Commission 2016). In short, it calls for a change in law-making processes. This involves going beyond the purely formal conception of formulating legal norms (formal legistics) and reflecting on building the substance of the norm (material legistics). This is a matter of linking projects such as those for good governance, better regulation and thus better legislation (Karpen 2017).

From a classical legal perspective, creating legislation is generally described as a longitudinal process whose stages are formalized and laid down in other laws. This process begins with a pre-parliamentary phase during which general, abstract norms that take the form of legal rules are drafted as part of a project. These norms are subject to an internal and external consultation procedure before being validated by the Federal Council. In the case of draft legislation, the bill will be sent to the Federal Assembly, where it will be debated in committee and then put to a vote in both legislative chambers. This is the parliamentary phase. At the end of this phase, in the specific case of Switzerland, the law is published in the Federal Gazette, which marks the beginning of the referendum period, during which the people can contest the proposed legislation. This is the referendum phase. Once the referendum deadline has passed, the legislation is published officially and comes into force. This process, which emphasizes the legislative procedure dictated by law, is however no longer sufficient to meet the expectations of good governance.

The better-regulation movement, building on studies of public governance, proposes a much more highly developed programme of action. It argues for placing the public problem to be resolved at the centre of the legislative intervention, thus attempting to provide a framework for the issue of interests that is inherent in any deliberation. To this end, this programme recommends beginning by understanding the various facets of the problem in question. Empirical data serve to document the problem. This evidence-based approach must make it possible to identify the problem's dimension and dynamics. The causes and consequences must next be analysed. Analysis is used to define the objectives to be pursued and to identify the means to be mobilized in order to attain them. To avoid the danger of glossing over certain points, and that of an intervention simply creating more problems, the analysis process must include a risk analysis and must be participatory. The participatory dimension will bring to light the various interests and expectations of the addressees of the norm. It will also provide an opportunity for gathering the opinion of experts. The risk analysis will allow an assessment of the legal, political, economic, social and even environmental dimensions. From a legal point of view, this is a matter of ensuring, for example, that the state is competent to act, that the means for action respect the principle of proportionality, and that there is no contradiction between the draft legislation and existing legal obligations. All these elements form a preliminary stage which must then guide the organization in its reflections about the norm that it intends to develop. They will enable it to formulate the norm. Adoption of the norm can then take a definitive or experimental form (Ranchordás 2014). In either case, its application will require a further *a posteriori* evaluation to assess its relevance for resolving the public problem. Lastly, the idea that the legislative solution is adopted once and for all is called into question. Proponents of the better-regulation movement advocate the use of experimental legislation, overseen by a scientific protocol, that in time allows a decision on whether the legislative response should be made permanent or adapted. They also argue that laws should have a limited lifetime. This is the assumption behind the sunset legislation that was adopted by the federal legislature concerning the application of contact tracing for COVID-19.

Swiss jurists did not wait for the better-regulation movement to tackle the question of producing relevant legislation, that is, laws likely to attain the desired goals, with reasonable use of available means and without producing disproportionate collateral effects, and being sufficiently comprehensible to be enforceable. Indeed, the development of the field of legisprudence from the 1980s onwards (Mader 1985) followed by the creation of the Swiss Evaluation Society shows that the Swiss Confederation has been one of the forerunners in this field and that the legislative process involves not only legal competences, but also competences in the fields of project management and evaluation. The production of legislation guides testifies to this commitment (Federal Office of Justice 2019). Although all the steps of the better-regulation project are featured in these guides, they have not yet fully incorporated the cyclical perspective of better legislation (Flückiger 2019).

Key concepts

- Decision (*décision, Verfügung, decisione*): in the legal sense, the term designates a measure taken unilaterally by a public authority in respect of a specific case for the purpose of creating, modifying or withdrawing the rights or obligations of a private individual. Such a measure must follow the procedural rules to be legitimate.

- Legal rule (*règle de droit, Rechtssatz, stato di diritto*): a term in Swiss law that designates laws which, in a general, abstract manner, grant rights, create obligations or determine competences.
- Principle of legality (*principe de la légalité, Legalitätsprinzip, principio di legalità*): a legal term designating a general rule of binding scope whose purpose is to assert that the activities of public authorities must be based on a clear, precise law.
- Soft law: a term that designates behaviour-oriented norms without legally binding force that may take various textual forms.
- Sources of law (*sources du droit, Rechtsquellen, fonti di diritto*): a term that, as used by jurists, designates the formal constituents of law (legislation, case law, established doctrine and customary law).

References

Ayres, I. & Braithwaite, J. (1992). *Responsive Regulation: Transcending the Deregulation Debate.* Oxford University Press.

Baldwin, R. (1990). Why Rules Don't Work. *The Modern Law Review, 53*(3), 321–337. Retrieved from http://www.jstor.org/stable/1096474 (accessed 17.11.2022)

Black, J. (2001). Decentring Regulation: Understanding the Role of Regulation and Self-Regulation in a 'Post-Regulatory' World. *Current Legal Problems, 54*(1), 103–146. https://doi.org/10.1093/clp/54.1.103 (accessed 17.11.2022)

Bundesamt für Justiz. (2019). *Gesetzgebungsleitfaden. Leitfaden für die Ausarbeitung von Erlassen des Bundes.* Schweizerische Eidgenossenschaft.

European Parliament, The Council of the European Union, & The European Commission. (2016). *Inter-institutional Agreement on Better Law-Making.*

Flückiger, A. (2019). *(Re)faire la loi. Traité de légistique à l'ère du droit souple.* Schulthess.

Karpen, U. (2017). Introduction. In U. Karpen, H. Xanthaki, L. Mader, W. Voermans, & R. Cormacain (Eds.), *Legislation in Europe: A Comprehensive Guide for Scholars and Practitioners* (1st ed., pp. 1–16). Hart Publishing.

Mader, L. (1985). *L'évaluation législative. Pour une analyse empirique des effets de la législation.* Payot.

Morgan, B. & Yeung, K. (2007). *An Introduction to Law and Regulation: Text and Materials.* Cambridge University Press.

Ranchordás, S. (2014). *Constitutional sunsets and experimental legislation: a comparative perspective*: Edward Elgar Publishing.

Tanquerel, T. (2018). *Manuel de droit administratif* (2nd ed.). Schulthess.

References for further study

Flückiger, A. (2019). Le droit souple cantonal : quand les conférences intercantonales recommandent, les réglementations s'harmonisent. In M. Hottelier, M. Hertig Randall, & A. Flückiger (Eds.), *Etudes en l'honneur du Professeur Thierry tanquerel : entre droit constitutionnel et droit administratif: questions autour du droit de l'action publique* (pp. 109–126). Université de Genève.

Moor, P., Martenet, V. & Flückiger, A. (2012). *Droit administratif / Vol. 1, Les fondements* (3rd ed., completely revised, updated and expanded). Stämpfli.

Waldmann, B. & Wiederkehr, R. (2019). *Allgemeines Verwaltungsrecht*. Schulthess.

6 Ethics

Sophie Weerts

6.1 The importance of ethics for public administration

Philosophically speaking, ethics involves reflecting on values, that is, on the set of perceptions that guide individual behaviour in a given society. Ethics is thus closely linked to the field of morality, with emphasis on the process of discussion that leads us to reflect on what is right and just. It can therefore be understood as "reflection that leads to choices, based on prioritized values and standards" (Lacroix 2011: 108).

In the academic field of ethics, a number of approaches are found: normative ethics, descriptive ethics, theoretical ethics and applied ethics. The first of these approaches, normative ethics, examines values that should guide individual behaviour. It is very close to morality. The second, descriptive ethics, seeks to discover the moral principles underlying ethical opinions, without taking a position on them. For this, descriptive ethics needs theoretical ethics, which sets out the various philosophical theories behind our decisions and positions. The fourth approach, applied ethics, is based on the idea that, at a more operational level, a deliberative framework can be formulated to support action and decision-making. The purpose of applied ethics, then, is to articulate a coherent conception of morality that can generate these responses and justify them with a reflective approach (Wyser 2016).

Generally speaking, it can be said that both normative ethics (concerned with the definition of values) and applied ethics (aimed at promoting a reflective approach) are more important than ever in the field of public administration. There are a number of reasons for this. The first is the need for citizens to be able to trust public organizations (Dobel 2005). The development of the information society since the 1990s has led to greater awareness of scandals and misconduct inside public authorities and organizations. Situations like these are liable to create a climate of mistrust towards those whose job it is to act for and in the name of the general interest, and could ultimately call democracy into question. This explains the development of calls for more morality, more ethics, in the public space. The second reason is administrative reform and the changing role of the state, which have brought about many changes, including decentralization, greater budget autonomy and a networked approach to public goods and services. These elements have changed not only the internal workings of public administration, but also its framework for action. These changes have been seen as blurring the values that are central to the professional identity of those serving the state. Here, it is the question of redefining values and implementing them in day-to-day management that justifies a focus on ethics. A final factor is the role of legislation and the law in general in managing social, economic, technological and environmental issues. Beginning in the 1990s, the law—the instrument of reference for governing in the context of Weberian administration—began to mutate slowly. Other forms of governance emerged with the principle of accountability, risk- or benefit-analysis approaches, and public and social values (Bennett & Raab 2018). This explains the renewed interest in ethics in many fields, including medical sciences, environmental protection and data protection.

The need for a high level of probity in the performance of public duties, the loss of reference points in terms of public values and, finally, the wider margin of discretion given to those engaged in public tasks are all factors that help to explain the importance given to the subject of ethics in public administration. In this transformed public administration, ethics becomes a resource that complements the law.

6.2 Key points of ethics

In this section devoted to key points, we begin by reviewing the reasons why, regarding public administration, the resurgence of interest in ethics is justified (§ 6.2.1). We then turn to the two models of ethics management found in public administration: compliance with norms, and integrity (§ 6.2.2). The second—integrity—has developed substantially since the late 2000s, warranting closer attention. We will show how this is reflected on the normative level (§ 6.2.3).

6.2.1 Reasons for the renewed interest in ethics in public administration

An institutional discourse on ethics developed in the 1990s. Two elements, linked to two moments in the history of public administration (▶ IDHEAP Model of Public Administration: Overview), explain this renewed interest in ethics in public administration (Hijal-Moghrabi & Sabharwal 2018).

Hybridization of public-sector values

The first element to rekindle reflection on the values underlying public administration was the deployment of administrative reforms aimed at introducing New Public

Management (▶ 1 Values). Some have stressed the negative impact of these reforms on the ethics of public administration, given the weakening of control mechanisms in favour of greater decentralization of powers and responsibilities, which is perceived as bringing a risk of increased corruption. Others considered that it would in fact bring the benefit of a reduced risk of corruption. In any case, empirical research has shown that this period of administrative reform has resulted in the values of public administration being rearranged, leading to a form of hybridization of values (Emery & Giauque 2014; Wyser 2016).

Hybridization reflects the idea that public administration has found itself at the confluence of two organizational models. On the one hand stands the Weberian model, predominant in public administration in the institutional sense throughout the 20th century, which is characterized by its rational-legal approach. In practical terms, this means that all public action is viewed through the prism of the law. Respect for legal rules (and hence the rule of law), respect for hierarchical power, the sense of public interest and the principles of neutrality and equal treatment are the defining elements of the organizational line of conduct of those who serve the state. All these elements are reflected in the value of legality. In this context, those who work for the administration are executors. On the other hand stands the corporate organizational model, to which New Public Management subscribes. In this case, the reference value is efficiency. Results are the ultimate goal. In the corporate model, it is important for individuals to have the leeway to mobilize the resources they need to attain an objective, while accommodating the constraints of the environment. Respect for the law then becomes another constraint to be worked with. The administrative reforms implementing New Public Management led to the increasing power of the value of efficiency.

The Weberian model had the advantage of providing a particularly clear framework for action: the law and the hierarchical order guided those in the service of the state. Through a series of reforms such as management by budget and the public-policy perspective, the New Public Management model increased state employees' room for manoeuvre, generating a degree of confusion as to the limits of their action and decision-making power. It is therefore understandable that this situation led people to imagine a frame of reference other than that of the law, which had been the point of reference in the Weberian model.

Overlapping of public and private sectors

The second reason for the renewed interest in ethics in 21st-century public administration is the deployment of this functional conception of public administration. The tasks involved in guaranteeing or strengthening access for all to public goods and services have become so diverse and so complex that the state is no longer able to pursue its public missions in an environment marked by budgetary and human-resource constraints. In this context, formal and informal collaborations and partnerships have developed between administrative units, private companies and associations.

However, in this new context, not all those involved in the provision of access to public goods and services have the same degree of adherence to the notion of public interest. A private company involved in or performing public tasks remains an organization based on the idea of profit. A foundation will also have an interest in getting involved for the purpose of obtaining grants. As a result, and as Dominique Hänni rightly points out, government employees find themselves in an environment where interactions with the private sector are becoming much more frequent. This may involve representation on boards of directors, negotiations in public or semi-public projects, piloting prevention or information campaigns, or control and monitoring of private actors involved in the pursuit of public tasks. Added to this is the fact that their margin of discretion has been significantly extended by the development of laws that are increasingly taking the form—especially in the field of public policy—of programme standards or rules containing legal concepts that are unclear (Hänni 2019).

The environment in which public administration operates has altered the limits of an organizational framework based on the hierarchical line, further highlighting employee responsibility. This second reason, then, explains the emergence of the need to establish a frame of reference that complements legal rules to guide the behaviour of all. As we shall see, the discourse on ethics in public administration seeks to respond to the risks resulting from this new environment.

6.2.2 Ways of promoting ethics

Studies on ethics in public administration (Graycar 2020) have highlighted two approaches to improving ethical behaviour in public administration: compliance with standards, and integrity. The second of these—integrity—has come to the fore in the development of functional public administration. It advocates the implementation of a series of formal, informal and organizational measures, which are now expressed through the concept of ethical infrastructure, to address the risks of influence that those who have to make decisions in the context of public administration may have to face.

The distinction between compliance with standards and integrity

The question of ethics in public administration was first seen from the angle of the behaviour of public servants and the determination of the rules that should govern their behaviour. This initial conception was perfectly aligned with the Weberian model. It postulated the formalization of rules of behaviour, procedures and control mechanisms. This approach aligns with the idea of disciplinary law, a sub-branch of public-service law, or deontology (Bodiguel 2002). It echoes a particular conception of the legal relationship between the state and its agents. It also evokes the initial conception of behaviour regulation, based on control and sanction. In so doing, it seeks to go beyond ethics, in that legal rules are what set out the (ethical) behaviour to be followed. These rules are based on initial values such as protecting the public's trust and upholding the reputation of the state. They thus reflect some elements of normative ethics. Concretely, however, the moral legitimacy of behaviour is assessed in the light of existing criminal and disciplinary rules. In terms of substance, normative ethics focuses on the fight against corruption, fraud and abuse of power, and on discipline and neutrality. In terms of form, this conception takes a repressive approach and relies on legal instruments such as laws and ordinances.

A second approach to ethics in public administration has emerged. It is more closely aligned with the field of applied ethics. In his book *Ethics for bureaucrats*, Rohr (1989) argued the need to evolve from an approach aimed at avoiding scandals to one in which those who govern must develop a sense of virtue, the need to move from a culture of repression to one of promotion. This idea echoes the "reflective equilibrium" exercise advocated in 1971 by Rohr's compatriot, the American philosopher John Rawls (Rawls 1971). This new approach is founded on the idea of integrity, which can be defined as "a quality or characteristic of the behaviour of actors in accordance with relevant moral values, norms and rules" (L. Huberts & van Montfort 2020: 450). Here, therefore, public administration is called upon to promote a philosophy encouraging the development of appropriate behaviour. Such a philosophy implies creating an environment characterized by incentives rather than repressive measures. It utilizes informal means and organizational measures rather than focusing solely on inappropriate behaviour. Also, integrity is based on the premise that not everything is dictated in advance, that those who work in public organizations are subject to ethical dilemmas and that, as a result, they need specific help, which must be provided through various measures.

A more holistic, reflective perspective of integrity has been deemed better suited to 21st-century public administration. It moves beyond the traditional regulatory, legal approach focused on penalties. It favours a mode of governance that can call on a wide range of instruments to influence the behaviour of individuals, but is also able to adapt, given the reflexive dimension, to the changing context of organizations.

Risk analysis and ethical infrastructure

The concept of ethical infrastructure was proposed by the OECD in its work on ethical behaviour in public administration in the late 1990s (OECD 1997). The idea of infrastructure here refers to a panoply of regulatory tools and processes to prevent undesirable behaviour and encourage good conduct. These tools are independent elements, but they must all be deployed to provide public administration with a strong infrastructure that will enable it to prevent undesirable behaviour. In this way, they are aimed at responding to risks that can be identified in the way public organizations operate.

The goal of developing an ethical infrastructure is to deal with potential ethical risks. Accordingly, the first step is to identify decision-making centres where one or more risks may be present. This can be done by identifying the processes and functions within public organizations in which government employees may have to make decisions that are binding on the organization. The aim is to identify sources of vulnerability. For example, Maesschalk (2008) identified processes involved in purchasing goods and services, promoting staff, and inspecting and monitoring.

The ethical infrastructure that each organization must develop will therefore include a series of instruments, procedures and measures to guide those involved in public administration. These measures fall into three categories: orientation, management and control.

An *orientation towards ethical behaviour* is aimed at promoting and raising awareness of ethical issues and ethical behaviour among employees of public entities at an early stage. Awareness can be raised directly by reminding staff of the criminal and ethical rules applicable to public officials and private organizations performing public tasks. It can also be instilled by the adoption and dissemination of a specific code of conduct for a public authority or organization. Training contributes directly to raising awareness of ethical behaviour and to developing the skills needed to resolve ethical dilemmas.

Management of ethical issues can be handled through an organizational and regulatory structure. On an organizational level, a special body or central management department can play a coordinating role. On the regulatory level, this can be enshrined in human-resources management policies and practices, which must guarantee job security, promotion prospects and fair remuneration.

Control of conduct will involve unwanted behaviours being criminalized and opportunities for independent investigation and prosecution of violations being set up, with effective accountability and control mechanisms that not only discourage problematic behaviour, but also enable it to be detected easily. Information and protection systems for whistle-blowers, and internal and external monitoring systems, can also contribute to this control dimension. This can be the work of a parliamentary management committee. Lastly, transparency rules also contribute to the establishment of the ethical infrastructure.

6.2.3 Normative framework of integrity

Deployment of ethics in public administration through the "integrity approach" began to take shape in the mid-1990s. In addition to the fact that the state is currently criticized for being slow, formalist and bureaucratic, a series of scandals have tarnished the reputation of public organizations. Scandals are seen by states as risk factors for democracy, because they gradually erode the trust of citizens that democratic institutions must enjoy in order to justify their political legitimacy. This situation has led to the widespread engagement of international organizations promoting liberal and democratic values, which have adopted a series of legal texts and political declarations with inevitable repercussions in Switzerland.

At the international level

In 1996, the United Nations General Assembly started the ball rolling by adopting its code of conduct for international public servants. It recommends that states use it as a model in their fight against corruption. In 2003, the UN adopted its first legal instrument: the United Nations Convention against Corruption.

The Council of Europe has also taken up the theme of ethics in public administration, considering it to be a key element in preserving trust in governments and respect for democracy, the rule of law and human rights. In 1999, it in turn adopted a legal text, its Criminal Law Convention on Corruption and, later, an additional protocol, to which Switzerland has acceded. The Group of States against Corruption (GRECO), set up within this framework, monitors the implementation of international anti-corruption commitments in member states, including Switzerland. In addition, a number of resolutions and recommendations have been adopted, such as the Committee of Ministers Resolution 97 (24) on the twenty guiding principles for the fight against corruption, Resolution 79 (1999) on the political integrity of local and regional elected representatives, Recommendation (2000) 10 on codes of conduct for public officials, Recommendation (2002) 2 on access to public documents, Recommendation (2007) 7 on good administration, Recommendation (2014) 7 on the protection of whistle-blowers and Recommendation (2017) 2 on the legal regulation of lobbying activities in the context of public decision-making.

The Organisation for Economic Co-operation and Development (OECD) has also been very active in promoting ethics in public administration. It has made the fight against corruption, and more generally the promotion of integrity, one of its main causes. In 1997, the Convention on Combating Bribery of Foreign Public Officials in International Business Transactions was signed. Under Swiss law, this convention came into force in 2000. The OECD has adopted several recommendations for its member states. In 1998, it published a recommendation on improving ethical conduct in the public service, which was updated and replaced in 2017 by the Recommendation on Public Integrity (OECD 2017). The OECD also adopted Guidelines for Managing Conflict of Interest in the Public Service in 2003, and a recommendation on strengthening integrity in public procurement (2008/2013). In 2010, it issued a recommendation to its member states on Principles for Transparency and Integrity in Lobbying.

All these international texts show that the discourse of international organizations initially focused on the issue of corruption among public officials, before widening to encompass supervision of their conduct in their duties (transparency, respect for integrity in the exercise of their functions), protection for those who denounce problematic conduct within the public service and the need to supervise lobbying.

At the national level

While Switzerland has demonstrated its determination to combat corruption by ratifying all the above-mentioned international conventions, it has also adapted its legal framework by adopting a series of normative rules.

Thus, the Confederation has made it a criminal offence to grant undue advantages (art. $322^{quinquies}$) and to accept undue advantages (art. 322^{sexies}). It also ensures that bribes and kickbacks can no longer be deducted from taxable income. Like the cantons, it adopted a law on transparency. It also made up for shortcomings identified by the GRECO by introducing transparency requirements for the funding of political parties and election campaigns. Measures are also included in the legal rules governing the employment relationship between public organizations and their employees, and in the legislation governing the organization of public services and public authorities. Furthermore, on 15 August 2012, the Confederation adopted a Code of Conduct for staff of the federal administration aimed at preventing conflicts of interest and the misuse of non-public information, and on 5 November 2014, an Aide-mémoire for members of the Federal Council and the Chancellor of the Confederation.

A series of normative measures have thus already been taken at federal and cantonal level. While it is not possible to give a complete picture of these measures here, it should be noted that regulations are disparate due to federalism. We can, however, identify the main themes. One is personal incompatibilities (whether due to family, institutional or economic ties), which are detailed in federal and cantonal laws relating to public officials or in special laws relating to specific public organizations. These laws must, however, be supported by recusal processes and verification mechanisms to prevent them from becoming a dead letter. The matter of ancillary activities has also been regulated in a series of texts, prescribing obligations to register, authorize or retrocede a share of the income earned. Prohibition or strict regulation of the acceptance of benefits and declarations and registers of interest are also part of the fight against corruption. Certain behaviours, however, can be seen as particularly tricky to decipher on the grounds that they may fall within the scope of criminal law. On the one hand, disclosure of information obtained in the course of one's work may constitute a breach of official secrecy, but on the other hand, it may be seen as necessary in a democratic, transparent society.

6.3 Future prospects and challenges

Public administration faces three challenges in the area of ethics. The first is to maintain an open conception of integrity in order to go beyond merely monitoring compliance with predefined standards of behaviour. This brings with it the second challenge, which is of an operational nature: the question of how, in practice, to reinforce ethics in a public administration that can no longer rely on a single organizational infrastructure. The third challenge is deploying the integrity approach beyond the bounds of administrative units, thus covering all stakeholders involved in public administration.

As we have seen, many points are now regulated with a view to guaranteeing the integrity of public administration. While a list of these points reveals a series of themes to be examined in public decision-making processes, they should be seen as a minimum standard, to be considered as evolving in line with developments in public administration. They must also be accompanied by protection and sanction measures, because the primary goal is to develop a public administration that inspires trust in citizens. This goal also demonstrates the normative reflex that accompanies integrity in public administration. While standards are important from an integrity perspective, they are not enough. In other words, for ethics to be a resource for public administration, adopting standards in formal or pseudo-formal texts is not enough. We cannot limit ourselves to integrity as a closed concept, but must rather accept its evolving, and therefore open, dimension.

Following on from this first challenge, the second challenge then arises, that of implementing other aspects of the integrity infrastructure, namely informal and organizational measures. As Fortier and Emery have pointed out, this is the fundamental issue of operationalization (Fortier & Emery 2015). In this respect, work on leadership and a commitment to exemplarity can be seen as key points for implementing ethical operation in public administration (▶ 9 Leadership). For example, a shift from strong leadership to participative leadership (one that emphasizes the democratic foundation of public administration) could strengthen a commitment to upholding and protecting the public interest. Another element that must not be lost sight of is ethics training (Wyser 2013). Provided that such training can successfully combine the sharing of theoretical knowledge with practical learning through the analysis of ethical dilemmas, it will contribute to strengthening ethics in public administration.

Given the functional line that public administration is taking in the first decades of the 21st century, expanding ethical principles and standards beyond the realm of public organizations is evidently necessary. Hänni (2019) has pointed to a number of elements that indicate that such a movement is well under way in Switzerland. The management committee of the Council of States has recommended that the Federal Council actively monitor the interests of directors of companies that have close ties to the Confederation. In the field of public procurement, the Federal Procurement Conference recommends that contracting authorities include an integrity clause in contracts with private companies, with the aim of preventing corruption. Any breach of this clause should lead to cancellation of the award and immediate termination of the public procurement contract, with the company being required to pay a contractual penalty. Regarding links of interest, in 2016 the Federal Supreme Court ruled that the private-law nature of the legal relationship between Swissmedic[11] and experts did not justify the withholding of information relating to links of interest between them, on the grounds that it was in the public interest to ensure that the experts had no problematic conflicts of interest, given that they were called upon to draft reports in the drug admission procedure (ATF 142 II 340). The 2018 Car postal scandal[12] and the 2020 Crypto AG scandal[13] showed that ethical issues go far beyond questions of corruption and personal advantage, but can also arise in the organizational conduct of an entity. It should also be borne in mind that, in the view of the Federal Supreme Court, it is not only problematic conduct *per se* that must be combated, but any conduct that has the appearance of a lack of integrity. Hänni also notes that in the area of transparency and administrative control, the results of the analysis are more mixed. Regarding the cantons, several cantonal transparency laws apply to centralized and decentralized units, as well as to legal entities and private-law bodies over which the state exercises effective control. On this point, then, some cantons have gone further than the Confederation, but as we have shown, an in-depth analysis should be carried out at every institutional level, just as a set of tools, processes and regulations should be deployed to prevent undesirable behaviour and encourage good conduct in keeping with the ethos of public administration.

11 Swissmedic, an autonomous public-law entity of the Swiss Confederation, is the licensing and supervisory authority for therapeutic products. It is empowered to contract freely with other legal entities, such as experts.

12 The Car postal scandal involved a public-subsidy fraud scheme. Through an accounting system, the state-owned company collected funding that was not due from the Confederation, cantons and municipalities. It repaid CHF 205 million to the injured parties. Car postal's management resigned in June 2018, its entire board of directors was dismissed and the unit was reorganized.

13 Crypto AG is a privately owned Swiss company that markets message-encryption solutions. In 2020, an international media investigation revealed that the company had been infiltrated by the American and German secret services, and was rigging its encryption systems to enable spying on countries that were clients of the Swiss company. A parliamentary investigation found that the Swiss intelligence services were aware of the espionage from Switzerland and had failed to inform the Federal Council.

Key concepts

- Conflict of interest (*conflit d'intérêts, Interessenkonflikt, conflitto di interesse*): a situation of proven or apparent interference between a public interest and public or private interests likely to influence the independent, impartial and objective exercise of a function.
- Corruption (*corruption, Korruption, corruzione*): in the legal sense, the act of soliciting, offering, giving or accepting, directly or indirectly, an undue advantage or a promise of such an advantage that affects the normal exercise of a function or the behaviour of its beneficiary.
- Integrity (*intégrité, Integrität, integrità*): a quality of a person or organization that acts in accordance with certain principles or values, such as impartiality, loyalty, responsibility or honesty.

References

Bennett, C. J. & Raab, C. D. (2018). Revisiting the governance of privacy: Contemporary policy instruments in global perspective. *Regulation & Governance, 14*(3), 447–464. https://doi.org/10.1111/rego.12222 (accessed 21.11.2022).

Bodiguel, J.-L. (2002). Pourquoi a-t-on tant besoin d'éthique ? *Éthique publique, 4*(1). https://doi.org/10.4000/ethiquepublique.2476 (accessed 21.11.2022).

Dobel, P. (2005). Public management as ethics. In E. Ferlie, L. Lynn & C. Pollitt (Eds.), *The Oxford handbook of public management* (pp. 156–181). Oxford University Press.

Emery, Y. & Giauque, D. (2014). The hybrid universe of public administration in the 21st century. *International Review of Administrative Sciences, 80*(1), 23–32. https://doi.org/10.1177/0020852313513378 (accessed 21.11.2022).

Fortier, I. & Emery, Y. (2015). L'éthos public en tant que processus social dynamique. *Pyramides, 22*, 83–114.

Graycar, A. (Ed.) (2020). *Handbook on corruption, ethics and integrity in public administration.* Edward Elgar Publishing.

Hänni, D. (2019). *Vers un principe d'intégrité de l'administration publique. La prévention de la corruption en droit administratif.* Schulthess.

Hijal-Moghrabi, I. & Sabharwal, M. (2018). Ethics in American public administration: A response to a changing reality. *Public Integrity, 20*, 1–19. https://doi.org/10.1080/10999922.2017.1419053 (accessed 21.11.2022).

Huberts, L. & van Montfort, A. (2020). Building ethical organisations: The importance of organisation integrity systems. In A. Graycar (Ed.), *Handbook on corruption, ethics and integrity in public administration* (pp. 450–462). Edward Elgar Publishing.

Lacroix, A. (2011). L'insuffisance du droit en matière d'éthique ou les lois sur l'éthique : voyage au pays de l'absurde ! *Éthique publique, 13*(1), 95–115.

OECD (1997). Creating an effective ethics infrastructure. *Focus Public Management Gazette*. 7, 1.
OECD (2017). *Recommendation of the Council on Public Integrity*. https://legalinstruments.oecd.org/en/instruments/OECD-LEGAL-0435 (accessed 21.02.2024).
Rawls, J. (1971). *A theory of justice*. Harvard University Press.
Wyser, C. (2013). Éthique. In A. Ladner, J.-L. Chappelet, JY. Emery, P. Knoepfler, L. Mader, N. Soguel & F. Varone (Eds.), *Manuel d'administration publique suisse* (pp. 541–558). Presses polytechniques et universitaires romandes.
Wyser, C. (2016). L'éthique publique : entre conformité et intégrité. In Y. Emery & D. Giauque (Eds.), *L'acteur et la bureaucratie au XXIe siècle* (pp. 303–327). Presses de l'Université Laval.

References for further study

Huberts, L. W. J. C. (2018). Integrity: What it is and why it is important. *Public Integrity, 20*(sup1), S18–S32. https://doi.org/10.1080/10999922.2018.1477404 (accessed 21.11.2022).
Kolthoff, E., Huberts, L. & Van den Heuvel, P. (2006). The integrity of new public management: is integrity at stake? *Public Administration Quarterly, (30)*3/4, 399–439.

7 Strategy

Oliver Neumann

7.1 The importance of strategy and its implementation for public administration

Strategic management is one of the key responsibilities of an organization's senior management. It serves to create a common direction within the organization, define general goals and formulate a plan to achieve them. Strategies can help members of an entity to understand the purpose of organizational action and indicate the direction to which common effort should be directed. They also make it possible to systematically measure success against objectives, and to make more targeted and therefore more efficient use of resources.

The origins of the word "strategy" date back to ancient Greece, where it roughly meant "commanding an army". It was not until the 1960s that the term came to be used in business contexts, to apply to competitive struggles rather than wars and battles.

In the public sector, strategy remained relatively unimportant until the 1980s. Things began to change with the introduction of reforms inspired by the New Public Management (NPM) movement. As a result, the management style of many public-sector organizations has come to resemble that of the private sector. These reforms, which originated in English-speaking countries and gradually spread to continental Europe, have strengthened the autonomy, flexibility and accountability of managers in public organizations. They have also laid the foundations for a new type of strategic management at the operational management stage—that is, at a level below that of political management (Stewart 2004). Consequently, it has become increasingly difficult to assert that the strategic direction of a public organization depends solely on political decisions.

Paradoxically, strategy as a management tool is still less widely used in the public sector than in the private sector. This is surprising, given that strategic management offers public organizations considerable opportunities. It allows an organization to be run more effectively and efficiently, by setting a common direction and making it possible to concentrate resources and strengths. Strategy also mitigates the risk of inertia in public organizations which, in the absence of competition or external pressure, might be tempted to simply maintain the status quo, thus becoming incapable of adapting to a constantly changing context. Strategy can therefore be an essential element in transforming a culture of pure management into one of future-oriented achievement within public organizations. A shining example of the full extent of the problems that can arise from a lack of strategy in public organizations is the discussion about the digitalization of public administration, with a large proportion of the population today expressing little satisfaction with the quantity and quality of digital services on offer (▶ 14 Digital transformation). Many public organizations simply failed to develop digitalization strategies early enough and implement them rigorously, whereas many private organizations had done so long before.

One possible explanation for this dichotomy between the public and private sectors lies in the absence of competition within public organizations, since developing strategies to "beat the opposition" generally proves simply pointless. Moreover, those who take a sceptical view of strategy implementation in public organizations claim that the approach is expensive and time-consuming, that strategic management quickly becomes purely bureaucratic, and that the organizations concerned lose flexibility. Added to this is the fact that alternatives and opportunities not defined in the strategy are more likely to be missed because of an excessively strict focus on the strategy. If ad-hoc instruments are properly implemented, however, these criticisms prove unfounded. Consequently, the importance of strategy in public organizations needs to be analysed in greater depth. This exercise must also consider the adaptation of existing strategies, based on the emergence of new instruments and research findings.

The purpose of this contribution is precisely to examine in detail the subject of strategy in public organizations. In the following section, we explore the key concepts of strategy and strategic management. We will then address the aspects of strategy and strategic management that specifically apply to public organizations, including the interrelationships between politics and administration, and the specific features of public authorities' target systems. We present the various existing strategies and identify the typical components of a strategy document. We also make concrete recommendations for managers of public-sector organizations to help them better grasp the growing demands of strategic management and thus lead their organizations on the path to success. In the third and final section, we discuss possible future developments and challenges for the strategic approach in the public sector.

7.2 Key points of strategy and strategic management

In a field of research as highly developed as strategy, it is hardly surprising that definitions abound. According to Porter (1996), the essence of strategy is the deliberate choosing of what *not* to do. This definition is special in that it underlines the importance of using limited resources sparingly. Applying a strategy thus means not only doing new things, but also no longer doing certain things. Johnson *et al.* (2020), on the other hand, define strategy as "the long-term direction of an organization". This relatively abstract conception purposefully allows for several ways of formulating a strategy, for example a written statement or a strategy which, although existing, remains implicit. This conception also underlines the importance of thinking actively about the future.

Mintzberg (1987) discerns five different conceptions of strategy, known as the five Ps: strategy as *plan*, as *ploy*, as *pattern*, as *position* and as *perspective*. Strategy as plan is "some sort of *consciously intended* course of action, a guideline (or set of guidelines), to deal with a situation" (Mintzberg 1987: 11). In this conception, strategy is a plan drawn up in advance, developed intentionally and purposefully. The purpose of such a plan is to define certain core objectives for an organization, so that they can then be put into practice. The plan can be formulated in a very general way or in a very specific way, to address a particular situation or issue. A classic example of this conception of strategy is the battle plan. In a public administration or a private company, this could be a digitalization plan aimed at making full use of the potential of new digital technologies to achieve the organization's core objectives.

The second conception, *strategy as ploy*, is in fact a subset of the first. It refers to a very specific manoeuvre in a concrete situation—one designed to get ahead of or neutralize a competitor, for example. Another example would be a city deciding to buy back a derelict industrial site to build social housing, rather than leaving the initiative to a private investor planning to build luxury housing.

The third conception, *strategy as pattern*, sees strategy as a "pattern in a stream of actions" (Mintzberg 1987: 12). Here, strategy is aimed at achieving consistency between decisions and practices, whether they are intentional or not. The pattern does not have to be written down and may simply emerge over time. This conception therefore differs significantly from those of plan and ploy. An example would be a public organization in which it is generally accepted that day-to-day activities are more important than innovation (▶ 17 Innovation). The result of this attitude is that no processes of innovation are launched, or that efforts in that direction are not supported, and the status quo remains the only strategic pattern. Mintzberg refers to this as "emergent strategy", as opposed to "plan" and "ploy", which he terms "intentional strategy". Both types can exist simultaneously, and together they form a "realized strategy" (possibly excluding certain elements that were included in the plan, but which were ultimately not implemented).

Mintzberg's final two conceptions are more abstract. *Strategy as position* involves attempting to position the organization successfully in its external environment. This might mean finding a niche for the organization's activities, so that only a minimum of competition needs to be faced, or making the organization irreplaceable. Available resources could then be focused on this niche.

Strategy as perspective involves creating an understanding of the external context or a shared philosophy within the organization, going beyond the organization's positioning. This cultural dimension can also be seen as an organization's "personality", which can be somewhat aggressive and progressive (Tesla, for example) or conservative and stability-oriented (like a public archive). For managers, it is especially important to understand that Mintzberg's conceptions are not mutually exclusive, but exist simultaneously and can complement or influence each other.

Now that the term strategy has been defined, let us turn to the notion of strategic management. Strategic management means the initiation and conduct of the entire strategic process, from strategic analysis of the situation, through the formulation of a strategy, the taking of appropriate measures to implement it, to the evaluation of the strategy's effectiveness and any necessary adjustments (▶ 16 Evaluation). Strategic management is therefore generally focused on an "intentional strategy", although it is also judicious to incorporate elements of an "emergent strategy". The different areas of strategic management should never be regarded as purely sequential, but rather as a continuous cycle, with numerous dependencies between the different tasks. In this sense, strategic management is an ongoing activity, not something that can be undertaken from time to time (see Poister 2010). As the term suggests, responsibility for strategic management lies with the managers in charge of the relevant areas. They can delegate specific strategic-management tasks, for example setting up task forces to develop a strategy for a specific area, in consultation with management, or handing over strategy-related communication to an outside agency.

Johnson *et al.* (2020) have developed a very useful matrix for practising strategic management. They divide the various tasks of strategic management into three circles: "strategic position", "strategic choices" and "strategy implementation" (see Figure 7.1).

The first circle, strategic position, encompasses the influence on strategy of external environmental factors, organizational resources and skills, overriding objectives and the culture of the organization. The questions that arise here, according to Johnson *et al.* (2020), are:

- What is the organization's *raison d'être* (▶ 2 Essential Functions)?
- What drives change in the external environment?

Figure 7.1 Elements of strategic management
Source: Johnson *et al.* (2020)

- How can the organization determine its competitive position or, in the case of the public sector, its distinguishing feature?
- What are the organization's specific skills?
- What are the expectations of the stakeholders concerned (▶ 3 Stakeholders)?
- Is the strategy suited to the organization's culture and ethical principles (▶ 1 Values)?

The second circle, strategic choices, covers options available for both the strategy itself and the approach required to implement it. The questions that arise here are generally:

- What operating strategy or business model should be applied?
- What areas of business should be part of the portfolio?
- Where should the organization be active (e.g. at the cantonal, national or international level)?
- Is sufficient importance given to innovation (▶ 17 Innovation)?
- Should the organization operate alone, or should it form alliances, or even merge, with other organizations (▶ 8 Governance)?

The third circle, strategy implementation, concerns the concrete, practice-oriented formulation and implementation of the strategy:

- Is the strategy appropriate, acceptable and realistic?
- What strategic development processes are needed?
- What organizational structures and systems are needed (▶ 10 Organizational structures)?
- How should the organization guide the needed change processes (▶ 15 Organizational learning)?
- Who should take on which tasks in the strategic process (▶ 9 Leadership)?

7.2.1 Strategy specifics in the public sector

In matters of strategy, there are probably more similarities than differences between the public and private sectors. That said, some differences are significant enough to warrant closer examination. The most obvious divergence lies in the objectives of private and public organizations: while the former are generally concerned with making profits, the latter serve the public interest (▶ 2 Essential functions) or aspire to create public added value (▶ 1 Values), which can take the most diverse forms. Another difference is the context. While private companies operate in a competitive environment, public organizations operate in a much more political (▶ 4 Institutions) and/or societal context, with a large number of groups involved (▶ 3 Stakeholders) (Alford & Greve 2017). Moreover, public organizations, and especially administrative entities, can rely on their executive power (▶ 5 Law) to achieve their objectives, although they are often in competition with other public organizations and units for resources whose allocation is determined by politics. Furthermore, the principle of rule-of-law action applies (▶ 1 Values and ▶ 5 Law). Consequently, the law sets the bases and the limits of state action, thus restricting the objectives that public organizations can set themselves. In this specific context, when it comes to strategy, managers in public organizations may have less latitude, or room for manoeuvre, than their counterparts in the private sector. However, the margin is generally sufficiently broad to make strategy an effective tool in the public sector too.

In this respect, examining the interactions between politics and the managers of public organizations is useful precisely because it enables an assessment of this latitude. For this purpose, Stewart (2004) draws a distinction between political strategy, organizational strategy and management strategy. The first of these, determined directly by politics, covers what the government and/or political authorities want to change (often in the form of policy plans, which can then be translated into legislation). However, this strategy can also be influenced by public administration, for example while a political strategy is being negotiated between several departments or offices, or while a piece of legislation is being formulated. Organizational strategy may be quite different from political strategy, but managers can build on the latter and exploit their room for manoeuvre to shape and direct their organization to best meet the needs of their stakeholders. Management strategy covers primarily technical and operational aspects, such as budgeting and reporting processes. While policy imperatives must be respected, management has some latitude to implement its own strategies in these areas. It should also be pointed out that public-sector organizations are particularly diverse, and their degrees of autonomy and proximity to politics vary widely: consider a parliamentary service unit, which is by definition closer to the political process than is a public museum. Regardless of these factors, strategy can have greater or lesser importance depending on the organization concerned.

7.2.2 Types of strategy and typical elements of a strategy document

From a practical point of view, the question often arises as to what types of strategy exist and how they interact. In public organizations, political strategies often take precedence, virtually defining the context for organizational and management strategies. Internally, however, the overall organizational strategy predominates, since it should define all subordinate strategies and/or those designed to give it concrete form. Let's take as an example a fictitious public-transport company adopting a global development strategy. Sometimes, additional strategies are also formulated at a general level, such as a digitalization strategy. More often than not, they are integrated into the overall strategy after a certain period of time. Since public organizations usually have a hierarchical structure, with compartmentalized departments, the next level up is that of departmental strategy—the area of passenger transport in our example. At this level, strategies may also be formulated for individual units, such as passenger-transport marketing, or for certain products and services, such as regional transport in a particular city. Beyond hierarchies, cross-functional strategies, that is, involving several departments—shared IT, human resources (▶ 12 Human-resources management) or even finance (▶ 13 Finance management)—can also be defined. While the structure of an organization's overall strategy usually takes the form of a hierarchical cascade, there are cases where important elements of subordinate strategies are subsequently integrated into the overall strategy.

Another question is what form a strategy document should take, and what elements it should include. A strategic document should be pleasant to read and easy to consult. A PDF document, a poster or a website can be used. In the case of a PDF document, the length should not exceed ten pages. If special details are required, it is best to use appendices. The principle that applies to the main document is "as much as necessary, but as little as possible", because strategies that are too long and difficult to understand complicate communication considerably. The following elements are typical of the highest strategic levels (there may be fewer for subordinate strategies):

- *Management summary*: what are the key strategy points? (maximum one page)
- *Motivation and context*: why is this strategy necessary?
- *Situation analysis*: e.g. what are the strengths, weaknesses, opportunities and threats (SWOT analysis)?
- *Vision*: what is the goal or specific ambition?
- *Mission*: what is the organization's role in achieving this goal?
- *Objectives*: what are the core elements of the mission, those that bring us closer to the organization's vision?
- *Measures*: what concrete measures should be implemented to achieve our goals?
- *Implementation plan*: who is responsible for which measure, what budget is allocated to which measure, what is the timetable?
- *Evaluation plan*: how can the progress of the strategy and/or the achievement of objectives be evaluated (▶ 16 Evaluation)?

It is important to understand that a strategy does not have to include all the above points. Depending on the context, it may make sense to omit or add certain elements. If, for example, a higher-level strategy already exists, we can forgo indicating our own vision and mission, and opt instead for a reference to the overall strategy. Space devoted to the various elements can also vary, although motivation, situation analysis, vision, mission and objectives are generally relatively short, and measures and implementation and evaluation plans tend to require more space.

In addition to these guidelines regarding the form of a strategy document, we set out below some concrete design principles for managers of public organizations, classified by phase of strategy development and implementation.

7.2.3 Design principles for strategy development

- For the situation analysis, and possibly for the entire development of the strategy, it is a good idea to involve as many members of the organization as possible, and even outside people, to get a complete picture of the situation.
- Any relevant political strategies should always form guidelines for an organizational or management strategy.
- Strategies should not be cluttered with unnecessary detail, but include only the essential points, stated as clearly as possible.
- Strategies should not only provide new directions, but also define what not to do in the future.
- Strategies should be flexible enough that they can be quickly adapted in the case of unforeseen events.

7.2.4 Organizational principles for strategy deployment

- To be implemented, a strategy must be communicated professionally and as widely as possible, both internally and, where appropriate, externally. Vision and mission should be the main motivational levers.
- Strategic management should be seen as an ongoing process, not a sequential task to be carried out from time to time.
- "Culture eats strategy for breakfast", said Peter Drucker. If a new strategy entails a change in culture, this transformation must be a priority for management, and the new culture must be passed on.
- Progress in deploying the strategy should be reviewed at regular intervals, and where appropriate, transparently communicated, even if setbacks are noted.
- Good practice in matters of strategy should be documented and made accessible.

7.3 Future prospects and challenges

In this final section, we look at two key challenges that public organizations will face as they develop their strategies. Research is currently focusing on these aspects. The first is that strategic cycles are becoming shorter and more flexible in a rapidly changing environment; the second, that the importance of open strategic processes is increasing. In the public sector, these two challenges are still being only timidly addressed in strategic practice. However, this is likely to change rapidly in an increasingly dynamic and complex context (Johnson *et al.* 2020).

Let's begin by looking at the length of strategic cycles. Traditionally, strategies are relatively stable management tools. The fact that strategic documents are often valid for five years or more testifies to this. During this relatively long period, the strategy undergoes only minor, if any, adjustments: the course is maintained. This can prove to be problematic when the context changes rapidly and complexity increases: sooner or later the strategy ceases to be relevant to new challenges. In the age of digitalization, where new technologies are almost constantly driving changes in society, the economy and other areas, strategic cycles of such length are simply no longer effective. Faster adaptation is essential. However, a strategy cannot be completely overhauled every month. This would involve a great deal of work, and besides, constant communications on new strategic orientations would end up discouraging the organization's members. So, a happy medium must be found. Strategic cycles could be shortened to two or three years. Another approach is to divide a strategy into a framework document, valid for a longer period and describing, for example, the overall vision and mission, and a basic document covering a shorter timeframe and including more concrete elements such as objectives, orientations and measures.

Instruments such as planning scenarios and decentralized forms of strategic development can also be valuable levers for better mastering dynamics and complexity (Johnson *et al.* 2020). Managers need to find the right balance between stability and relevance for their organization.

The other major challenge ahead is to assess whether strategy should remain an internal instrument, its formulation being strictly the prerogative of senior management, or whether more participative approaches should be adopted in the future. A central yet still relatively new concept in this area is that of open strategy (Whittington *et al.* 2011). It centres on the idea of *open innovation*, a process in which organizations can innovate by making use of the know-how, suggestions and resources of external partners and stakeholders (customers, companies, start-ups, universities, etc.). Where open strategy is concerned, innovation is the strategy itself. An open strategy has two distinct dimensions, which can relate to both the internal and the external context (see Table 7.1).

	Transparency	Inclusion
Internal	E.g. blogging about the strategy on the intranet	E.g. strategic workshops attended by a large number of employees, or even all members of the organization.
External	E.g. strategy updates on the website or via newsletters	E.g. crowdsourcing, i.e. gathering strategic ideas externally

Table 7.1 The dimensions of open strategy
Source: Whittington, Cailluet & Yakis-Douglas (2011)

The first dimension is the strategy's transparency in terms of how it is communicated. Internal transparency should be considered a minimum requirement. After all, a strategy of which members of the organization are not kept informed is unlikely to have any impact. Internal transparency can be ensured through the organization's own channels, such as the intranet or internal communication. External transparency, on the other hand, is a little rarer. It is achieved by addressing regular communications on the strategy and its progress to the general public or to certain groups outside the organization. Public administrations can afford to be transparent, because they have a special responsibility to the general public, and do not generally have to fear competitors who might take advantage of the fact that their strategy is open. External transparency can be provided by keeping the strategy up to date on the internet and social networks, or through newsletters, for example. The second dimension is the involvement of various stakeholders in the development of the strategy and in other related issues. With internal involvement, strategy development is thus not left to senior management alone: other members of the organization can also contribute substantially. This can be achieved by a variety of means, such as strategy workshops open to all staff, also known as "strategy jams", or an online consultation. As regards external involvement, the openness is even wider, since any interested party can, in principle, contribute to the development of the strategy on a voluntary basis. This open approach is sometimes called crowd-sourcing: online formats are particularly well-suited to it, as they minimize barriers to participation.

An open strategy is undoubtedly more complicated to develop than a purely internal strategy devised by management. Analysing the opinions obtained and integrating them into the strategy requires a lot of effort. Also, communicating externally rather than internally is a more complex undertaking. But open strategies enjoy a higher degree of acceptance among users thanks to their "quasi-democratic" genesis. They also improve the transparency of a public organization's actions and are therefore well worth the extra effort. In addition, open strategies potentially contain better ideas than their conventional counterparts, since more people, with very diverse viewpoints, contribute to their development. Of course, the decision to opt for an open strategy, like that concerning the length of the strategic cycle, always rests with the management of the organization concerned.

These questions come in addition to the many others that arise in the field of strategic management, and which we have addressed in this contribution. In conclusion, strategy is undoubtedly one of the most effective instruments that the reforms associated with New Public Management have brought to public administration. Many have criticized the public sector's wholesale adoption of concepts devised for private-sector management. However, much of the criticism is based on the observation that management in the private sector is focused on a short-term horizon. But actually, strategy contributes to long-term planning. It is therefore the very opposite of a short-sighted approach. Each public organization is free to choose to take up and adapt elements of NPM that it deems relevant to its own needs. This is why, in the future, strategy and strategic management will have their place within public organizations and should even gain in importance.

Key concepts

- Open strategy (*stratégie ouverte, offene Strategie, strategia aperta*): the creation of internal and external transparency by means of a strategy and the involvement of internal and external actors in the strategy development process.
- Strategic management (*gestion stratégique, strategisches Management, gestione strategica*): a continuous process of analysing the existing strategic position,

making strategic choices, implementing the chosen options by making the necessary resources available and evaluating the success of the strategy.

- Strategy (*stratégie, Strategie, strategia*): "the long-term direction of an organization" (Johnson *et al.* 2020).
- Strategy implementation (*mise en œuvre d'une stratégie, Strategieimplementierung, attuazione di una strategia*): the process of putting strategic plans into practice in order to achieve set objectives.

References

Alford, J. & Greve, C. (2017). Strategy in the public and private sectors: similarities, differences and changes. *Administrative Sciences*, *7*(4), 35.

Hautz, J., Seidl, D. & Whittington, R. (2017). Open strategy: Dimensions, dilemmas, dynamics. *Long Range Planning*, *50*(3), 298–309.

Johnson, G., Whitington, R., Scholes, K., Angwin, D. & Regnér, P. (2020). *Exploring strategy: Texts and cases* (12th ed). Pearson Education Limited.

Mintzberg, H. (1987). The strategy concept I: Five Ps for strategy. *California management review*, *30*(1), 11–24.

Poister, T. H. (2010). The future of strategic planning in the public sector: Linking strategic management and performance. *Public Administration Review*, *70*, 246–254.

Porter, M. E. (1996). What is strategy? *Harvard business review*, *74*(6), 61–78.

Stewart, J. (2004). The meaning of strategy in the public sector. *Australian Journal of Public Administration*, *63*(4), 16–21.

Whittington, R., Cailluet, L. & Yakis-Douglas, B. (2011). Opening strategy: Evolution of a precarious profession. *British Journal of Management*, *22*(3), 531–544.

References for further study

Johnson, G. & Scholes, K. (Eds). (2001). *Exploring public sector strategy*. Pearson Education Limited.

8 Governance

Laure Athias and Martial Pasquier

8.1 The importance of governance for public administration

Lausanne is one of the world's leading centres of cancer research. Immunotherapy, aimed at supporting the body's natural defences to destroy cancer cells, is the focus of cutting-edge research and experimental treatments. In 2015, the American Ludwig Foundation committed to investing over CHF 100 million over a ten-year period. Vaud canton[14] funds major real-estate investments to house the research, and supports the University of Lausanne and the Vaud University Hospital Centre (CHUV) in their contribution to this work, with which the École polytechnique fédérale de Lausanne and the University of Geneva are also associated. The ISREC foundation (supporting cancer research in Switzerland) has constructed a building (AGORA) on land made available by the State of Vaud to bring together multidisciplinary research teams. Start-ups have been created from all these efforts.

This convergence of efforts aimed at the public good raises central questions of governance: how should coordination between these different entities be designed? What are the risks that entities will have to face? Which organizational forms should be chosen? How much autonomy should they be given?

Governance[15] means the rules, conventions, principles and values that enable a community—generally an organization or group of organizations—to carry out activities, manage conflicts and develop coordination mechanisms to ensure coherent, orderly, sustainable development. For various reasons, the importance of this issue has grown considerably since the 1970s. The first of these has to do with the evolution of the principles and rules of public management. Public organizations had long been managed on the bureaucratic principles championed particularly by Max

14 One of the 26 states that make up the Swiss Confederation.
15 Governance between levels of government (Confederation-cantons-municipalities), commonly referred to as multilevel governance, is addressed in ▶ 4 Institutions.

Weber (▶ 3 Stakeholders). In the 1980s, in an essentially neo-liberal perspective, the functioning of administrative units was scrutinized in terms of their efficiency. The principles of New Public Management (NPM) embody a more entrepreneurial vision of public administration, with greater autonomy for the entities responsible for carrying out public tasks, and an expectation of results rather than processes. There has been a shift from a conception of the state as an actor and producer of services towards a state that regulates activities and services produced by third parties. This conception of public administration, more prevalent in English-speaking countries, has also fostered the development of additional requirements imposed on administrative systems, such as transparency and accountability. Administrative units are thus increasingly required to respect principles whose application can be contradictory: fairness, respect for procedures, effectiveness and efficiency, transparency, accountability and so on. As a result, it is important to clarify the rules governing competence, autonomy and communication, so that the administration can carry out its activities with clarity.

A second reason is that many public services are produced within a network (▶ 3 Stakeholders). Responsibility for the entire service lies not with any single actor, but with a whole range of public and sometimes private actors, who must coordinate their efforts. Sometimes, their interests do not converge, and major differences can arise. The implementation of regional-development policies is a good example. Organizations created around a territory[16], which does not necessarily correspond to an administrative unit, can bring together municipalities, associations of municipalities, private associations and private actors, whether profit-making or not. It is therefore important to establish clear rules regarding the setting of objectives, decision-making processes, financing and control.

A third reason for the increased importance of governance in public action is the multiplicity of possible organizational and legal forms. For nearly all of the 20th century, most public services were provided by administrative units or entities specifically created by the legislator, usually autonomous establishments under public law. Since the 1980s, executive or legislative authorities have chosen to delegate the provision of these services to bodies that sometimes have distinct legal forms. For example, the university hospital centre in Lausanne (CHUV) is a service of the department of health, the university hospitals in Geneva (HUGs) are an autonomous establishment under public law, while Lucerne Cantonal Hospital (LUKS) is a limited company. The autonomy conferred on these public organizations is a question of organizational governance, not of the provision of services which, in clinical terms, are similar.

16 The Communauté régionale de la Broye (Coreb) is a regional-development organization that brings together the AVRBV (Association vaudoise région Broye Vully) and Ascobroye (Association fribourgeoise des communes de la Broye) associations, as well as private members (www.coreb.ch).

This contribution begins by describing the various possible modes of governance for the provision of public services, with a presentation of the link between the mode of governance and organizational and legal aspects. A more normative approach follows to highlight trade-offs in the various governance and organizational choices. It concludes with a look at future prospects and challenges.

8.2 Key points of governance

8.2.1 Possible modes of governance

Modes of governance for the provision of public services are set out in Table 8.1.

Modes of governance	**Doing**			**Getting done**	
Governance models	Classic administration	Internal contracting	Handover to autonomous entities (agencies)	External contracting	Public-private partnerships
Legal and organizational forms	Administration	Target agreements, public-service mandates	Autonomous establishments, foundations, limited companies with (mainly) public capital	Forms provided for in the Code of Obligations	Contract or joint venture between the public and private sectors

Table 8.1 Modes of government

Among modes of governance, we can broadly distinguish those that enable public services to be provided in-house ("doing") from those that outsource them to the private sector ("getting done"). A simple example is snow clearance on public roads. This public task can be carried out by road-service departments ("doing"), but can also be entrusted ("getting done"), for example in small to medium-sized towns, to private contractors (farmers, transport companies, etc.).

The classic administrative model is still the most widespread, with tasks performed by an administrative unit. Services are provided by entities directly subordinate to an executive authority. These units have no legal personality, and their budget is drawn from the state budget. The rules that apply are those of bureaucratic administration, applied hierarchically.

Internal contracting can take place between an executive authority and an administrative authority, and can take the form of public-service contracts/mandates or target agreements. The Federal Administration's new management model

(NMG), introduced in 2017, favours the responsibility of administrative units in the provision of services, while increasing latitude in the use of resources (performance agreements, budget envelopes, etc.). In the same vein, the budget of the State of Valais includes a political performance mandate for each department, which includes political objectives to be achieved, priority measures, indicators for assessing the achievement of objectives, and the corresponding resources made available.

The classic form of agency is the creation of a legal entity to perform public tasks, within a specific legislative framework. For example, Fribourg canton made its automobile department independent by creating an "autonomous establishment under public law" (Office de la circulation et de la navigation, OCN). Its tasks differ little from those of automobile departments in other cantons, but the way it operates differs. Financially independent, it has to cover all its costs, can borrow from banks, invest without going through the state budget, and derogate in part from the law on state personnel, while remaining administratively attached to the Department of Security, and Justice and Sport (DSJS).

Contracting also takes place beyond the state's borders. This is the "getting done" principle. Here, the legislative and executive authorities define the services and access conditions, while implementation is entrusted to private entities. In Switzerland, unemployment insurance funds provide a very good example. Unemployment benefits are governed by federal law (Unemployment Insurance Act, UIA), which also stipulates that the cantons must have a public fund accessible to all (federalism of execution principle). The act also allows employers' or workers' organizations to set up private unemployment insurance funds (the main unemployment insurance fund in Switzerland is that of the UNIA trade union). The performance of a public task can thus be entrusted to public and private organizations which compete with each other insofar as they are remunerated primarily on the basis of the services delivered.

A final governance model is known as a public-private partnership (PPP). The state asks a private company to design, finance, build and manage an infrastructure for the provision of public services. In return, the government guarantees a pre-defined payment[17]. The Neumatt PPP in Burgdorf in Berne canton is a good example. The 25-year contract, signed in 2009 by the canton of Berne and the private project company Zeughaus PPP AG (made up of Marti Holding AG, BAM Deutschland AG and Hälg Facility Management AG), covers the design, construction, financing and maintenance of a new complex comprising a 110-bed regional prison, four administrative centres, a warehouse and an underground car park. Total investment for this project amounted to CHF 150 million. Under the contract the private project company, which is responsible for all tasks except those directly related to the prisoners, receives an annual contribution from the canton.

17 There are also PPPs in which the private operator's remuneration comes not from the state, but from the users of the service (see Athias et al. [2019] for a fuller description of the different types of PPPs).

Apart from the modes of governance set out in Table 8.1, the state can also intervene unilaterally through rules that apply equally to all providers in the sector (in other words, regardless of the governance choices made). When the state finances activities in the health, education, culture or sport sectors, it lays down rules for service providers, set out in legal provisions. For example, quality of life in Switzerland's nursing homes is governed by quality standards set out in cantonal regulations.

8.2.2 Choice of mode of governance

After the above descriptive review of the various possible modes of governance, the question naturally arises as to which one to choose. This question is linked to the more general question of "doing" or "getting done", which was addressed in the work of Ronald Coase (1937) and Oliver Williamson (1975)[18].

Two main coordination mechanisms: price versus hierarchy

What is the difference between "doing" and "getting done"? The answer lies in the coordination mechanism: within an organization, the coordination mechanism is the hierarchy[19] (through the employment contract and rules of subordination), whereas between an organization and its outside partners, coordination is mainly based on price. This is how, for example, we can distinguish the relationship an organization has with an employee from that which it has with a freelancer.

It should be noted, however, that other coordination mechanisms can complement price-based coordination, such as contractual clauses that stipulate how partners must adapt to unforeseen events, or that ensure the continuity of the relationship (e.g. exclusivity clauses). These are hybrid modes of governance, in that both coordination mechanisms (price and authority) are present.

Each mode of governance has its own coordination mechanism, which is what determines its ability to manage a given service and minimize the costs involved.

Production costs versus transaction costs

When only production costs are considered, the price-coordination mechanism is often assumed to do better than in-house supply with its associated hierarchical coordination mechanism. In other words, the "getting-done" solution would seem to provide an advantage in terms of production-cost minimization because of strong incentives for efficiency and potential competitive pressure to penalize poor performance. Another potential advantage lies in the market's ability to

18 Ronald Coase and Oliver Williamson were awarded the Nobel Prize in Economics, in 1991 and 2009 respectively, for work leading to the development of transaction-cost theory. This is the only theory that can answer the question about the optimal mode of governance for public services, in that it is the only one that distinguishes between "doing" and "getting done".

19 As Coase (1937: 387) points out: "If a workman moves from department Y to department X, he does not go because of a change in relative prices, but because he is ordered to do so."

aggregate demand, leading to economies of scale, whereas a public entity may be constrained by its size.

But the market's advantage in terms of productive efficiency can be called into question when the specific nature of public organizations is taken into account. This is because the primary objective of public organizations, unlike for-profit organizations, is to serve a mission (Wilson 1989; Tirole 1994; Besley & Ghatak 2005; Athias 2025), that is, to produce goods and services that benefit everyone without the possibility of exclusion (these are public goods and services ▶ 2 Essential functions). Some of those involved in the production of public goods and services take this collective impact into account when choosing how much effort to devote to their work. These "motivated[20]" workers are inclined to increase their efforts without financial compensation, leading to productivity gains at the organizational level (Perry & Wise 1990; Besley & Ghatak 2005; Athias & Wicht 2024).

Moreover, when considering efficiency, we need to take into account not only production costs, but also transaction costs—the costs incurred by using price as a coordination mechanism, which are often overlooked. Transaction costs are a direct consequence of the fact that contracts are incomplete. This is because, since actors have limited rationality (they are rational, but their cognitive capacities are limited), they are unable to perfectly assess all future performance trends in an uncertain world. Renegotiations will therefore be necessary to adapt service provision to unforeseen events. During these renegotiations, actors may behave opportunistically, seeking to exploit contractual weaknesses to appropriate a larger share of the gains. This type of behaviour is all the more difficult to sanction when there is a relationship of dependence between actors. As a result, transaction costs can be very significant. These are the costs—monetary and above all non-monetary (direct and indirect)—that can arise *ex ante*, before the contract is signed (costs of drafting and negotiating the contract, guarantees, etc.), but above all *ex post*, after the contract is signed (costs arising from poor suitability of the contract, renegotiations, implementation and monitoring costs, and possible breach of contract).

Determinants of transaction costs

One of the major contributions of transaction-cost theory is to demonstrate that, although these costs are unobservable, their magnitude can be estimated on the basis of the (observable) characteristics of the service in question. These characteristics, which constitute the determinants of transaction costs, are three in number:

- Asset specificity: can the necessary assets be redeployed at no cost for another use?

20 Examples are physicians seeking to save lives, researchers to advance knowledge, judges to promote justice and soldiers to defend their country.

- Uncertainty: is it easy to anticipate future demand or future operating conditions for the service in question?
- Complexity: can service quality be easily observed, measured and verified by a third party?

The greater the asset specificity, the more the contracting parties are locked into a situation of dependence, which increases the risk of opportunistic behaviour, and therefore transaction costs. Similarly, uncertainty often means that renegotiation is required to adapt public services to changing circumstances. Lastly, the more complex the service, the more the existing supplier organization can cut production costs to the detriment of service quality without being penalized. Transaction costs, arising out of the discrepancy between the service provided and that expected, will therefore be all the higher.

The optimal mode of governance is one that minimizes total costs: transaction costs as well as production costs. With higher transaction costs, the hierarchical coordination mechanism becomes preferable, with its powerful means of control and its internal mechanisms for conflict resolution and decision-making in unforeseen situations.

8.2.3 Choice of legal and organizational form

Once the mode of governance has been chosen, the question of which legal and organizational form to adopt depends primarily on the incentives to be given to service providers. As highlighted above, one of the market's advantages in terms of productive efficiency lies in strong incentive schemes.

Similar incentives could be introduced within public administrations to encourage employees to increase their efforts[21]. However, such schemes are often very difficult to design, given the multiplicity of decision-makers and the objectives assigned to public administrations (Tirole 1994). One solution is to create public agencies charged with the execution of a task including performance targets. This is known as the phenomenon of agentification. The power of incentive schemes depends on the way in which the state exercises its responsibility as owner, directly through its organizations, and indirectly through its representatives.

21 The problem that arises is the influence of asymmetric information on employees' level of effort (Laffont & Martimort 2002). As Laffont (2000: 127) notes: "The government is incapable of observing the effort levels of its agents. At most, it observes results that depend not only on effort, but also on a set of random circumstances, which make interpreting the results difficult. Poor results can be due to a lack of effort, but also to unfavourable circumstances. The absence of incentives (for effort) is characterized here by remuneration that is independent of performance. This is optimal when agents work in good faith: a good level of effort can be taken for granted, and they are exposed to no unnecessary risks. In contrast, if agents have private objectives, they must be given incentives to work hard by making their remuneration dependent on their results."

Unlike countries such as France, which have categories of public establishments[22], Swiss public authorities use, in addition to the status of "autonomous establishment under public law" created by statute, the legal forms provided by the Code of Obligations to create agencies:

- Simple partnerships: many structures are created through an agreement between several public entities; they have no legal personality and are generally managed by one of the partner public entities. In the higher education sector, many cooperative ventures between institutions take the form of a simple partnership.
- Autonomous establishments under public law: the Hôpital Riviera-Chablais was recently created on the basis of an intercantonal agreement and has a legal personality.
- Associations: the cantons of Fribourg and Jura have created the iGovPortal.ch association to facilitate a unified, coordinated "eGovernment" strategy between a canton and its municipalities. Other cantons such as Graubünden, St. Gallen and Solothurn have joined them.
- Foundations: these can be public-law foundations such as Pro Helvetia, or private-law foundations such as the Manufacture-Haute École des arts de la scène.
- Limited companies: RUAG Holding AG is an aerospace and defence company whose sole shareholder is the Swiss Confederation.

Within these different forms of agency, the choice of a legal form and its organizational implications often depends on several criteria, even if ideological and political positions always feature strongly in the corresponding debates. One criterion involves the nature of the activity. If the activity is commercial and subject to the laws of competition, the classic limited-company form should be favoured. This is because such a structure must be able to act with the same resources as its competitors, or risk being either advantaged (state responsibility) or hindered (lack of flexibility regarding salaries, for example). Economic risk is another important criterion. Many activities present significant risks whose financial impact must be limitable. For example, the limited-company structure of Agno airport (Lugano Airport SA with capital of CHF 4 million), owned by the canton of Ticino and the city of Lugano, was put into ordinary liquidation in May 2020, and employees were able to be made redundant. In contrast, abolishing an autonomous establishment under public law would have required the involvement of the corresponding legislative authorities. Political control and accountability rules are also key criteria in the choice of a legal form. The closer the nature of the activity is to the state's sovereign tasks, or the more politically sensitive it is, the more the authorities will want to ensure that they can

22 France distinguishes between public administrative establishments, public industrial and commercial establishments, independent administrative authorities, public interest groups and departments of national competence. In addition to these categories, there are public enterprises under private law and semi-public companies.

control the entity and be able to obtain any information they require. Both the conventional solution and the creation of an autonomous establishment under public law allow the necessary arrangements to be made relatively easily; the process is more complex with the forms provided for in the Code of Obligations.

In conclusion, to understand the legal form chosen for agencies, one must be aware of the historical context in which they were created. While most of the cantonal banks created at the end of the 19th century are still autonomous establishments under public law, their governance is currently more akin to that of limited companies. In contrast, the Swiss National Bank is a limited company founded in 1906 with both public and private shareholders, but whose activities are governed by the National Bank Act of 2004.

8.3 Future prospects and challenges

We have discussed the different modes of governance for the provision of public services, and highlighted the trade-offs involved, which are technical and not ideological. Thus, while it is now common practice to carry out cost-benefit analyses when choosing investments, the same should also apply to choices of governance, since each mode of governance has its own advantages and disadvantages. It is important to understand that there is no perfect solution to the governance problem, no one optimal mode of governance: it all depends on the service in question and its environment. This message runs counter to the aspirations towards standardization that we see in practice.

Also, certain characteristics of public services change over time, in response to technological innovations for example, and this may call into question the mode of governance initially chosen. Similarly, in an increasingly globalized and interconnected world, the complexity and uncertainty surrounding the provision of some public services (particularly in the fields of health, education and the environment) are intensified. However, as emphasized in this contribution, where asset specificity and high levels of complexity and uncertainty are present, the preference should be for more hierarchical modes of governance, with their greater capacity for control and adaptation.

Beyond considerations of the technical aspects, public-sector organizations are faced with another challenge: that of preserving their mission as an organizational objective, distinct from the goal of maximizing profits. Although, in the collective unconscious, private for-profit organizations always outstrip public organizations in terms of organizational efficiency, public organizations can rely on motivation rather than (costly) monetary incentives to generate a given level of effort. The challenge for every public organization is therefore to achieve the closest possible match between its employees' motivation and its mission, without lapsing into bureaucratic conservatism or resistance to innovation. The tendency over recent decades to give public organizations profitability objectives could therefore prove counter-productive.

Key concepts

- Accountability (*accountability/imputabilité, Rechenschaftspflicht, responsabilità*): the obligation to answer for the performance of a task to an authority and, more generally, to all stakeholders.
- Agency (*agence, Agentur, agenzia*): a public entity carrying out public tasks, enjoying considerable management autonomy but with a requirement to achieve performance targets.
- Motivation (*motivation, Motivation, motivazione*): an individual predisposition to take into consideration the overall value of the good or service produced for society in deciding what level of effort to put into producing it.
- Opportunism (*opportunism, Opportunismus, opportunismo*): opportunism by actors involves disclosing incomplete or distorted information in order to appropriate part of the benefits that were supposed to accrue to the other party to the exchange. This hypothesis is advanced not with the idea that all actors are necessarily opportunistic, but that they can potentially act opportunistically. Thus, the choice of a mode of governance cannot be made without taking it into account.
- Transaction costs (*coûts de transaction, Transaktionskosten, costi di transazione*): the costs of using the market to complete a transaction. They break down into *ex-ante* costs, but above all *ex-post* costs (i.e. before and after a contract is signed). *Ex-ante* transaction costs are those associated with finding a partner and drafting, negotiating and securing an agreement. *Ex-post* transaction costs, on the other hand, include control costs, renegotiation costs, costs arising out of a discrepancy between the performance delivered and that expected and possibly the costs of breaking off agreements. Transaction costs are mainly non-monetary and unobservable.

References

Athias, L. (2025). *On the normative motivation of states: Universalism in Western post-enlightenment societies.* Working Paper.

Athias, L. & Wicht, P. (2024). Make or Buy for Public Services: Culture matters for efficiency consideration. *Quarterly Review of Economics and Finance*, 99, 1–12. https://doi.org/10.1016/j.qref.2024.101899.

Athias, L., Macina, M. & Wicht, P. (2019). Public Private Partnerships: A Swiss perspective. In A. Ladner *et al.* (Eds.). *Swiss public administration: Making the State work successfully* (pp. 187–204). Springer International Publishing.

Besley, T. & Ghatak, M. (2005). Competition and incentives with motivated agents. *American Economic Review*, *95*(3), 616–636.

Coase, R. H. (1937). The nature of the firm. *Économica*, *16*(4), 386–405.

Laffont, J.-J. (2000). Étapes vers un État moderne: une analyse économique. In *État et gestion publique*. La Documentation française, 117–149.

Laffont, J.-J. & Martimort, D. (2002). *The theory of incentives: The principal-agent model*. Princeton University Press.

Perry, J. L. & Wise, L. (1990). The motivational basis of public service, *Public Administration Review*, *50*, 367–373.

Tirole, J. (1994). The internal organization of government. *Oxford Economic Papers*, *46*, 1–29.

Williamson, O. E. (1975). *Markets and hierarchies: Analysis and antitrust implications*. Free Press.

Wilson, J. Q. (1989). *Bureaucracy: What government agencies do and why they do it*. Basic Books.

References for further study

Saussier, S. & Yvrande, A. (2007). *Économie des coûts de transaction*. La Découverte.

Williamson, O. E. (2017). *Contract, governance and transaction cost economics*. World Scientific. https://doi.org/10.1142/10316

9 Leadership

Yves Emery and David Giauque

9.1 The importance of leadership for public administration

For over a hundred years, leadership has been one of the major themes in management, both in terms of its practical implications and in terms of scientific literature. The concept seeks to identify the practices, tools, skills and behaviours that enable managers to influence the actions of their subordinates for the purpose of achieving specific organizational objectives. Leadership is all the more important because of the prevalence today of goal-oriented and results-oriented management, and the qualitative and quantitative evaluation of public services. Some specialists speak of performance management, while others stress the importance of achieving results. In this regard, the Swiss Constitution requires that state actions be subject to evaluation (▶ 16 Evaluation), which again highlights the need for objectives that the legislator, and then the political authority, must specify, steer and achieve. These new management arrangements require managers to be able to lead the workgroups for which they are responsible. This involves rallying teams around concrete projects, maintaining a high level of motivation among members and inspiring both respect and trust. Hence the importance of these new managerial figures, leaders, in contemporary organizational realities. Showing leadership in Swiss public administration is no easy task—especially since, in the Weberian tradition, the administration is often seen as a neutral organ executing political objectives. This vision leaves little room for a form of embodiment of power implied by exercising leadership.

Numerous studies have shown that the actions of leaders can have a great effect on the teams they manage and, ultimately, on an organization's ability to achieve its goals (Bass *et al.* 2003). This underscores the need to better understand this phenomenon and to identify the foundations of the type of leadership that best motivates people and respects public values, complementing modern human-resource management practices (▶ 12 Human-resource management). An interest in leadership thus calls for a better understanding of the organizational, structural and individual levers that politicians and senior administrative staff use to steer public action, based on concrete objectives pursued by teams.

In this contribution, we focus on administrative leadership, leaving aside political leadership, which is a theme in its own right (Moynihan & Van Wart 2013; Denhardt & Campbell 2006). By administrative leadership, we mean the kind exercised by administrative executives, not elected officials. Note that for a long time little thought was given to the idea of leadership within an administration, the main mission of senior managers being seen as limited to the technical implementation of decisions made by political authorities. The advent of New Public Management (NPM) put the question of administrative leadership on the agenda and, in its wake, the skills expected of managers and the leadership styles they practise. Today, men and women in managerial positions in public administration are clearly expected to show leadership and succeed in mobilizing their teams around objectives that are defined—admittedly not always clearly—by the political authorities.

The verb *to lead* means to give direction, to indicate the course towards which the action of a team or entity is to be steered. Leadership has often been associated with a person, a charismatic leader capable of influencing others[23]. It may also be associated with a function: a management position is assumed to confer leadership on the holder. But we need to understand leadership in the public sector, or public leadership, more broadly. In the context of this contribution and drawing on the work of Denhardt & Campbell (2006: 563), we see leadership as an "interactional process that seeks to mobilize personnel, and more broadly stakeholders, towards shared goals, founded on a complex moral relationship based on trust, obligation, involvement, emotion and a shared vision of the common good."

We first present specific features of the Swiss context that are important to consider in terms of public leadership, before sketching a historical portrait of the dominant conceptions of leadership, in order to focus on elements that are relevant in today's context. We conclude by stressing the importance of looking at public leadership not only as a matter of individual leaders, but also as a collective phenomenon, a property of public organizations that are agile and capable of change.

9.2 Key points of leadership

Since leadership always develops in a specific context, which may be more or less receptive to certain practices, it is important to touch on some particularities of the Swiss public context.

23 For better (Gandhi) or for worse (Hitler), to cite examples often mentioned in the literature on leadership, alongside prominent business leaders such as Steve Jobs.

9.2.1 Specific features of the Swiss context

The importance attached to leadership differs from country to country, depending in particular on culture. This may explain why leadership in organizations has long been a central theme in English-speaking countries, which are culturally more individualistic. Switzerland's highly hierarchical, even paternalistic, corporate culture is perhaps not the most fertile ground for advances in leadership, especially in public organizations. A recent survey on public innovation (Boukamel & Emery 2018) highlights a characteristic that is hardly conducive to the development of leadership. The authors point out that "heads that rise above" are disliked (the "tall poppy" syndrome), indicating the importance of sober leadership, and echoing the Swiss political-administrative culture characterized by the search for compromise and concordance (Giauque 2013). These principles are conducive to the emergence of consensus, but may not appeal to the generally ambitious nature of a person with leadership qualities.

Another point that is key to understanding administrative leadership is the importance attached to technical expertise, particularly in Switzerland. Generally, senior executives (both political and administrative) are expected to be experts in their field and hence able to answer the most specialized questions. Technical leadership is therefore still predominant in management profiles today: this "technical leadership" is sometimes to the detriment of managerial and leadership qualities and the social and communication skills needed to motivate and involve staff.

9.2.2 The leader's and the manager's role

Leadership is not synonymous with management. Management involves the planning, organization and control of activities, with the aim of optimization. Leadership calls on the human dimension of managing, the energies and motivations that can be summoned to shape and achieve shared goals. These two roles of "manager" and "leader" are indispensable in any management team, and are sometimes summarized as follows. Managing means laying the foundations of cooperation and setting up organizational tools and processes for the purpose of achieving assigned organizational goals—often referred to as the "hard" factors of management. Leading, showing the way, on the other hand, consists in ensuring, through communication and day-to-day relationships, that employees are involved and motivated. Management is essential to the smooth running of an organization, because without structures and ground rules, there can be no collaboration. But leadership is just as important, because employee involvement and motivation are essential to organizational sustainability, and even to organizational learning (▶ 15 Organizational learning) and innovation. Good leadership will thus induce staff to become more involved in achieving organizational goals, with a foundation of a healthy collaborative climate that fosters mutual trust. The psychological mechanism at work here is known and has been studied by specialists. Leadership that inspires trust helps to increase the legitimacy of management practices and tools, as well as organizational goals. These conditions are conducive to calm and collaborative social relations, encouraging employees to make sustained efforts to attain a high level of performance. Social-exchange theory studies this mechanism and shows that if employees perceive that their organization and hierarchy provide them with adequate resources and working conditions, they will tend to want to "give back", particularly through greater involvement at work (Gould-Williams & Davies 2005).

9.2.3 Leadership styles and levers of action

Many organizations have chosen their executives from among the best specialists, particularly in public administration, which is characterized by the merit principle, paving the way for the technical leadership mentioned above. This type of leadership is important, as it allows those under supervision to know *how to do* their job. It is called *instrumental leadership* (Day & Antonakis 2012), and is an integral part of the most current conceptions of leadership. Although we now know that it is not always best to choose the most expert person in a team to lead it, doing so does have obvious advantages, since it guarantees technically impeccable work. It also meets a key expectation of political decision-makers running the administration: that their objectives should be fully attained, in accordance with the state of the art and the rules and procedures in force, while respecting a strict division of responsibilities.

In the early 1990s, the New Public Management movement emphasized the importance of managerial skills in conjunction with more entrepreneurial behaviour (Osborne & Gaebler 1993). The motto "steering not rowing" is essential in a public administration in search of greater performance from resources that are tending to diminish. Management by objectives (MBO) has thus become a new managerial standard, and has been introduced in a number of Swiss public administrations, including the federal government. What specialists call *transactional leadership* involves setting goals for staff, then monitoring the attainment of these goals and, depending on the result, sanctioning or rewarding (hence the link with pay for performance, ▶ 12 Human-resources management). In short, this means answering the question of "what" to do? Many analysts point out that steering by objectives, or even by results, implies a change in the psychological contract, which becomes above all *transactional* and less *relational*. In this case, it is a matter of all the members of an administrative entity producing results, justifying the validity of their employment and, where appropriate, obtaining an extension of their contract, or even a salary increase. This represents a radical change in the traditional conditions of employment in the public sector. This transactional leadership approach involving the setting of objectives has become a classic ingredient of training courses for administrative executives. The acronym SMART is often used to summarize the criteria that good objectives must meet: specific, measurable, achievable, relevant and time-bound.

The highly rational vision underlying MBO was counterbalanced from the outset by leadership specialists (Bass 1985) referring to the manager versus leader roles evoked above. According to these specialists, the leader's role is characterized by a form of *transformational leadership*, focused on developing and sharing a common vision capable of mobilizing the organization's staff by developing their skills. Thus, transformational leadership seeks to work on the meaning, the purpose, the "why" of collective action, and not just the "what" that MBO focuses on. In public-sector organizations in particular, transformational leadership is of particular importance. This is because public servants are driven by a specific motivation, linked to public-service values, which specialists have termed *Public Service Motivation* (PSM) (Giauque *et al.* 2010). This very particular type of motivation requires public employees to be stimulated and motivated, with care given to promoting the meaning, values and aims of the public action they are working to achieve.

Transformational leaders build a relationship of trust with their subordinates, help them to develop, and show them how they can contribute to making goals a reality—goals that are defined, at least in part, in a participatory way. In recent years, many public administrations have drawn up "charter" documents (*charte, Leitbild*) for the purpose of sharing a vision of the managed entity, often in interaction with external stakeholders (▶ 3 Stakeholders).

These three forms of leadership—instrumental, transactional and transformational—are useful for leading a public entity effectively, but they do not necessarily require charisma (Moynihan & Van Wart 2013). However, few executives are able to juggle all three registers of leadership. This is why, in our view, contemporary public leadership must be seen as primarily collective, especially in the Swiss context, where discretion and modesty are regarded as great managerial qualities. We will return to this point later.

While it may seem unimaginable for a symphony orchestra to function without a conductor, such orchestras do exist and operate successfully. To pull this off, all the musicians must feel they are co-creators of the collective performance, of the work being played. By analogy, and backed up by a growing number of authors, we contend that public administration in the 21st century will only be able to meet the ever-increasing challenges ahead if it succeeds in developing *distributed leadership*, or *collective leadership* (Ospina 2017).

This type of leadership results from empowering all staff (and not just managers) to achieve the administrative entity's objectives. We can also use the term *leaderful organization* in this respect: an environment supporting collective leadership to collaborate effectively and produce results together.

We see this approach as very promising, particularly in Swiss public-sector organizations (see § 9.2.1), since it goes beyond leadership approaches centred on the person of the leader, to reach a more collective, organizational sense of leadership, one that incorporates the multilevel, multi-actor network perspective that characterizes modern extended-governance and public-action-network approaches. First, this means taking into account all levels of the organization, not just the "top floor". Of course, it is important that the management team should be highly competent in the three registers of leadership mentioned earlier: technical mastery of the field of activity, transactional management and transformational leadership. That said, the executive team needs to give less importance to concentrating and holding on to power, instead seeing themselves more as catalysts for leadership initiatives throughout the action network both inside and outside their entity. In particular, it is important that front-line actors (the "street-level bureaucrats") are empowered to make decisions at their level with a view to optimizing the provision of public services. Externally, the beneficiaries of public services must also be able to participate in improving those public services, in agreed-upon ways.

Distributed leadership of this kind can only be achieved if interpersonal relations at all levels are imbued with respect and trust, in order to free people's capacity for action. "Benevolent leadership", which some practitioners see as necessary to create a social bond of trust between actors, is a complementary (and likely indispensable) approach (Cohen 2019). In this model, the construction of collective action, strategic plans and organizational culture is seen as a collective undertaking, where each person has a role to play within a flat structure in which formal hierarchical responsibilities are reduced to a minimum. This enables every member of an administrative entity to exercise a form of leadership, within their area of expertise or in the running of a project entrusted to them. We are aware that this model may seem far removed from the way that public administrations operate today, with their reputation for vertical action and a limited capacity to reform their structures. But the increasing complexity of the challenges faced by administrations and the speed at which changes are unfolding mean that the vertical model, which concentrates power at the top of the pyramid, is becoming obsolete. A leaderful organization is therefore not simply a theoretical construct or the expression of a more democratic model of organizational values. Rather, it is a functional necessity brought about by the evolution of our society. And in this area, public administration should play an exemplary role.

9.3 Future prospects and challenges

Over the past ten years, practical and theoretical reflections on leadership and its various forms have grown exponentially, clearly showing the intense interest in this driving force for improving organizational performance.

But some voices are warning against overvaluing leadership in the quest for organizational performance. Some studies point out that at best 10% of organizational performance is actually influenced by the leadership dimension, and that other variables—organizational, structural, cultural and environmental—could explain the remaining 90% (Pfeffer & Sutton 2007). This suggests that much of an organization's success or failure owes nothing to the style of leadership practised. This idea opens up an interesting field of research into the human qualities and skills required for effective management of a workgroup; but it is probably currently overestimated, to the detriment of other organizational realities. The linkage between leadership and other management practices and mechanisms is clearly a work in progress in terms of scientific research, but also in more practical terms. Thus, future avenues of investigation could be opened up, particularly in order to reach a better understanding of the most effective ways of coordinating and integrating leadership and organizational (managerial or management) approaches. At this stage, it seems clear that leadership cannot be the sole answer to contemporary organizational challenges, regardless of the qualities of the people exercising that leadership.

On the other hand, studies of leadership have a natural tendency to highlight its beneficial effects for organizations. A more critical reading would also be desirable in the future. Some leaders can be toxic, and their conduct can have a lasting negative effect on their subordinates—and their organization's results. Talking about these negative experiences can make important practical and intellectual contributions to the definition of altruistic, benevolent leadership. As regards public-sector organizations, continued exploration of the concept of leadership and its characteristics would be useful, because it seems to be able to foster an increase in employees' motivation in the cause of public service. This is a fruitful avenue for adapting leadership to the specific context of public administrations.

Ultimately, the most promising path is probably one that moves away from an excessively individualistic perspective on leadership towards a collective, organizational reading of running or steering an organization. Leadership is fundamentally associated with the ability to steer or lead an organizational dynamic—one that increasingly is going beyond the organization's boundaries to include key stakeholders. Both literature and practice show that without clear goals and directions, without a minimum of shared trust, and without empathy and altruism, there can be no organizational cooperation, and which jeopardizes any managerial desire for organizational change or innovation. Leading an organization therefore requires managerial, transactional and transformational skills, as well as a great deal of benevolence, but above all a collective, almost "anthropological" vision of organizational mechanisms.

Key concepts

- Leaderful organization (*organisation emplie de leadership, eine von Leadership angereichte Organisation, organizzazione leadership*): a leadership style that is not associated with a particular individual (the leader), but with an organization, where leadership is collective and distributed.
- Leadership (*leadership, Führung, leadership*): the skills, qualities and behaviours that enable a leader to mobilize subordinates to achieve organizational goals.
- Public leadership (*leadership public, für den öffentlichen Sektor angepasster Leadership, leadership pubblica*): a leadership style compatible with the characteristics of an environment specific to public-sector organizations and conducive to the strengthening of a collective orientation towards public value.
- Transformational leadership (*leadership transformationnel, transformationales Leadership, leadership trasformazionale*): a leadership style oriented towards the development of individual and collective skills enabling organizational learning and evolution.

References

Bass, B. M. (1985). *Leadership and performance beyond expectations.* Free Press.

Bass, B. M., Avolio, B. J., Jung, D. I. & Berson, Y. (2003). Predicting unit performance by assessing transformational and transactional leadership. *Journal of Applied Psychology, 88*, 207–218.

Boukamel, O. & Emery, Y. (2018). Les freins culturels à l'innovation dans l'administration publique : spécificités helvétiques. *Gestion et management public, 6*(4), 25–44.

Cohen, R. H. (2019). *Les leviers de l'engagement.* Eyrolles.

Day, D. V. & Antonakis, J. (2012). *The nature of leadership.* Los Angeles: SAGE.

Denhardt, J. V. & Campbell, K. B. (2006). The role of democratic values in transformational leadership. *Administration & Society, 38*, 556–572.

Giauque, D. (2013). L'administration publique fédérale suisse en comparaison internationale : à la recherche d'une tradition administrative. In A. Ladner, J.-L. Chappelet, Y. Emery, P. Knoepfel, L. Mader, N. Soguel & F. Varone. (Eds.), *Manuel d'administration publique suisse* (pp. 31–45). Presses polytechniques et universitaires romandes.

Giauque, D., Ritz, A., Varone, F. & Anderfuhren-Biget, S. (2010). Public service motivation. First empirical evidence in Swiss municipalities. *Yearbook of Swiss Administrative Sciences, 1*(1), 159–170.

Gould-Williams, J. & Davies, F. (2005). Using social exchange theory to predict the effects of HRM practice on employee outcomes. *Public Management Review, 7*(1), 1–24.

Moynihan, D. P. & Van Wart, M. (2013). Lessons from leadership theory and the contemporary challenges of leaders. *Public Administration Review, 73*(4), 553–565.

Osborne, D. & Gaebler, T. (1993). *Reinventing government: How the entrepreneurial spirit is transforming the public sector*. Penguin Books.
Ospina, S. M. (2017). Collective leadership and context in public administration: Bridging public leadership research and leadership studies. *Public Administration Review*, *77*(2), 275–287.
Pfeffer, J., & Sutton, R. I. (2006). *Hard facts, dangerous half-truths, and total nonsense: Profiting from evidence-based management*. Harvard Business Press.

References for further study

Lindorff, M. (2009). We're not all happy yet: Attitudes to work, leadership, and high performance work practices among managers in the public sector. *The Australian Journal of Public Administration*, *68*(4), 429–445.
Miao, Q., Newman, A., Schwarz, G. & Cooper, B. (2018). How leadership and public service motivation enhance innovative behavior. *Public Administration Review*, *78*(1), 71–81. https://doi.org/10.1111/puar.12839 (accessed 23.11.2022).
Tang, G., Chen, Y., van Knippenberg, D. & Yu, B. (2020). Antecedents and consequences of empowering leadership: Leader power distance, leader perception of team capability, and team innovation. *Journal of Organizational Behavior*, *41*(6), 551–566. https://doi.org/10.1002/job.2449 (accessed 23.11.2022).

PART III

Organization and processes

Introduction

Tobias Mettler

1 Purpose of the "organization and processes" dimension

When the term "organization" is used in scientific literature or in everyday language, it can refer to a variety of aspects, leaving room for many interpretations and meanings. While the previous contributions mainly describe the institutional and functional perspective of public administration, the purpose of this dimension is to focus primarily on the *instrumental perspective* (how the public administration "organizes"). The aim here is to define effective and efficient mechanisms (processes) and structures (organization in the sense of how things are organized) and perpetuate them (Bleicher 1981; Hunziker 1999).

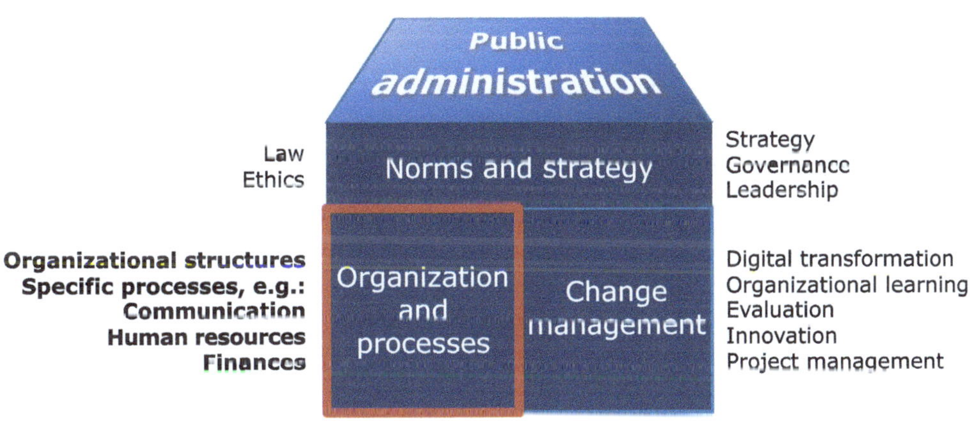

Figure III.1 The "organization and processes" dimension in the IDHEAP model

2 Components of the "organization and processes" dimension

When seeking to define the term organization using an instrumental approach, public administration is generally seen as a set of various value-creating activities. In the value-chain approach defined by Porter (1985), a distinction is made between primary activities, which are directly necessary for the provision of a service, such as consulting and communication (▶ 11 Communication management), and supporting activities, such as public procurement, personnel management (▶ 12 Human-resources management) or financial management (▶ 13 Financial management). If these activities are grouped together logically and occur roughly in an established order, they are often referred to as processes. The complete set of an organization's processes is also referred to as the process landscape.

Beyond the definition and perpetuation of effective and efficient processes, structural aspects also play an important role. Should service provision be centralized or decentralized? Should activities be carried out in-house or outsourced? In this age of digitalization and hybridization of the world of work, isn't it better to create networked structures? Are fixed workstations still necessary? Answering these and many other questions falls within the remit of the process-based organization, because it—among other things—must define and implement optimal forms of collaboration, communication channels and hierarchical levels (▶ 10 Organizational structures). The well-known management-science principle that "structure follows process follows strategy" (Chandler 1990) teaches us, however, that hierarchical and structural considerations must come after an organization's processes have been configured, which is rarely the case in reality. This often leads to problems such as isolated solutions, redundancy, or manual data re-entry resulting from missing or incompatible data exchange interfaces, amongst others.

But it is not always necessary to fully optimize processes to eliminate all inefficiencies and redundancies. Unlike the value chains of private companies, whose purpose is to increase the organization's competitiveness, those of public administration are designed to coordinate various processes with the aim of providing and distributing a specific public service, and thus to generate a social and/or political benefit (Dorobek *et al.* 2009) that contributes to improving the common good (Meynhardt 2019).

References

Bleicher, K. (1981). *Organisation - Formen und Modelle.* Gabler.

Chandler, A. D. (1990). *Strategy and structure: Chapters in the history of the industrial enterprise.* MIT Press.

Dorobek, S., Eßig, M. & Klein-Schmeink, S. (2009). Besonderheiten öffentlicher Wertschöpfungsketten. In M. Eßig & M. Witt (Eds.), *Öffentliche Logistik* (pp. 151–196). Springer.

Hunziker, A. W. (1999). *Prozessorganisation in der öffentlichen Verwaltung: New Public Management und Business Reengineering in der schweizerischen Bundesverwaltung*. Haupt.

Meynhardt, T. (2019). Public value: Value creation in the eyes of society. In A. Lindgreen, N. Koenig-Lewis, M. Kitchener, J. D. Brewer, M. H. Moore, & T. Meynhardt (Eds.), *Public value: Deepening, enriching, and broadening the theory and practice* (pp. 5–22). Routledge.

Porter, M. E. (1985). *Competitive advantage: Creating and sustaining superior performance*. Free Press.

10 Organizational structures

Oliver Neumann

10.1 The importance of organizational structures for public administration

We often ask participants in the continuing-education seminars we organize whether they have been affected by a reorganization during the past year. The proportion of those who come forward (usually close to a quarter) never ceases to surprise us. These people almost always, work in very different public organizations. This means that many public-sector entities are frequently engaged in a process of transformation, actively considering how to adapt their organizational structures to current circumstances. The events underlying these changes are many and varied: a political intervention, a reshuffle in the management team, a new strategic direction or a major crisis facing the organization, for example. Reorganizations also bring their share of worries and disruption to an organization. They may even have the effect of hobbling the capacity for action of the units concerned, until such time as the new structures are well established and staff have found their feet and become accustomed to operating within a new hierarchy. The frequency of changes in organizational structures, and their possible undesirable effects, underline how important it is to consider them from a theoretical point of view before proceeding with their implementation.

In addition to frequent reorganizations, public entities are known for their highly hierarchical structure. As a result, decisions often have to be referred to higher echelons for ratification, before coming back down the hierarchy, which is time- and energy-consuming. Another characteristic of public-sector organizations is their strict compartmentalization between areas of activity (e.g. environmental, transport or economic departments). In addition, these units frequently have few connections with one another and answer to heterogeneous political interests, since they are headed by different political managers. Thus, in a way, they form juxtaposed silos. This configuration also leads to difficulties, especially when a complex societal problem (such as climate change) concerns several departments. Nonexistent or laborious consultation processes, jurisdictional disputes, redundancies, wasted resources and ineffective action are often the result. As early as 1922, in his book *Economy and Society*, German sociologist Max Weber described the organizational aspects of an ideal bureaucracy (i.e. administrative organization) as follows: a hierarchical form of organization, a formal division of power and authority, a fixedly defined field of activity, a strict division of tasks and professionalism (Weber 2002). A century later, these characteristics are still omnipresent. But is it still necessary and appropriate, in the age of digitalization and major societal challenges, for public organizations to have a strictly hierarchical silo structure? Because in today's world, responsiveness, speed and customer focus play an essential role. Citizens rightly expect such changes to take hold. Recent years have indeed shown a trend towards more interconnected, less hierarchical forms of organization, which we discuss in the following pages.

This contribution therefore sets out to explore the theme of organizational structures in greater depth. In the next section, we first look at the notion of organization, and examine three typical forms of organization: functional, divisional and matrix. Their respective advantages and disadvantages are discussed. We also formulate a number of design principles that can serve as benchmarks for public-sector managers in the context of a reorganization. In the third and final section, we look at current perspectives and future challenges, with a focus on trends away from traditional organizational structures, issues concerning more open forms of organization and agility principles and their implications for organizations. These various aspects will be illustrated with concrete examples.

10.2 Key points of organizations

10.2.1 The concept of organization

The term organization has two meanings (Schreyögg & Geiger 2020). On the one hand, it refers to systems as a whole—companies, administrations, schools, churches and so on. In this sense, the more specific notion of "institutional organization" is often used. On the other hand, the term organization—in the sense of "manner of organizing"—covers the various characteristics of the internal structure of such a system, such as its degree of centralization. In this case, we speak more specifically of "instrumental organization", which will be the main focus of this contribution. An essential objective of organization defined in this sense is to configure work processes to ensure that services can be provided with maximum reliability and efficiency. Work processes are brought together in a structure that constitutes organization. However, this aggregation does not take place in an uncontrolled manner. Guiding this process—in other words, organizational design—is the job of management. Seen in this light, organization is a tool for management and performance management, alongside other instruments such as strategic planning, monitoring and evaluation. Of course, these instruments are often interdependent, especially organization and strategy. Organization must be aligned with strategy if implementation is to be successful (▶ 7 Strategy). For example, if a new strategy prioritizes innovation, but organization is based on a hierarchical, silo-structured model, the cross-functional creativity and responsiveness required for innovation is unlikely to be achieved.

In concrete terms, what elements should be considered before those responsible for organizational design choose a form of organization, be it functional, divisional or matrix? They must consider three main areas of tension. First comes the balance between subdivision and coordination, with, on the one hand, the process of subdividing tasks into sub-areas, each with its own management mechanisms (known as "differentiation") and, on the other hand, the process of coordinating these sub-areas (also known as "integration") so that the expected main tasks can be accomplished jointly. If differentiation is insufficient, task management will be hampered. If it is too great, integration may be compromised, mainly due to a lack of consultation. The organization then risks disintegrating. Second, managers need to pay attention to the sharing of power and decision-making competencies within the organization. These can be either concentrated and centralized at the top of the hierarchy, or decentralized and distributed along the chain of command. A high concentration of power makes for more consistent decision-making, with authority in the hands of fewer people. Decentralized power speeds up the decision-making process and ensures that decisions are made by those who are directly involved in the field of activity concerned, and therefore have greater knowledge. Third, consideration must be given to the prevailing degree of normativity within the organization: this may range from a strong emphasis on general rules and guidelines to a high degree of self-organization, with problem-solving and regulatory arrangements varying between different teams. A highly standardized environment prevents incompatibilities and redundancies, and promotes fairness; self-organization brings greater flexibility and openness to alternative approaches. In the face of these three areas of tension, the context and culture of the organization (in the institutional sense) always play an important role and must be taken into consideration.

10.2.2 Functional organization

Functional organization is based on the idea of structuring an organization around specialized subtasks (Schreyögg & Geiger 2020). In this form of organization, functions of a similar nature are grouped together in departments at the second level of the hierarchy. This type of structure is generally found in organizations providing a relatively homogeneous range of products or services. An example of this type of organization is Swissmint, the company responsible for producing the Confederation's coins. Its organization chart is shown in Figure 10.1. Swissmint has a clear mission, which is to mint current coins for payment transactions in Switzerland, as well as various coins for collectors and hoarders. Below the general manager and a support unit attached to him or her, called "Management systems", this organization of quite modest size has the functional divisions "Marketing and Sales Management" (with the subdivisions "Sales/Administration" and "Marketing") and "Technical Management" (with the subdivisions "Tool Production" and "Production"). None of the departments can function properly independently of the others. For example, if the "Tool Production" department were to disappear, the "Production" department would no longer be able to manufacture coins, making sales and marketing impossible or useless.

The main advantage of functional organization lies in a rigorous separation of tasks (differentiation) and thus in a high degree of specialization of departments. It is conducive to a high degree of professionalization and hence to the effectiveness and efficiency of each department. Synergy effects can also be achieved in the handling of similar tasks, for example when administration is handled by a single department. The main disadvantage is the amount of coordination required between departments (integration), which can lead to internal management problems and generate a silo mentality.

As a result, the mission of the organization as a whole risks taking backstage to the subtasks of individual departments, resulting in suboptimal overall performance. Coordination between departments is handled at the top of the hierarchy, with a high concentration of power. The risk of management burnout increases with the

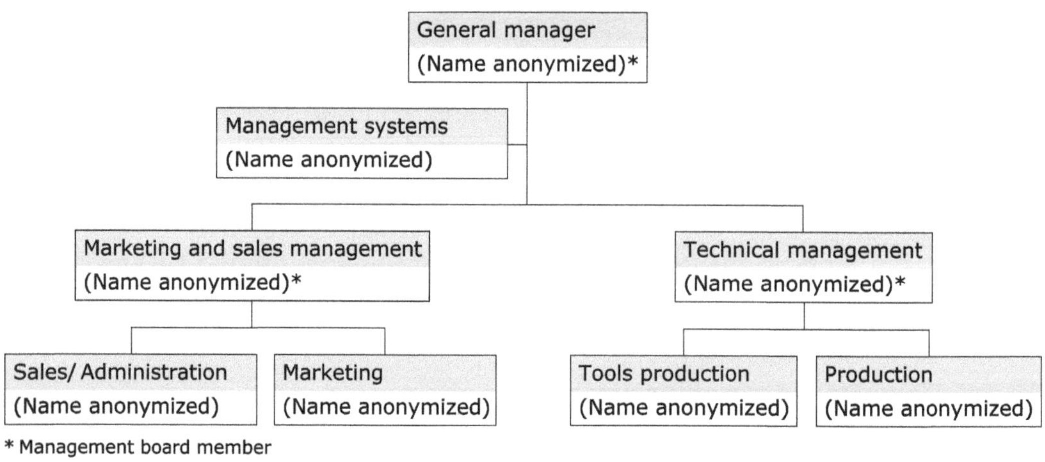

Figure 10.1 Swissmint organization chart (status: February 2023 © Swissmint)

size of the organization. Achieving good cooperation between departments generally requires highly formalized standards, but this can penalize innovative solutions.

10.2.3 Divisional organization

Divisional organization is based on relatively independent elements, such as various products, public policies, markets or regions (Schreyögg & Geiger 2020). A department will therefore group together a number of skills that will all be needed to produce or supply a service. This focus is reflected, at the second hierarchical level, in divisions that enjoy relative independence. Each division has significant autonomy and provides a wide range of services to its external stakeholders. This type of organizational structure is therefore often only found in relatively large organizations operating in several fields. An example of this type of organization is the administration of the city of Biel, in the canton of Bern, whose organization chart is shown in figure 10.2. The administration is headed by an executive body, the municipal council, with five members drawn from the world of politics. The council is chaired by the mayor. Each member is responsible for one of five departments, each dedicated to different areas of public policy, such as "Education, Culture and Sport" or "Social Action and Security". If one of the departments were to disappear, the others would be able to continue their activities (with the exception of the Finance Department and the City Hall Department, which, as central departments, provide

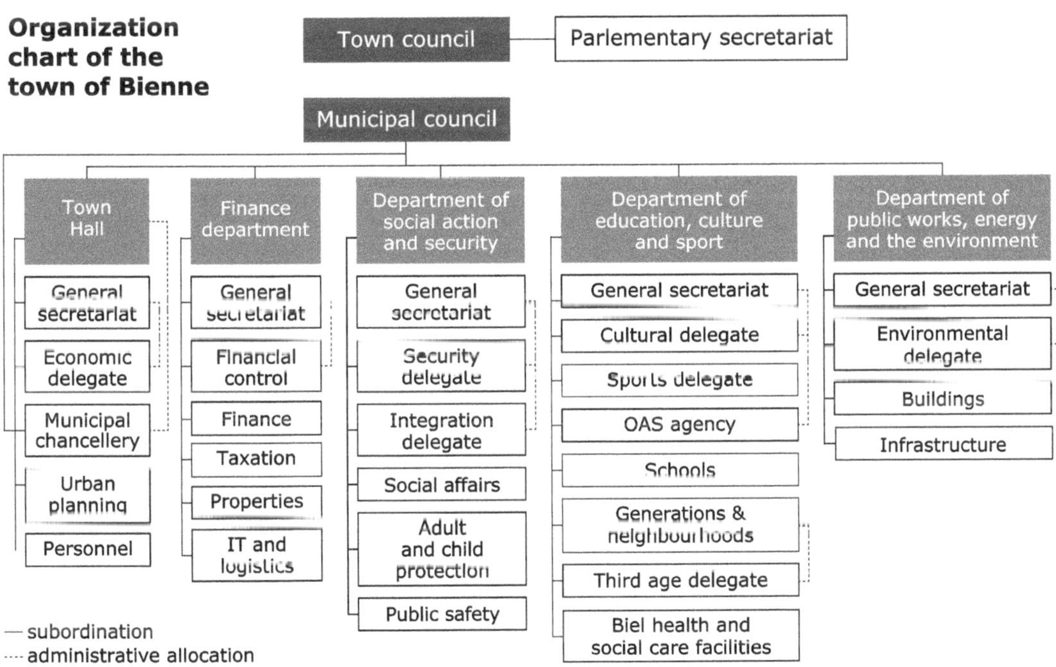

Figure 10.2 Organizational chart of Biel Municipal Administration (status: September 2022 © City of Biel)

essential services to the other departments). This is a characteristic property of divisional organization.

The main advantage of divisional organization is the substantial autonomy allowed to divisions. This gives them greater speed and efficiency of action. As a result, dependencies (and hence differentiation) are reduced, simplifying integration. Increased autonomy can also help to increase employee motivation and identification with the division. With power distributed along the chain of command, the weight of decision-making is spread over more shoulders. Generally, all divisions are subject to a low level of formal standards, which gives them greater flexibility. Disadvantages include a loss of efficiency due to redundancies between departments and a profusion of management positions. Like functional organization, divisional organization also carries the risk of silo mentality. In addition, management of the reporting system that ensures supra-divisional control can become very cumbersome. Finally, from the customer's point of view, finding a contact person can be confusing in an organization where each division has its own contact channels.

10.2.4 Matrix organization

Matrix organization combines the characteristics of both functional and divisional organization. Like the latter, it is structured vertically around divisions (administrative units) focused on a particular field, each with a high degree of autonomy in terms of products, markets or regions. But there is also a horizontal dimension that cuts across divisions and, just like functional organization, is organized into specialized functions such as personnel, finance, research and development and information technologies. Employees are thus simultaneously assigned to two departments, one divisional and the other functional, and are therefore subordinate to two managerial structures. In this configuration, functional departments enjoy a status similar to that of divisions. Their purpose is not, as it is in divisional organization, to be merely centralized departments providing services for other units. As a result, in matrix organization, the people in charge of functional departments are often also members of general management. Functional departments ensure that their services are provided efficiently and effectively across all divisions. But since it is very complex to implement, matrix organization is generally only found in very large structures covering a broad spectrum of activities. Swiss Post, whose organizational chart is shown in figure 10.3, provides an example of matrix organization in the public sector.

Within the Swiss Post Group, the Board of Directors and Executive Management oversee the following divisions (administrative units, or "strategic subsidiaries" in the terminology used by Swiss Post): Logistics Services, Communication Services, PostalNetwork (access points), Mobility Services (including the Postbus), as well as PostFinance (retail bank), which is somewhat separated from the rest of the group. The heads of these areas are members of Executive Management (with the exception of PostFinance). Functional departments ("function units" in Swiss Post terminology) such as Finance & Real Estate, Informatics/Technology, Communication, Human Resources and Corporate Services are simultaneously responsible for all divisions (administrative units, strategic subsidiaries), and some of their managers are also members of Executive Management.

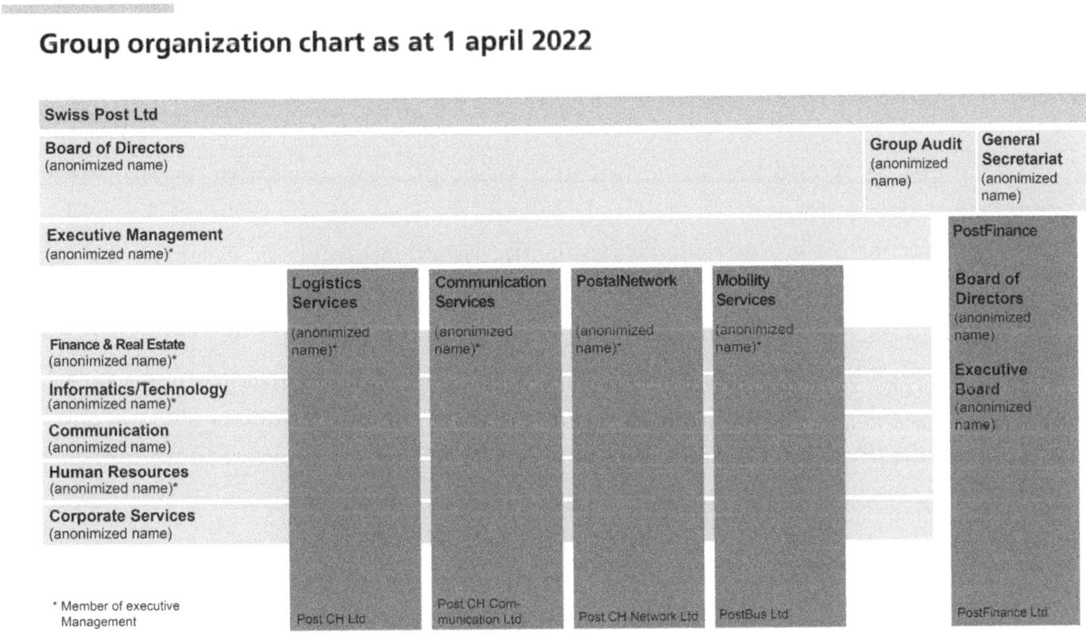

Figure 10.3 Organizational chart of Swiss Post Ltd (status: April 2022 © Swiss Post
Source: https://www.post.ch/en/about-us/profile/swiss-post-group-structure (accessed 12.12.2023)

The greatest advantage of a matrix organization is its ability to counteract silo mentality thanks to the strong interlocking of divisional and functional departments, making good integration possible despite relatively high differentiation. This allows a more assertive global vision to be instilled throughout the entire organization. In addition, the cross-cutting nature of functional departments means that general resources (such as IT) can be allocated more efficiently. These two aspects contribute to improving overall performance. For customers of functional departments, the shared access simplifies the search for a contact person. The intensified interactions between different departments can also be a vector for innovation (Schreyögg & Geiger 2020). Power is fairly evenly distributed along the chain of command, and the burden of decision-making is spread over many shoulders. Nevertheless, vertical and horizontal cooperation often requires a highly standardized framework. This brings us to the disadvantages of matrix organization. Chief among these are the extreme complexity and enormous amount of coordination required, supported by a high level of bureaucracy. The number of managerial positions is even higher than in divisional organization, and this can multiply rivalries in terms of decision-making powers. On the human-resources side, the dual hierarchical structure is not only a source of conflict, but also of burnout. At the same time, a dilution of competences can occur, compromising the sense of responsibility for problems encountered. Lastly, complexity can slow down decision-making processes, which can be severely taxing for senior management.

10.2.5 Design principles for an appropriate organizational structure

At this point we would like to set out nine principles for successful organizational design in public entities:

- When structuring, or restructuring, an organization, it is essential to take into account key contextual factors such as the organization's size, culture and stakeholders.
- In large organizations, not all hierarchical levels need to be structured in the same way (e.g. only divisionally, or only functionally). Mixed forms are also possible.
- Reorganizations must be carried out judiciously and at a measured frequency to avoid excessive disruption to the organization, or even paralysis for an extended period.
- The reorganization process must be supported by clear communication of the rationale and timetable for the reorganization. Comments and concerns should be taken seriously.
- Subdivision of tasks (differentiation) should cease where the effort of coordination between sub-areas required to ensure concerted execution of core tasks (integration) becomes difficult to maintain.
- The sharing of power and decision-making depends on the organization's mission. In principle, however, decentralized power offers a number of advantages, including greater speed and flexibility.
- The degree of normative constraint within the organization should be as low as possible, but also as high as necessary. Superfluous standards should be subject to regular review.
- Today, instrumental organization no longer necessarily stops at the door of institutional organization. When designing an organization, thought must also be given to how interfaces with external actors and stakeholders can be arranged as efficiently as possible (see also the next section).
- Agile organization methods are attracting increasing attention in the public sector. It is therefore worth asking whether the benefits of agile working (e.g. increased customer focus and innovative capacity) might justify, within one's own entity, the transformation of certain sectors (see also next section).

10.3 Future prospects and challenges

In recent years, organizational design in the public sector has had to face two new challenges. First, it is becoming increasingly difficult to draw the line between an organization seen as a system and its environment. Second, questions are still being raised as to whether the fashionable discourse advocating more agile organizational structures, as seen in software development for example, can be of practical use in public entities. These two issues are currently the subject of intense debate in scientific circles.

Debate regarding the boundary between an organization and its environment is focused on the network-governance model (Klijn 2008). In this approach, the role of public entities changes in that they no longer bear sole responsibility for providing public services. Provision of these services is instead ensured by creating a network of state and non-state actors, who together tackle societal problems or implement public policies. In this model, the main protagonist is often a public organization responsible for coordination and steering, but which is also itself involved in the provision of services. Although the debate about governance is not entirely new, this model is being used more and more frequently, including by a growing number of public organizations. The move towards networked collaboration is a response to the growing complexity of issues facing society, such as climate change. Responding to such challenges requires multi-dimensional approaches from experts from various disciplines. If the necessary expertise or resources are not available within the organization, adopting a network-governance approach is an appropriate course of action. Under these conditions, a public organization's interfaces with the outside world play an increasingly important role, essentially becoming a constituent element of the organizational structure. Organizations must strive to become more open, if only to enable intensive collaboration within networks of state and non-state actors (▶ 8 Governance). Designing these interfaces raises a number of questions, such as how to arrange them to ensure that collaboration is as efficient and effective as possible. Beyond the organizational aspects involved, this often challenges the organization's culture and identity. The response to these questions will come from collaboration between the scientific community and those in the field, leading to a reciprocal transfer of knowledge and experience.

The second challenge for public-sector organizational design concerns agile working methods and their implications for organizational structure. These working methods, initially used for software development, have revolutionized the IT sector (▶ 14 Digital transformation). But agile principles can also be applied in other fields, particularly to organizations aiming to offer innovative products and services. This explains why this new approach is attracting interest from many public organizations. However, there are as yet few examples of successful agile transformation in public organizations. Agile organization is based on four fundamental values: 1) individuals and the interactions between them are more important than work processes and tools, 2) products and services that work are more important than comprehensive documentation, 3) collaboration with customers is preferable to contract negotiation, 4) it is better to respond to change than to follow a pre-established plan (Mergel *et al.* 2020). In terms of organizational structure, an agile entity is very different from the three typical forms described earlier. It is focused above all on teams. As far as possible, teams should bring together all the skills needed to develop or deliver a product or service (or part of it). The optimum size for a team is around seven people who organize themselves, work in the same place if possible, and preferably concentrate on a single task. This approach virtually abolishes any kind of hierarchy. Integration arises out of a strong shared vision to which everyone contributes. Managers become coaches or "servant leaders" who attempt to iron out difficulties that teams encounter. Decision-making hierarchy and control give way to autonomy and trust. The normative framework is limited to a strict minimum, and focuses on rules of cooperation, inspired by existing frameworks from the IT world, such as Scrum and Crystal. Agile methodology generally works well in small entities, but can also be scaled up to large organizations (Rigby *et al.* 2018). In the Swiss public sector, for example, the Swiss Federal Railways (SBB) are currently experimenting with this approach. Agile teams and organizations often work in a more flexible, customer-oriented, efficient and cross-functional way. However, bringing teams of this type into a hierarchical organization comes up against significant obstacles. A public organization is unlikely to be able to transform itself completely into an agile organization. Instead, it will initially limit the changeover to a few isolated departments. Interfaces between the old and new systems (usually in the form of a manager with an understanding of both worlds) then become necessary to guarantee cooperation. But trying to integrate an agile team into existing structures is doomed to failure. Agile working methods are incompatible with the power structure, reporting systems and decision-making channels of traditional organizations. It is interesting to note that, in organizations whose activities and products are not limited to information technology, agile practices first appear within the IT department before spreading to other areas of activity. However, since this trend is still relatively recent in Switzerland, it will be exciting to monitor how it evolves and to draw potentially generalizable lessons.

Key concepts

- Agile organization (*organisation agile, agile Organisation, organizzazione agile*): a trend stemming from software development, attracting increasing interest in the public sector, focused on self-organized, cross-functional teams, autonomy, trust and customer orientation. This new approach represents a challenge for organizations operating with traditional structures, however, due to its partial incompatibility with these structures.

- Divisional organization (*organisation divisionnaire, divisionale Organisation, organizzazione divisionale*): a form of organization in which the structure is based on relatively autonomous objects such as products, public policies, regions or markets, and in which departments are responsible for providing services autonomously.
- Functional organization (*organisation fonctionnelle, funktionale Organisation, organizzazione funzionale*): a form of organization in which the structure is subdivided into partial, specialized tasks, with tasks of the same nature grouped together within a single department.
- Matrix organization (*organisation matricielle, Matrixorganisation, organizzazione a matrice*): a form of organization combining aspects of functional organization (horizontal structure) and divisional organization (vertical structure), with both dimensions generally having similar importance.
- Organization (*organisation, Organisation, organizzazione*): a term designating, on the one hand, complete systems pursuing a given goal (institutional organization), and on the other, various characteristics of the internal structure of such a system (instrumental organization).

References

Klijn, E. H. (2008). Governance and governance networks in Europe: An assessment of ten years of research on the theme. *Public management review, 10*(4), 505–525.

Mergel, I., Ganapati, S. & Whitford, A. B. (2020). Agile: A new way of governing. *Public Administration Review, 81*(1), 161–165.

Rigby, D. K., Sutherland, J. & Noble, A. (2018). Agile at scale. *Harvard Business Review, 96*(3), 88–96.

Schreyögg, G. & Geiger, D. (2020). *Organisation: Grundlagen moderner Organisationsgestaltung*. Springer Verlag.

Weber, M. (2002). *Wirtschaft und Gesellschaft: Grundriss der verstehenden Soziologie*. Mohr Siebeck.

References for further study

Carnevale, D. (2002). *Organizational development in the public sector*. Westview Press.

Christensen, T., Lægreid, P. & Røvik, K. A. (2020). *Organization theory and the public sector: Instrument, culture and myth*. Routledge.

11 Communication management

Martial Pasquier and Vincent Mabillard

11.1 The importance of communication for public administration

Communication is becoming increasingly important in the public sector. Whatever the institutional level, public bodies have a duty to inform the general public—sometimes with the aim of influencing their behaviour. With the multiplication of communication channels, in particular through new technologies, new possibilities for interaction between administrations and the population are opening, bringing authorities closer to residents. The need to communicate has been greatly amplified by the frequency and scale of the crises facing our societies. In these circumstances, the Federal Council and the administrative bodies concerned are multiplying press conferences and publicity campaigns. These communication campaigns are particularly aimed at promoting desirable behaviours or supporting the people and businesses concerned. New technologies have prompted organizations to create applications, which are promoted through a wide range of traditional and digital media (press releases, advertisements in newspapers and on posters, banner ads). The use of more playful tools, such as challenges launched on social media, is also on the rise.

All the tools of communication are used on a daily basis to present public-policy issues, explain the decisions made by governments and administrations, promote values or behaviours, facilitate access to public services, highlight the activities of organizations or reinforce recruitment. Communication has thus become essential to the running of public organizations owing to the need to keep the entire population informed and to the growing value placed on dialogue between governors and governed.

11.1.1 Characteristics of public communication

Public communication can be defined as all activities of public institutions and organizations undertaken for the purpose of exchanging and transmitting information. Above all, public communication seeks to present and explain public actions and decisions, promote their legitimacy, help to maintain social ties and uphold values recognized by the community (Pasquier 2017). It is mainly focused on institutions (parliament, government, courts) and public organizations, which can take a wide variety of forms (administration, autonomous agencies, etc.). It pursues two objectives: on the one hand, transmitting information, by disseminating it or making it available in a clear, structured way to all those concerned; on the other, exchanging information in order to gain a better understanding of people's expectations and level of knowledge, and to involve them more in public decisions.

There are several types of communication specific to the public sector. *Government communication* seeks to inform and explain government decisions and actions. The presentation of a legislative programme, major projects or the budget, which usually brings together all the members of the government, are high points in government communication. *Communication in connection with the rights and obligations of citizens* includes making available all existing legal bases (systematic compilation of laws), opening up the debates of legislative and judicial authorities (control of the exercise of power) and making available information produced by the administration (principle of transparency, see below). The promotion of popular rights is also part of this type of communication. *Communication as an instrument of public policy* includes all awareness, prevention (smoking, AIDS, etc.) and promotion campaigns. These communication activities are usually explicitly included in legal provisions as specific measures to achieve public-policy objectives, like other tools.

Institutional communication seeks to enhance the value of organizations beyond their own activities. For example, it may involve publicizing an organization and its missions, or reinforcing their legitimacy. The publication of activity reports or the organization of open days are part of this type of communication. The purpose of *communication in connection with public services* is to provide information on services offered by the administration (conditions for obtaining a service, documents to be submitted, prices, etc.). *Project communication* is focused on major projects, especially infrastructure projects (bridges, metro systems, etc.). *Internal communication* is aimed primarily at an organization's employees. This type of communication has seen strong development with intranet sites, in-house newspapers, etc. Finally, *crisis communication* involves the dissemination of information in times of crisis or unrest affecting the population as a whole. Although public communication uses the same tools as private and political organizations, it differs from them significantly. A number of studies equate traditional public-communication activities with those of the private sector, particularly in view of the spread of digital communication (chiefly websites and social networks). But public communication obeys different rules and serves different functions. Above all, public organizations have a legal and sometimes moral obligation to communicate that is absent in the private sector. In addition, the generally lower budget in the public sector, the greater political pressure than in the private sector, and the growing demand from citizens for information result in quite marked differences in the way that public and private organizations communicate on a daily basis (Liu *et al.* 2010).

The distinction between public and political communication is essential, because there is a high risk of funding personal, private or partisan interests with public money. In this sense, the communication activities of public organizations must first and foremost serve collective interests. Although they are often lacking in detail on the rules to be followed, a number of legal provisions governing public-communication activities allow them to be differentiated from communication for political purposes, which primarily serves the "conquest of power" (Cotteret 1997). In this respect, the Huchon case in France is worthy of note. The Île-de-France regional council, whose president was Jean-Paul Huchon, ran a poster campaign promoting regional transport and related major achievements at a cost of €1.6 million. This campaign was launched six months prior to the 2010 regional elections. Following a complaint from a member of the opposition, the Conseil d'État (administrative court) ruled that the campaign constituted a promotional activity for Huchon's candidacy, and demanded that the candidate reimburse the regional authority for this cost.

It should also be noted that the communication activities of public organizations, as addressed in this contribution, are generally qualified as active communication, in that they are planned, organized and carried out by the corresponding entities. This differs from passive communication, which consists in making existing information and documents available at the request of a natural or legal person outside the administration (access-to-information or transparency laws). This principle of *transparency*, long established in countries such as Sweden (1766) and Finland (1951), has only more recently been codified in Switzerland at the federal level (2004). The characteristics of these laws are quite similar: they specify what information can be consulted, give exceptions, indicate how the state must provide information, and so on. The adoption of access-to-information laws marked the transition from the principle of secrecy to that of transparency in government.

11.1.2 The development of public communication

The growth in public communication can be explained by changes in our society and in representations of the political-administrative system. The latter has indeed evolved considerably since the 1980s, with the emergence of, first, the New Public Management model, and then *democratic governance* (Sørensen and Torfing 2007).

One immediate consequence is that organizations must increasingly demonstrate their ability to deliver results with the resources they are given, and thus take every opportunity to communicate about outcomes. Our society has also undergone considerable change, moving towards *hyperreality*. The tendency to comment on every word, every action, every sign—all scrutinized in an attempt to identify hidden intentions, inflections, support or decisions—has resulted in greater professionalization of communication activities, aimed at mastering and winning the "war of symbols".

The growing demand for information from constituents, the move towards transparency, increased media pressure and the need to secure public support in times of crisis make these communication activities essential to managing public organizations and strengthening the bond of trust between governors and governed. For example, if authorities can get the population to support its projects, they no longer need to use force; communication therefore plays a major role. In addition, the need for accountability (not just from a legal standpoint towards political institutions, but also towards other administrations, the media and the general public) is part and parcel of the need to communicate clearly and regularly about decisions made by public bodies. Lastly, citizens, political parties, associations and journalists cannot help make democracy function properly without a regular exchange of information.

The growing importance of public communication can also be explained by the arrival of new media, and more generally by the omnipresence of the media in our professional and private lives. The fact that electronic media enable ongoing exchanges between senders and receivers means that public organizations must now be able to communicate and control messages continuously. Digital technology is therefore an integral part of the communication toolbox (Doutrellot *et al.* 2012). Reaching people involves generating interaction around their interests on the web, and the message delivered must meet the personal biases expressed by internet users. On top of this phenomenon comes the increasing mediatization of our society: every person, event or organization gains exposure, and sometimes overexposure, in the media. For all these reasons, public organizations would be extremely ill-advised to neglect their communication activities.

11.2 Key points of public communication

The key points here focus on the main functions and rules of public communication, on the development of digital technology and lastly on professionalization and evaluation issues, on which recommendations will be given at the end of the section.

11.2.1 Functions of public communication

Communication activities are central to the conduct of administrative activity: they fulfil functions that are essential to creating and maintaining trust and social ties between public organizations and the population. These functions cover several types of action:

- providing information to the public to underpin the state's democratic functioning (information brochures at the time of referendums, detailed budgets, etc.);
- explaining and giving background information on decisions; this requires pedagogical skills to convey often complex information to a non-professional audience;
- upholding values and promoting responsible behaviour through days dedicated to certain rights and values, or through awareness-raising campaigns (brochures, for example); and
- promoting dialogue between public organizations and citizens to enable the latter to understand the complexity of public policies.

Public-communication activities are also aimed at welcoming and listening to users of administrative services, promoting the legitimacy of organizations, and helping to maintain social ties between members of the community—particularly those who are physically, geographically and/or socially marginalized. Municipal gazettes or magazine often fulfil several of the functions mentioned above (providing information on government decisions and activities, maintaining social connections and dialogue between institutions and citizens, etc.).

11.2.2 Rules of public communication

While these various functions are a key feature of public communication, the rules it obeys are also of central importance, since they fundamentally differentiate public communication from political communication and the communication of private organizations. These rules are derived from the Constitution, which stipulates that the Federal Council "informs the general public fully and in good time about its activities..." (article 180, paragraph 2), and from the Government and Administration Organisation Act (GAOA), which specifies that the Federal Council "ensures that consistent information on its assessments, plans, decisions and provisions is provided promptly and regularly" (article 10, paragraph 2).

A first important rule concerns the continuity of information provided: partial results and news of ongoing projects must be communicated to the public. This continuous dissemination of information facilitates the work of elected representatives and the media, and informs democratic debate. Next, communication must be objective, comprehensive and tailored to the target audience. It must not suppress criticism and must ensure that information is balanced. It must also be able to react immediately in order to guarantee equal access to official information, while providing communication that is accessible to the entire population.

Another essential rule is that communication must be consistent and coordinated between the various institutional levels (between the Confederation and the cantons, for example) and between administrative departments. Confusion must be avoided at all costs, especially in crisis situations, although this can prove difficult in the case of political controversies. In addition, all issues relating to institutional affairs and current projects must be dealt with in a proportionate manner. Treatment of these subjects must be targeted so as to establish an effective partnership with the public. Lastly, dialogue-based communication encourages interaction with the public. In this respect, citizens' involvement in the actions and decision-making of the authorities seems to be increasing with the development of digital public communication.

11.2.3 "Traditional" and digital communication

Another key aspect of public communication is the development of digital tools and the online presence of government agencies. The creation and use of websites, newsletters and social-media accounts, already well established in the private sector, has greatly changed the way information is produced, managed, distributed and consumed. Digital public communication also enhances some of the functions described above, particularly the capacity to listen to the public and to engage in dialogue using platforms with greater interactive potential. While it might seem that the entire population has access to information, citizens without internet access and those who don't know how to use new means of communication must be taken into account. As a result, it is essential to ensure that the means and channels used to disseminate information to the public complement each other.

Similarly, it must be borne in mind that applications for smartphones and tablets are web-dependent, which means that not all users of public services can be reached, sometimes in very sensitive cases. For example, weather alerts sent by SMS have been replaced by push messages on the application created by the Federal Office of Meteorology and Climatology (MeteoSwiss). It has been shown that this app does not always alert people in real time. This tension between immediacy and reaching the entire population shows that while the new means of communication have undeniable advantages, they also have a number of limitations. These will be discussed in the "Future prospects and challenges" section below.

Despite the reservations expressed above, digital communication tools are being used increasingly, and are generally making it easier for administrations to share information with their users. Today, websites appear to be an essential means of providing content on the main activities of the various levels of government. The web can also be used to quickly provide direct information about planned activities, elected representatives and their interests or current legislation. However, the extent of online information provision differs greatly, especially at the local level, and depends very much on the size of municipalities and the resources available to them (Mabillard and Keuffer 2020). Social networks are also being used in a very heterogeneous way. It is not uncommon for certain public organizations to be more active than municipalities or cantons, owing to their grassroots activities. Frequently cited examples include the police, the fire department, etc. Here again, what matters is ensuring consistency and coordination between the various actors so as to avoid creating confusion in the minds of the public.

But traditional communication channels have not disappeared with the arrival of new technologies. Far from it: brochures and newsletters remain (or are once again becoming) central to communication, especially at the local level. This is perfectly in line with the need to ensure that the various methods used to reach target groups complement each other. While there are no statistics in Switzerland, a recent French study found that 78% of respondents preferred to get their information from the local authority's print magazine (Cap'Com 2018). Added to this are events (e.g. open days), trade fairs and exhibitions and media relations (press releases, interviews, participation in debates).

However, these relationships increasingly involve online content, which means that public organizations need to be well equipped to stay on top of the flow of information on the web. Internally, speeches and oral messages, personal interviews and training seminars also remain important, even if working sessions are increasingly becoming virtual, a phenomenon accentuated by the COVID-19 crisis. In addition, the digitization of administrative acts, including the mandatory electronic invoice for all suppliers to the Confederation (above CHF 5000), and the development of E-government are leading to more widespread electronic interactions with the authorities (Swiss Confederation 2019).

11.2.4 Practical recommendations

To conclude this section on key points in public communication, we offer some recommendations. First of all, in addition to guaranteeing a clear identity and delivering a clear message, communication must be citizen-centric: users must be able to find information easily, based on their own needs, without having to go from one department's website to another. Moreover, new communication technologies are reshaping the role of two-way exchanges between authorities and citizens. This means moving on from the simple dissemination of information to dialogue, by promoting participative platforms and processes.

Next, communication requires increasingly sophisticated skills. This necessitates a greater capacity for adaptation and teamwork than in the past. New communication technologies pose a strong challenge to the practice of working in silos. Technology must make it possible to anticipate certain requests and adopt a more proactive attitude, making for more effective communication. A frequently cited example is posting of content online after its publication on other media or in the context of other exchanges. The ability to communicate directly, favouring the principle of proactive transparency and capitalizing on the digital tools available to administrations, generates effective and better integrated communication.

Lastly, prioritizing and targeting messages (observing the principle of proportionality) makes the "storytelling" effort more successful. Identifying priorities and assessing the message's impact make it possible to measure and, where necessary, improve a prevention or awareness campaign, for example. Increased exchanges and feedback provided by users improve an administration's or public organization's ability to judge the effectiveness of its communication. Beyond measurement tools, to improve the effectiveness of communication, the following questions should always be asked:

- Which projects and public-policy objectives should be prioritized in my organization's communication?
- How does my organization's communication contribute to better understanding and improvement of projects and public policies under development?
- What opportunities and risks does my organization encounter in its day-to-day communication?
- Who are the priority targets of my communications, and what tools can I use to reach them? How does this fit into my organization's communications strategy?
- If I could change only one thing about my organization's communication, what would it be?

Ultimately, evaluation practices, based on objective measurements, must make it possible to reflect on both the tools and the communication strategy—all the more so because resources are becoming scarce, while digital communication platforms are flourishing.

11.3 Future prospects and challenges

Today and in the future, public organizations face a number of challenges regarding their communication activities. The main features of these challenges are set out in Table 11.1.

To begin with, the general framework of communication has changed considerably since the turn of the century. Digital media—whether traditional media transposed onto the internet, or forms specific to the digital world such as social

General communication framework	Constraints	Expectations
Digital media development	Numerous public actors at all levels of governance	Accurate real-time information
Community development and individualization of society	Numerous public policies	Information tailored to the addressee
Importance of information in our society	Rules of public communication	Dialogue and ability to interact
	Limited resources	

Table 11.1 Characteristics of the communication challenges facing public organizations

media—offer opportunities both for continuous interaction with the public or with particular target groups, and for disseminating a great deal of information that is very difficult to transmit through conventional channels. In the early 2000s, it was not possible for a cantonal government to broadcast a press conference. Today, with YouTube channels, any government can communicate core information on a region at any time (e.g. by press conferences).

The society we live in is tending towards a degree of individualization or towards grouping people into communities (virtual or physical), whose behaviours and expectations are differentiated. Although the state must ensure that it observes the principles of fairness and non-discrimination, including in its communications, the available means of communication make it possible to target individuals or defined groups more specifically based on their needs. Society has become very demanding in terms of the disclosure of information by a state that collects an enormous amount. Information must be organized and structured in such a way that anyone can access both information that concerns them (personal information) and useful information (drinking water quality, for example).

The constraints on communication are also many. More and more organizations at the international, national, interregional, regional, inter-municipal and municipal levels are focusing to some extent on the same themes. Ensuring that messages are consistent is becoming increasingly complex. Added to this is the fact that public policies are less and less isolated from one another and that the corresponding communications need to be coordinated.

Public communication is also facing growing demands regarding transparency and capacity for interaction, in a context in which other stakeholders (organizations, communities, individuals) use the full range of digital tools (emails, tweets, posts, etc.) without having to respect the criteria of objectivity and adaptation to target groups. The task of managing this mass of information, with limited resources, and with the attendant risks of misinformation, makes it absolutely crucial to find a suitable form of communication: one that is both diversified in terms of media and integrated in terms of message consistency, in line with the values promoted by public authorities and administration.

Lastly, the expectations not only of the public but also of all target groups (such as elected representatives, businesses and nonprofit associations) are increasing, making the task of administrations very difficult: information must be provided quickly, accurately and in a coordinated way, while at the same time being suited to the capabilities of the addressees. For example, in October 2020 the municipality of Bourg-en-Lavaux decided to translate its website into simplified language. Communication must also allow interaction between an administration and the people it serves. Not only does the administration have to communicate, it also has to be attentive to the questions, answers and comments of addressees. An organization that is active on social media needs to maintain a constant watch and have the resources to react to messages that are erroneous, contrary to values or malicious.

Key concepts

- Democratic governance (*gouvernance démocratique, demokratische Regierungsführung, governance democratica*): a model of administrative conduct that introduces new obligations in terms of transparency and accountability, and assigns a more active role to stakeholders, promoting participation in public decision-making in particular (Pasquier and Weiss 2017).
- E-government (*e-gouvernement, E-Regierung, governo elettronico*): the use of information and communication technologies in public administrations to increase the accessibility and quality of services provided by public organizations (Pasquier and Weiss 2017).
- Hyperreality (*hyperréalité, Hyperrealität, iperrealtà*): the inability to distinguish the real from the imaginary, often accompanied by an enhancement of reality; simulation of something that never really existed (Baudrillard 1981).
- Transparency (*transparence, Transparenz, trasparenza*): the right to know applied to relations between the administration and individuals, codified in access-to-information laws (Pasquier and Weiss 2017).

References

Baudrillard, J. (1981). *Simulacres et simulation*. Editions Galilée.

Cap'Com (2018). Baromètre de la communication locale (5e vague). https://www.cap-com.org/sites/default/files/field_file/BarometreCommunicationLocale2018.pdf (accessed 24.11.2022).

Schweizerische Eidgenossenschaft (2019). E-Government-Strategie Schweiz 2020–2023. https://www.newsd.admin.ch/newsd/message/attachments/59197.pdf (accessed 24.11.2022).

Cotteret, J.-M. (1997). *Gouverner c'est paraître*. PUF.
Doutrellot, O., Mabi, C. & Moreau, R. (2012). La communication des collectivités à l'épreuve du numérique. *Pyramides 24*(1), 93–111.
Liu, B. F., Horsley, J. S. & Levenshus, A. B. (2010). Government and corporate communication practices: Do the differences matter? *Journal of Applied Communication Research 38*(2), 189–213.
Mabillard, V. & Keuffer, N. (2020). What drives online transparency practices at the local level? Evidence from 2222 municipalities in Switzerland. *Schweizerisches Jahrbuch für Politische Wissenschaft 11*(1), 158–170.
Pasquier, M. & Weiss M. (2017). *Kommunikation öffentlicher Organisationen*, Schulthess Verlag.
Sørensen, E. & Torfing, J. (2007). *Theories of democratic network governance*. Palgrave Macmillan.

References for further study

Canel, M. J. & Luoma-aho, V. (2018). *Public sector communication*. Wiley & Sons.
Canel, M. J. & Luoma-aho, V. (2020). *Handbook of public sector communication*. Wiley & Sons.
Mégard, D. (2017). *La communication publique et territoriale* (2nd ed.). Dunod.

12 Human-resources management

Yves Emery and David Giauque

12.1 The importance of human-resources management for public administration

Human-resources management (HRM) has always been an essential responsibility for every manager. Long before the creation of "personnel departments" in Switzerland in the 1970s, line managers were expected to motivate their teams and ensure that work was carried out efficiently. This responsibility may not have been clearly formalized, however, because technical aspects (being an expert in one's professional field) were at the heart of their mission (and were often the reason for promotion to a management position).

By HRM we mean "all the processes, procedures and tools needed to deal with personnel issues. These processes may be limited to administrative aspects or may include *human resources* aspects" (Emery & Gonin 2009: 10). The term "human resources" has gradually replaced "personnel". It refers to all people active within a public organization, whether they have permanent status or not. According to the Swiss Federal Statistical Office[24], over 318,000 people work in the Swiss public sector (in the narrow sense of the term: the Confederation, cantons and municipalities).

Of the various areas of modernization in the public sector, HRM is unquestionably one of those that has undergone the greatest changes over the past 25 years, especially in Switzerland (Emery *et al.* 2019). Clearly, political leaders have realized that public-sector modernization cannot be achieved without in-depth HRM reform. Heads of department often insisted on greater latitude in human-resources (HR) management. Even the citizens voted in favour of these reforms: the new regulations regarding federal-administration personnel, put to the vote following a

24 STATENT statistics, 2015

referendum, was approved by almost two-thirds of voters[25]. From simple administrative management of personnel files, public-sector HRM is now moving towards strategic management aimed at developing human potential, which places substantial responsibility on the shoulders of both top-level managers and administrative-unit managers (▶ 9 Leadership).

12.2 Key points of HRM

Before presenting the key points of HRM from the specific perspective of executives, a few particularities of the Swiss public-sector context need to be highlighted.

12.2.1 Specific features of the Swiss context

Switzerland has undertaken very extensive reforms of the status of public-sector employees, previously known as "functionaries" (*fonctionnaires* in French). It has brought employment conditions into line with those of the private sector, both at Confederation level and in a majority of cantons (Bellanger & Roy 2013). The Swiss public-service system can thus be described as a hybrid, combining values and practices from both the public and private sectors. After more than 30 years of applying the principles of New Public Management, current HRM systems in public administrations now happily mix public-sector specificities (e.g. mandatory advertisement for vacant positions[26]) with practices typical of the private sector (e.g. performance-related pay).

The profound changes in the legal framework alone illustrate the hybrid nature of the post-civil service era. This framework most often provides for the *public-law contract*, a legal form long regarded by public-sector doctrine as heresy. Such a contract offers greater flexibility in HRM, particularly as regards the employment-termination process. Another hallmark of Swiss modernization is the considerable autonomy enjoyed by public-sector employers in defining their staff regulations. This gives Swiss public regulations a remarkable heterogeneity (▶ 5 Law). This is the opposite of unified career systems, where a single legal framework applies to all public servants.

Lastly, it should be remembered that Switzerland has a so-called "open" public-service system, allowing considerable permeability between the private and public sectors. This *de facto* places the public employer in competition on the job market.

25 https://www.admin.ch/ch/f/pore/va/20001126/det473.html (accessed 24.11.2022).
26 This rule has been relaxed, however, since many staff regulations provide for "on-call" recruitment, circumventing this sacrosanct rule from the public service.

12.2.2 Success factors in contemporary public-sector HRM

Line managers: key players in HRM

The first point to understand is this: line managers are key players in the HRM system within public entities. Of course, it is the job of the HR department, the technically specialized unit, to set policies and define the applicable HRM processes and tools. But managers are the central players, since HRM primarily plays out in the field, in the day-to-day relations between the hierarchy and subordinate staff. This fact of life in HRM (Emery & Gonin 2009) becomes all the more obvious when we consider that, for many years, many Swiss administrations have defined department heads as the *hiring authority*. This means that they are responsible for all HRM decisions, from hiring to dismissal[27]. This empowerment of senior managers in matters of HRM is a decisive point for women and men with managerial responsibilities. They therefore must have not only a high level of HR skills, but also the motivation (and the time!) to take charge of all HR issues for their unit. This is all the more important because they will be assessed on their ability to manage their staff, whether as part of the regular evaluation process or during internal satisfaction surveys[28]. Consequently, line managers need to take regular training on HR issues in order to acquire the skills needed to play this complex role. Most public employers offer their managers HR training programmes, of varying degrees of sophistication, with compulsory modules for new managers.

Mobilizing professional support from HR specialists

In exercising this responsibility, managers can turn for support to "HR respondents" (known in the private sector as "business partners"). These are HR specialists whose job is to advise line management, covering as far as possible the basic requirements of staff regulations and the specific needs and expectations of the departments concerned. In large administrative units, HR respondents can be integrated into the management team to enable it to develop "made-to-measure" solutions. However, optimizing "local" HRM in this way demands a relationship of trust between management and the person assuming the role of HR respondent, because this will give the latter real room for manoeuvre.

But if there is greater HR latitude at the local level, it is important for line managers to act in accordance with the HR policy (or strategy) defined for the whole entity (▶ 7 Strategy). And this applies to the Confederation, to cantons and to municipalities. Determining an HR policy forces an employer to define its priorities and make use of its specific assets. This is in line with the legislator's wishes in ceding some of its power to the executive, and by delegation, to the HR department. The Confederation's new personnel strategy thus sets out the main areas of work for the period

27 See, for example, the new personnel law for the State of Vaud, which came into force in 2012. Lpers-VD (172.31).
28 The Federal Administration has been conducting such a survey annually for many years.

2020-2023. These are particularly focused on preparing employees, managers and HR specialists for the profound changes brought about by digitalization[29].

Recruiting the best candidates

Today's challenges require a highly qualified workforce, and the first step is to identify the HR needs of the unit in question: this is the process of *provisional HR management*, which has developed considerably in recent years. The job of the manager in charge of the unit is to forecast staff needs over the next two or three years (with help from HR specialists, and in line with strategic-development priorities for the entity as a whole and the unit specifically). This is a matter of considering future staffing needs in the light of known staff movements and probable departures. Once this analysis has been done, the profiles of the positions to be filled, in terms of skills, personality and motivation, can be defined. In today's hybrid environment, it is important to find people who are motivated as much by public missions and values (Giauque *et al.* 2011) as by the new requirements of productivity and innovation. Finding them involves the use of specialized websites and social media as well as traditional recruitment channels. These efforts must be supported by a promotional strategy that positions the public sector as an employer of choice in the job market.

The professionalization of recruitment places greater demands on all functions that hire staff. Evaluating candidates' skills requires the increasingly frequent use of tools to assess personality and even leadership style using simulations (psychological assessment). Managers' human qualities are now decisive factors in their professional success and career development: seniority and technical competence alone are no longer enough. Managers are expected to practise a cooperative, empowering, motivating leadership style (► 9 Leadership).

Optimizing the performance of teams

Personnel performance management is undeniably one of the major themes in the modernization of Swiss public-sector HRM. This issue is directly linked to the performance orientation advocated by contemporary reforms. For a long time, apart from compliance with established rules and the general principles of public action (equal treatment, proportionality, etc.), there were no specific criteria for evaluating the work of public servants, and no work assessment was carried out except in special cases (e.g. in the event of conflicts or serious breaches).

Optimizing the performance of public servants requires defining the performance they are to deliver, together with objectives and criteria for assessing them. Many public administrations require all managers to set objectives for their staff, and then monitor their achievement over the course of the year. This calls for specialized

29 https://www.epa.admin.ch/epa/fr/home/themes/personalstrategie_bundesverwaltung.html (accessed 24.11.2022).

know-how to which many in-house training courses are devoted. If objectives were not difficult enough to set already (see the now well-known SMART+[30] acronym), they must also be consistent with the major challenges facing the organization and the department, and not contradict each other. This strategic alignment of objectives is one of the major challenges facing public-sector managers. Sometimes it highlights the inconsistency, or even non-existence, of higher-level political objectives.

Enhancing and developing the human potential of an entity

Valuing human potential starts with an appreciation of work done (both how the work was delivered and the *results achieved* [Brun & Laval 2018]). Today, a majority of public administrations have introduced a performance-evaluation tool, based on criteria common to all staff and, frequently, objectives specific to the person being evaluated. This practice is generally well accepted, even if it is not always conducted optimally. It is a complex process, from both the technical and the human point of view.

The feedback provided through evaluation (which includes self-evaluation—important in getting the person concerned to take ownership of the evaluation's conclusions) allows managers to assess the level of performance attained and to set objectives for the coming period. Performance evaluation is also central to learning, both individual and collective, which is why it is essential that evaluations provide both positive elements (successes) and points for improvement in a balanced way (▶ 15 Organizational learning). Unfortunately, many managers feel that their role is primarily to identify their staff's problems and weaknesses, which is detrimental to motivation.

Recognition of good performance calls for tangible signs of appreciation, both financial and non-financial. Recognition is crucial for motivation and involvement at work. The Swiss public sector was a pioneer in the introduction of performance-related pay. The Federal Administration introduced this practice a long time ago, as did most of the German-speaking cantons (far fewer in French-speaking Switzerland) (Bellanger & Roy 2013). As a result, there is already a great deal of experience and hindsight regarding such practices, which has made it possible to introduce necessary adjustments (Atkinson *et al.* 2014).

Financial recognition of public servants is an important area of modernization, even if the budgets made available for this purpose have often fallen short of expectations. If a strong perception of organizational justice (sense of fairness) is to be maintained, all managers must evaluate the performance of their employees as accurately as possible. This is after all the determining factor in salary increases, as well as any end-of-year bonuses. This shows that the range of this type of recognition is

30 Specific, measurable, achievable, relevant and time-bound. The "+" is added for the ethical dimension of the objective.

often broad, even if the scale (sums awarded) is limited by internal guidelines (they rarely exceed 5% of salary).

Line managers should deploy other forms of recognition, particularly opportunities for ongoing training, the allocation of specific roles and stimulating projects, flexibility in managing working hours and, last but not least, different ways of saying "thank you" for work done! This is a vital management skill, one that is all too often overlooked.

For most employees, acquiring new skills and career development are essential motivations. Today's working environment is highly dynamic, and job security is a thing of the past. It should also be remembered that the possibilities for career development within public administration are far more diverse than the traditional hierarchical promotion. Organizational charts have been flattened, reducing the number of management positions to be filled. On the other hand, the desire to assume hierarchical responsibilities is diminishing. People today are looking for interesting work and a satisfying work-life balance, making climbing up the hierarchical ladder less of a priority.

Thanks to internal mobility schemes, cross-functional career paths are encouraged, with a view to decompartmentalizing organizational units (services, departments, etc.). But mobility between professional bodies is also encouraged, allowing for a career dynamic. The most relevant career-development paths are highlighted and communicated internally.

Confronting HR issues and finding solutions

Lastly, the HR responsibilities of managers involve, albeit a good deal less popularly, confronting and resolving HR issues arising in their unit. Such issues include two key areas: managing conflicts of all kinds (lasting disagreements within a team, so-called "toxic" behaviour by unmotivated people, psychological or sexual harassment, etc.) and dealing with under-performance.

Handling these problems requires line managers to name the issues, on the basis of established facts, and then reiterate the professional requirements that must be met (both for the work to be done and for relations with working partners). This reframing often takes place during a "a management meeting", with the manager setting out the problems in a factual manner and giving those concerned the opportunity to remedy them. Sometimes, specific resources, such as support from internal or external HR specialists[31], or ad-hoc training, may be offered. This kind of support has been identified in the literature as decisive for engagement at work (Kim *et al.* 2016). Despite these various tools, it is sometimes necessary to take action of a more

31 The resource people called on to resolve conflicts are often external, in order to provide a form of neutrality that is necessary for conflict resolution or mediation.

disciplinary nature—a warning, or even dismissal[32]—but always in a professional and ethical manner (▶ 6 Ethics).

12.3 Future prospects and challenges

Digitalization is certainly one of the most important HRM-related challenges in public administration, along with the associated technological and organizational challenges (▶ 14 Digital transformation). The advent of digital administration (e-government, e-administration), which has been discussed in the literature for many years (Dunleavy *et al.* 2005), was given a boost by the 2020-2021 pandemic, particularly in the HR field, where telework became an overnight reality for a majority of public employees. Rethinking the way that public administration operates by digitizing the services it provides to its citizens entails considerable efforts in terms of HRM. The *Justitia 4.0* project is very edifying in this respect: it is aimed at dematerializing all judicial records, thus profoundly modifying the work of all those involved in the justice system, starting with judges, who are seeing their working habits turned upside down. From trivial issues such as know-how about the use of new technologies, to more complex questions concerning the ethics of public action, digitalization impacts virtually all HRM processes, including the acquisition or development of skills and the recruitment of suitable candidates in a highly competitive market.

But the biggest challenges lie in the new possibilities for control that digitalization now offers to employing organizations and their line managers. Integrating sensors into work tools, or even directly into employees' arms to monitor their biological data, poses ethical problems the scale of which we are only just beginning to grasp. Similarly, for many professionals, working anywhere and at any time has become a reality. While this sounds very appealing at first, many people can no longer clearly delimit their work and prevent it from encroaching on their private lives. This increasingly blurred boundary can lead to burnout and generate problems in relationships with partners and family.

In the face of all these changes, managers' responsibility as role models means that they must be comfortable with new technologies and help to disseminate relevant innovations within their entities, while being alert to the ethical implications involved. Digitalization is not merely a matter for specialists in new technologies: it highlights the innovative capacity of managers at all levels of the hierarchy, and their openness to experimentation and to taking (reasonable) risks (Boukamel & Emery 2018).

32 If a position is eliminated, the public employer should offer a comparable position, if one exists, within the administration concerned.

Public-sector employers are increasingly competing in the job market. Becoming an employer of choice is not a matter of course, despite the very favourable employment conditions in Swiss public administrations. They need to improve their image on the market, by developing real *public-employer branding* to secure clear, aggressive, positive positioning on the job market (Emery & Kouadio 2017). Publishing an HR policy full of tempting promises is not enough. They must be accessible to existing staff. And here, the role of line managers is crucial: they must be able to offer work that is motivational because a) the missions pursued are meaningful (contributing to the progress of society and to collective wellbeing), b) the entity's projects are rich and dynamic, and c) the management style combines a spirit of innovation with respect for staff. With expert advice from HR professionals (who should not be confined to a purely administrative role), all this is possible! So... take action.

Key concepts

- Development of human capital (*valorisation du potentiel humain, Personalentwicklung, valorizzazione del potenziale umano*): a set of processes designed to leverage the skills of staff and to serve the organization.
- HR rewarding system (*reconnaissance du personnel, Personalhonorierung, riconoscenza del personale*): all types of formal recognition, both financial and non-financial, dispensed within an administrative entity.
- Performance management (*gestion des performances, Leistungsmanagement, gestione dei risultati*): a process by which employee performance is defined, evaluated and improved.
- Human-resources management (*Gestion des ressources humaines, Personalmanagement, gestione delle risorse umane*): a broad term encompassing all the processes, procedures and tools required to deal with personnel issues (or HR issues).
- Public-employer branding (*promotion de l'employeur public, öffentliches Personalmarketing, promozione del datore di lavoro pubblico*): process by which an administrative entity defines and promotes its assets, as an employer, on the job market.

References

Atkinson, M. M., Fulton, M. & Kim, B. (2014). Why do governments use pay for performance? Contrasting theories and interview evidence. *Canadian Public Administration, 57*(3), 436–458.

Bellanger, F., & Roy, C. (2013). Évolution du cadre légal et réglementaire de la fonction publique suisse. In Ladner, A., Emery, Y., Chappelet, J.-L., Knoepfel, P., Mader, L., Soguel, N. & Varone F. (Eds.), *Handbuch der öffentlichen Verwaltung in der Schweiz* (pp. 461–480). NZZ Verlag.

Boukamel, O. & Emery, Y. (2018). Les freins culturels à l'innovation dans l'administration publique : spécificités helvétiques. *Gestion et management public, 6*(4), 25–44.

Brun, J.-P. & Laval, C. (2018). *Le pouvoir de la reconnaissance au travail : 30 fiches pratiques pour allier santé, engagement et performance.* Eyrolles.

Dunleavy, P., Margetts, H., Bastow, S. & Tinkler, J. (2005). New public management is dead. Long life digital-era governance. *Journal of Public Administration Research and Theory, 16*(3), 467–494.

Emery, Y., Giauque, D. & Gonin, F. (2019). *Gestion des ressources humaines. Pour le meilleur et pour le pire* (vol. 137). Presses polytechniques et universitaires romandes.

Emery, Y. & Gonin, F. (2009). *Gérer les ressources humaines.* Presses polytechniques et universitaires romandes.

Emery, Y., & Kouadio, A. B. (2017). Marque employeur et stratégies RH pour les employeurs publics. Le cas du bassin d'emploi Franco-Valdo-Genevois. *Management international, 21*(2), 47–59.

Giauque, D., Ritz, A., Varone, F., Anderfuhren-Biget, S., & Waldner, C. (2011). Putting public service motivation into context: a balance between universalism and particularism. *International Review of Administrative Sciences, 77*(2), 227–253. https://doi.org/10.1177/0020852311399232 (accessed 24.11.2022)

Kim, K. Y., Eisenberger, R. & Baik, K. (2016). Perceived organizational support and affective organizational commitment: Moderating influence of perceived organizational competence. *Journal of Organizational Behavior, 37*(4), 558–583. https://doi.org/10.1002/job.2081 (accessed 24.11.2022).

References for further study

Berman, E. M., Bowman, J. S., West, J. P. & Van Wart, M. R. (2019). *Human resource management in public service: Paradoxes, processes, and problems.* CQ Press.

Martory, B. & Crozet, D. (2016). *Gestion des ressources humaines : pilotage social et performances.* Dunod

Pichault, F. & Nizet, J. (2013). *Les pratiques de gestion des ressources humaines : conventions, contextes et jeux d'acteurs.* Points.

13 Financial management

Nils Soguel

13.1 The importance of financial management for public administration

Freedom from financial constraints: a prospect for public administration to dream of. Drawing up a budget, making budget requests and fearing refusals, monitoring the budget, keeping and presenting financial reports: all these steps that mark time for public entities would no longer be necessary.

The reality is more prosaic. Reforms of all kinds may come and go, but financial management remains central. It is a concern for every manager. It affects the entire range of public services and projects. The availability of budgetary resources determines the ability to pay salaries, acquire goods and services, and have an infrastructure within which to operate. Lastly, presenting the past year's financial reports is an act of accountability that public administration cannot escape.

Drawing up a budget and presenting financial reports are two key stages during which public administration must engage in dialogue with its stakeholders (▶ 3 Stakeholders), foremost among them the legislature. To illustrate the importance of financial management from a democratic point of view, we could go back to the Magna Carta in 1215. Infuriated by King John's spending and his military failures, English barons demanded that he submit his tax demands to the consent of the people. Closer to our time, the French Revolution of 1789 enshrined in the Declaration of the Rights of Man and of the Citizen that "All citizens have the right to ascertain, by themselves or through their representatives, the need for a public tax, to consent to it freely, to know the uses to which it is put [...]" (art. 14).

The right to authorize and control budgets thus became, in principle, the prerogative of the sovereign people, through their representatives in the legislature. This prerogative stands at the crossroads of sound management of public affairs, financial legislation, accounting techniques, partisan politics and legislative control over government activity. However, a paradox emerged: parliaments claim these budgetary prerogatives, but are barely able to assume them and impose their will on budgets. It is true that the amounts involved are increasingly huge. We are talking millions, billions. Choices between different areas of expenditure or receipts are becoming increasingly difficult to make. The budget is seen more and more as a complex overarching structure whose individual elements cannot be altered without jeopardizing the whole.

In this context, administrative units have a significant capacity to intervene in financial management. But they must observe a number of rules. Here, we look at the most important ones, focusing on those that specifically concern operational financial management in the Swiss context[33].

13.2 Key points of financial management

13.2.1 Legal framework

Like the Confederation, each canton has its own legal framework for financial management. The same applies to the financial management of municipalities and, where applicable, other public bodies[34]. These requirements are set out in the Constitution (federal or cantonal), the Financial Management Act of Parliament or Municipalities Act of Parliament and in their subordinate legislation.

More specifically, the Constitution—whether federal or cantonal—sets out the powers of the various authorities (legislative, executive). It sets out the conditions for tax levies (constitutionality, legality) and lists the sources of financing that can be used. It also provides for the fundamental steps of financial management, including financial planning and budgeting. The legal provisions governing the authorization of expenditure (known as the regulation of appropriations: *Kreditrecht* or *droit des crédits*), is also found there (Lienhard et al. 2017: 152-170).

The Financial Management Act is intended to enable entities falling within its scope to manage their finances in accordance with constitutional provisions[35]. Traditionally, it sets out the principles of financial management (see below), and the content of the financial plan, budget and accounts. It regulates the timetable for the budgetary process, and the types of appropriations the executive can request. It also sets out the financial responsibilities of the legislature, the executive, the finance department (or ministry or service) and the various administrative units.

33 See Soguel (2020) for strategic and global aspects at the level of a whole entity, be it the Confederation, a canton or a municipality.

34 For example, in the Canton of Berne, the legal provisions apply to all public-law entities within the meaning of the Municipalities Act of Parliament, such as political municipalities, bourgeois municipalities, parishes, unions of municipalities and regional conferences.

35 As far as the municipalities are concerned, in most cantons the Municipal Act of the cantonal Parliament lays down the procedures applicable to this institutional level.

The financial responsibilities of administrative units—ministries, departments or services—are generally as follows:

- Prepare their appropriation requests before submitting them.
- Ensure that they have sufficient appropriation available before incurring an expenditure.
- Use the resources at their disposal sparingly, efficiently and effectively, especially financial resources.
- Keep their accounts and inventories as prescribed.
- Invoice for services provided, in accordance with legal provisions.

13.2.2 Principles of financial management

Administrative units must observe various principles when managing their finances[36]. Table 13.1 lists the most common principles that have a direct impact on units. Some concern budget preparation, others the presentation of financial reports.

Budgeting principles	
Universality	Every item of expenditure and revenue, whether operating or capital works, is shown in the budget document and then in the accounts. No expenditure or receipt item is omitted or evaded.
Unit	All the entity's expenditure and receipt items are set out in a single physical or electronic document submitted to the legislature for approval in the same debate. For administrative units, this means being subject to a strict budget-preparation schedule. In accordance with this principle, consolidated financial statements should also be drawn up to give an overview of all third-party entities controlled by the entity concerned (in the case of public bodies, this includes autonomous establishments under public law).
Caution	Expense items are recognized in the budget and accounts as soon as they are foreseeable and probable. Revenue, on the other hand, is not recognized until it is certain.
Qualitative specification	A budgeted amount can only be used for the intended purpose. Consequently, budgeted amounts must be broken down by aim and by nature (see accounting categories below).
Quantitative specification	Spending authorization is given up to the ceiling set by the budgeted amount. The ceiling cannot be exceeded without further authorization.
Period specification	Spending authorization is valid only for the reference year and not beyond, i.e. during the period from 1 January to 31 December
Annuality	A budget must be requested and voted every year. Financial reports must be presented every year.

36 This sentence could be written in the conditional tense: should observe. Liberties are regularly taken in applying the principles in question. See in particular Soguel (2020: chapter 8) on political finesse in financial reporting.

Financial-reporting principles	
Gross recognition	Condensing receipt and expenditure items so as to present only a net figure is not allowed. Every receipt and expenditure item must be recognized and presented separately.
Accrual accounting	An expense item must be recognized in the period for which it is due and not when it is paid. Revenue is recognized as soon as the entity is economically entitled to it, for example when it is invoiced, and not when it is received. This may require recognizing provisions or accruals.
Materiality	Any item of information likely to influence judgment or a decision is important. It must be included in the financial statements.
Understand-ability	Information must be presented in a way that is easy to access and understand.
Reliability	Information must accurately, faithfully and sincerely reflect reality.
Permanence of methods	To ensure comparability of figures over time, information recognition, measurement and presentation methods must be applied consistently.

Table 13.1 Some budgeting and financial-reporting principles

13.2.3 Financial process

Whatever the entity in question, the financial process comprises three major steps: budgetary process, budget execution and preparation and presentation of financial reports.

Budgetary process

The budgetary process comprises five phases, as shown in Figure 13.1. Its timetable is constrained by the need for the executive to submit its draft budget to the legislature on time (often by mid-September when the Financial Management of Parliament Act is explicit on this point)[37]. This gives the legislature sufficient time to review and vote the budget before the end of the year.

The first phase, that of preparing the process, therefore starts early in the year, sometimes as early as January. The executive makes an initial estimate of expected revenues. In some places, the executive sets spending ceilings—envelopes—for each administrative unit (e.g. ministry, department, division or service). This phase often lasts two months. It ends with the dispatch of the executive's budget guidelines to the units.

37 The duration of the budgetary process largely depends on the extent to which operations have been digitalized (▶ 14 Digital transformation) and, obviously, on the size of the entity. It takes longer to draw up a budget for the Confederation than it does for a municipality (FFA 2019). The Federal Financial Management Act of Parliament requires the Federal Council (executive) to submit a draft budget by the end of August (art. 19 para. 1).
The multi-year financial plan is updated as part of the same process, so that it can be brought to the attention of the legislature during the same parliamentary debate that leads to a decision on the budget.

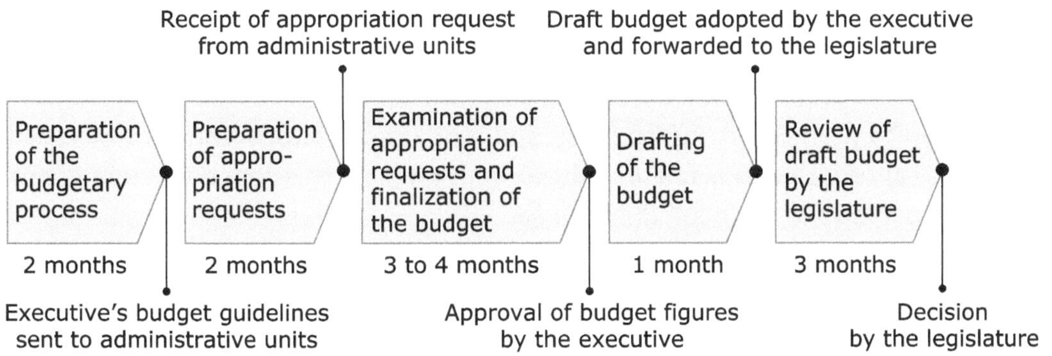

Figure 13.1 Phases of the budgetary process

In the second phase, administrative units determine the resources they need to carry out their mission. On this basis, they draw up their requests for budgetary appropriations. Requests may relate to a current expense, such as the payment of salaries or the purchase of goods and services. They may also relate to capital expenditure—expenditure that will be useful over several years—for example, on infrastructure construction. Units must justify their requests. In addition to requests for expenses, revenue items must also be presented in the documents forwarded to the finance unit (ministry, department or service). This phase also lasts about two months.

The third phase is the longest, taking three to four months. It includes an in-depth examination of appropriation requests by the finance department. The sum of requests made by the various administrative units generally exceeds the amount of expected revenue. This leads to intense discussions between administrative units. The choices to be made may be delicate, and may eventually involve members of the executive. When this phase is complete, the executive approves the budget figures.

Based on these figures, the finance department draws up the draft budget (i.e. the executive's budget request). The document is sometimes referred to as a "message on the draft budget" or "explanatory statement in support of the draft budget". At the end of this fourth phase, which lasts approximately one month, the document is adopted by the executive and forwarded to the legislature. Parliament reviews the proposed budget, first in committee(s), then in plenary sessions. The legislature votes on the budget before the end of the year[38].

Budget execution

Once approved, the budget must be implemented. This stage runs from 1 January to 31 December. The executing agent is the executive and, by delegation, the

38 In principle, the Financial Management Act includes a provision in case the legislature fails to adopt a budget for the following year by 31 December. Thus, depending on the canton, the executive is authorized to commit either: only those expenses that are essential to administrative activity and to the realization of current capital expenditure; or expenses as they appear in the budget approved for the previous year; or expenses in proportion to the amounts appearing in that approved budget, according to the principle of "provisional twelfths".

administrative units. There is an essential difference between receipt and expenditure items in the budget. The executive and the units concerned are obliged to collect taxes in accordance with current legislation. Here, then, budgetary authorization is not a permission, but an obligation. But as far as expenditure is concerned, budgetary appropriation is not an obligation. It gives permission: the amounts provided do not *have* to be spent; they *can be*.

In the units, execution of the budget is handled by two kinds of public servants. These are authorizing officers and accountants. The authorizing officer prepares the execution of the receipts or expenditure. Then he or she gives the order to collect or pay. The accountant only intervenes on receipt of this instruction to receive or pay money. He or she is responsible for completing the execution of the budget. These kinds therefore complement each other. But from a governance and control perspective, they must be clearly distinguished.

The authorizing officer is a person who is empowered, on behalf of the entity concerned—Confederation, canton, municipality—to contract, acknowledge and settle a commitment or debt or to order the recovery of a debt. Having this responsibility, he or she must observe the principle of the specification of budgetary appropriations. The chief authorizing officer is a member of the executive. For practical reasons, his or her power—the right to sign—is delegated to secondary authorizing officers (the heads of administrative units) within clearly defined limits as to amount and nature. In the specific case of an order for materials or equipment, these secondary officers are responsible for signing and placing the order, verifying delivery, checking and approving the invoice (which often requires a double signature) and forwarding the invoice for payment.

On this basis, the accountant performs the final act. This person is therefore materially responsible for public funds. He or she is responsible for collecting receipts, paying expenditure (again often requiring a double signature) and holding the entity's securities. He or she keeps accounts of all these operations.

Preparation and presentation of financial reports

The preparation of financial reports for presentation to the legislature is a matter for the finance department, which includes closing the accounts. The executive approves the financial reports and forwards them to the legislature for adoption.

Of course, the finance department does more than just close the accounts. It is deeply involved in the budgetary process, as we mentioned earlier. During the year, it supports, monitors and advises on budget execution. In addition, it manages the entity's cash and debt, particularly by arranging the necessary loans and investments. It also plays a cross-functional role well upstream of the financial process since it is consulted and takes a position on the cases of other entities whenever there is a financial issue involved.

13.2.4 Accounting categories

To implement the principle of qualitative specification, a particular system for classifying operating expenses and revenues, as well as capital expenditures and receipts, must be followed. This system is prescribed by the accounting model valid for all Swiss public authorities, which includes a detailed chart of accounts (CFM 2008)[39]. It shows the economic nature of transactions, and also identifies which public administration task a transaction serves. The system includes numerous categories. Here we will confine ourselves to categories that concern the operations performed most frequently by administrative units[40].

Operations or capital works

The classification system draws a fundamental distinction between transactions that concern day-to-day operations and those that concern capital works. This distinction is based on the duration of use, as illustrated in figure 13.2. Only expenditure contributing to the provision of services for more than one year may be budgeted or recognized as capital expenditure, together with the corresponding receipts. Expenditures that are useful for one financial year or less should be treated as current expenditures, together with the corresponding current receipts[41].

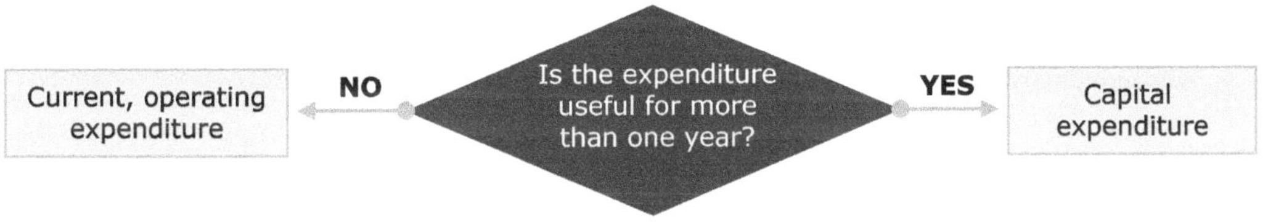

Figure 13.2 Distinction between operating and capital expenditure

Economic classification

Table 13.2 shows the headings used in the accounting model to classify operating transactions according to their economic nature[42]. It also indicates their percentage share of total expenses or revenue in 2019. Transfers (heading 36) account for more than half of the CHF 230 billion of expenses incurred by the Swiss

39 This model is now known by the abbreviation HAM2, which stands for harmonized accounting model, second generation.
40 Details and the most up-to-date version of the harmonized classification are available on the Swiss Public Sector Financial Reporting Advisory Committee website: https://www.srs-cspcp.ch/en. This Committee is responsible for updating these categories in line with the needs of a constantly changing society and public sector.
41 In practice, capital expenditure that represents only a small, i.e. immaterial, amount (in the sense of the materiality principle) is accounted for as current expenditure. This reduces the administrative burden.
42 Items beginning with 3 are current expenses and those beginning with 4 are current revenue. Capital expenditures are classified under headings beginning with 5, while corresponding receipts are classified under headings beginning with 6.

general-government sector[43]. These expenses include compensation paid to other entities, financial-equalization transfers and grants. Personnel expenses (30) are generally the second-largest item. Note that certain headings are reserved for expenses with no cash outflow, i.e. purely accounting items. An example is depreciation, which reflects the wear and tear and obsolescence of infrastructure (33).

The right-hand column shows tax revenues (item 40). Unsurprisingly, they account for the bulk of the CHF 238 billion revenue of the Swiss general-government sector in 2019. Levies and fees collected (42) represent the second largest item. But their volume is considerably smaller.

3	**Expenses**	**100.0%**	4	**Revenue**	**100.0%**
30	Personnel expenses	23.3%	40	Tax revenues	83.3%
31	Goods and services and other operating expenses	11.3%	41	Patents and concessions	1.6%
32	Federal defence expenses	0.4%	42	Levies and fees	7.5%
33	Depreciation of administrative assets	4.6%	43	Other revenue	0.5%
34	Financial expenses	1.3%	44	Financial revenue	5.6%
35	Allocations to special financing and funds	0.9%	45	Withdrawals from special financing and funds	0.7%
36	Transfer expenses	54.9%	46	Transfer revenue	0.3%
37	Redistributed grants	=	47	Grants to be redistributed	=
38	Extraordinary expenses	3.3%	48	Extraordinary revenue	0.5%
39	Internal service charges	=	49	Internal service revenue	=

Table 13.2 Classification by economic nature of operating transactions
Source of percentages for 2019: Federal Finance Administration, financial statistics, publication date: August 2021

Classification by task, by function

Table 13.3 shows headings used to classify transactions according to the performed task or function. Like the classification by nature, the functional classification is harmonized at the national level. It is useful for comparisons and for information on the cost of services. This classification comprises ten main functions, numbered from 0 to 9. Percentages indicate each function's share in total current and capital expenditure.

43 The financial statistics compiled by the Federal Finance Administration include four subsectors within the scope of the general-government sector: (a) Confederation, (b) cantons or intercantonal concordats, (c) municipalities or intermunicipal associations and (d) compulsory social insurance funds.

0	General administration	7.0%
1	Public order and safety, defence	7.8%
2	Education	17.8%
3	Culture, sports and leisure, church	3.3%
4	Health	7.2%
5	Social security	39.9%
6	Transportation and telecommunications	7.6%
7	Environmental protection and land-use planning	2.8%
8	Public economy	4.2%
9	Finances and tax	2.4%

Table 13.3 Classification by function.
Source of percentages for 2019: Federal Finance Administration, financial statistics, publication date: August 2021

Systematic numbering

Throughout the year, transactions must be recorded by economic nature and function using the systematic classification system. In addition, every entity runs its specific institutional classification, which reflects its own organizational chart. Each transaction is allocated using an account-assignment code made up of several digits (including those mentioned in the preceding tables): the first three digits assign the transaction to the institutional classification, the next four according to the economic nature, and the last three to the functional classification. Table 13.4 shows how this system works, taking as an example the expense for purchasing educational supplies.

Classification…												
… by institution	Department:	Public education	5									
	Division:	Schools		2								
	Service:	Elementary school			1							
… by nature	Account class:	Expenses				3						
	Account group:	Goods and services					1					
	Subgroup:	Materials and goods						0				
	Account:	Printed matter, publications							2			
…by function	Function:	Education								2		
	Task:	Compulsory schooling									1	
	Subdivision:	Elementary level										2
Number to be entered for account assignment:			5	2	1	3	1	0	2	2	1	2

Table 13.4 Numbering and assignment

This system provides the financial information needed to answer various management questions: how much is spent on what task? By which administrative unit? Through what type of expenditure?

13.3 Future prospects and challenges

In any public entity, financial management is a cumbersome process, involving a considerable number of interlocutors and stakeholders. Long before the "New Public Management" movement, attempts were made to relax certain financial principles. The aim was to reduce the budgetary incrementalism brought about by the traditional process and the explosive year-end spending caused by periodic specification. Decades ago Wildavsky (1978) showed that repeating the process year after year resulted in the renewal of existing budget allocations. Adjustments are only incremental within each budget heading. This prevents in-depth reflection on needs in terms of government tasks. In other words, allocations are frozen between administrative units, between government functions and between types of expenditure.

To break the hold of budget incrementalism, proposal followed proposal: planning, programming, budgeting system (PPBS), zero-based budgeting (ZBB), management by objectives (MBO) (Kong 2005). However, none of these proposals lived up to expectations, the cost of these clumsy administrative processes far outweighing the benefits they brought.

More recently, the New Public Management movement has introduced the idea of service contracts associated with lump-sum budgets. With lump-sum budgets—sometimes called global budgets—a budgetary appropriation is no longer split between various headings of the economic-nature classification. Units can organize their administrative processes more freely. They are no longer obliged to use particular resources within the limits of the appropriation specifically granted (for example, in-house production, with the associated payroll costs, or outsourcing, with the corresponding purchase of goods or services). This relaxes the principle of qualitative specification. In some cases, the gross-recognition principle is also abandoned. The lump-sum budget must be respected in net terms. In other words, an increase in expense can be offset by additional revenue, in order to conform to the principle of quantitative specification. The principle of period specification remains. However, the appropriation period is determined by the service contract, and it can exceed one year. Consequently, each global budget has its own temporality.

Such a change decentralizes organizational decisions, including financial ones, to the administrative units. It clarifies the distribution of roles. In theory, the administrative units, within the public-administration system, should benefit from greater operational latitude. The legislature, for its part, should focus on the strategic steering of public administration. The primacy of citizens and their representatives over public administration—in accordance with the Declaration of the Rights of Man and of the Citizen—is reaffirmed. However, it faces several obstacles, including asymmetry of information and even of skills.

This prompts us to remember that financial management, even when it appears to be a well-adjusted mechanism, remains a process influenced by human and power relationships (▶ 3 Stakeholders). This being so, in order to succeed in this particular game, it is best to know the rules.

Key concepts

- Budget (*budget, Voranschlag/Budget, preventivo*): the budget of a public entity is a legal document, drawn up by the executive and approved by the legislature, which forecasts and defines the expenditure and receipts that the entity is entitled to incur and collect for the coming year. The notion of budget is sometimes used in the sense of "household" or financial standing. The size of a public authority's budget, for example, is a proxy for its financial standing.
- Economic classification (*classification par nature, Artengliederung, classificazione per genere di conto/per natura*): classification of current revenue and expenses, as well as expenditure and receipts, according to their economic nature. This classification provides information on the type of resources used (personnel, goods and services, infrastructure, etc.). It also shows how financing is organized (taxes, levies, etc.). This is a harmonized classification for all Swiss public entities.
- Financial reports (*comptes, Staatsrechnung, consuntivo*): in Switzerland, the financial reports of a public entity comprise the statement of financial performance (income statement), the statement of capital works, the statement of financial position (balance sheet) and notes. They include current revenue and expenses, as well as capital expenditure and receipts for the year, together with a statement of assets and liabilities as at the end of the year.
- Functional classification (*classification fonctionnnelle, funktionale Gliederung, classificazione funzionale*): classification of current revenues and expenses, as well as expenditure and receipts, by government tasks. This classification is harmonized for all Swiss public entities, modelled on the international government financial statistics (COFOG).
- Institutional classification (*classification organique, organische Gliederung, classificazione istituzionale*): classification of current revenue and expenses, as well as expenditure and receipts, according to the organizational chart of the entity

concerned. Items are classified based on administrative units (departments, divisions or services). This classification makes it possible to clearly allocate and recognize the amounts for which units are responsible. As each entity has its own organization, this classification is not harmonized between Swiss public entities.

References

CFM – Conference of Cantonal Finance Ministers / Konferenz der kantonalen Finanzdirektorinnen und Finanzdirektoren (2008). *Manual – Harmonised accounting model for cantons and municipalities / Handbuch – Harmonisiertes Rechnungsmodell für die Kantone und Gemeinden [HAM2]*. CFM.

FFA-Federal Finance Administration / Eidgenössische Finanzverwaltung (2019). *Ökonomische, rechtliche und organisatorische Grundlagen der Haushaltsführung des Bundes.* Bundespublikationen.

Kong, D. (2005). Performance-based budgeting: The U.S. experience. *Public Organization Review*, 5(2), 91–107. https://doi.org/10.1007/s11115-005-1782-6.

Lienhard, A., Mächler, A. & Zielniewicz, A. (2017). *Öffentliches Finanzrecht*. Stämpfli Verlag.

Soguel, N. (2020). *Comprendre et gérer les finances de ma collectivité*. EPFL Press.

Wildavsky, A. (1975). *Budgeting: A comparative theory of budgetary processes*. Little, Brown and Co.

References for further study

Müller-Marqués Berger, T. (2018). *IPSAS explained. A summary of international public sector accounting standards*. John Wiley & Sons Ltd.

Pfäffli, S. (2011). *Budgetierung im öffentlichen Sektor: ein Handbuch für Studium und Praxis aus finanzwissenschaftlicher Sicht*. Haupt Verlag AG.

Soguel, N. (2009). Impact de la budgétisation descendante et des règles budgétaires contraignantes sur l'« argent » à disposition des politiques substantielles. In: P. Knoepfel (Ed.), *Réformes de politiques institutionnelles et action publique*. EPFL Press.

PART IV
Change management

Introduction

Tobias Mettler

1 Purpose of the "change management" dimension

"The wheels of bureaucracy turn slowly." This common view is readily asserted by citizens confronted with the organizational inertia of public administration. For many years now, business, society and politics have been faced with the need for substantial changes in response to societal, economic and technological shifts.

Organizational inertia is not confined to government departments: it is also a constant challenge for large private companies. Because of their size and complexity, large entities tend to formalize their organizational structure and processes. While this brings them greater stability and professionalism, it also carries the risk of hampering their ability to innovate and react.

Figure IV.1 The "change management" dimension in the IDHEAP model

To counterbalance aspects presented in the other dimensions of the IDHEAP model, where the primary aim is stabilizing public administration, this dimension deals with managing change. It sets out to show that organizational transformation should be welcomed rather than resented.

2 Components of the "change management" dimension

What is meant by "change management" and how is this dimension perceived by the various actors involved? How does one actively design organizational transformation? These are the central questions that organizational research seeks to answer. For many years, two opposing positions have been put forward (Robbins 1994).

The "calm waters metaphor" conceives of change as a process necessary to stabilize the situation following a transitory imbalance: "*[...] relatively long periods of stability [are] punctuated by compact periods of qualitative, metamorphic change*" (Gersick 1991: 12). The "social-change model", often used in project management (▶ 18 Project management), has largely contributed to popularizing this way of understanding change (Lewin 1952). It sees organizational transformation as a succession of three phases: *unfreeze* (allow the prospect of change), *move* (change), *freeze* (stabilize). Unfreezing is triggered by internal or external developments in an organization (new environmental conditions, societal trends, technological advances, changes in employees, etc.). The result is an imbalance that can be corrected in a lasting fashion by targeted measures. The evaluation of projects, programs, initiatives and activities (▶ 16 Evaluation)—systematically measuring the impact of the efforts undertaken and communicating them transparently to the various stakeholders—is of great importance in this approach.

In contrast, the second view of organizational transformation is the "white-water rapids metaphor". This sees change management as an ongoing task: "*[...] transformation is seen here to be an ongoing improvisation enacted by organizational actors trying to make sense of and act coherently in the world*" (Orlikowski 1996: 65). While the first approach assumes temporary imbalances, the second considers that an organization invariably strives to be consistent with its environment (Lindberg & Berger 1997). Continuous change in structures, processes, culture and technology (▶ 14 Digital transformation) is seen as an ongoing task, necessary to ensure that administration can function properly and to minimize risks (Alchian 1950; Brown & Duguid 1991). In this context, learning from successes and mistakes (▶ 15 Organizational learning) is a proven means of keeping the organization on track for success.

The contributions about this dimension of the IDHEAP model see organizational transformation as both a reaction to imbalance and as an ongoing task. They therefore present various concepts and solutions for gradual or radical transformation—depending on the case—of public administration. Innovation (▶ 17 Innovation), for example, often leads to radical change within an organization. The aim is to give public administration a significantly different direction by eliminating what is outdated and creating new structures and behaviours. The stages of change are then relatively short and intense. This can lead to strong opposition and disorganization, and poses a risk of the entity losing its identity (Jarvenpaa & Stoddard 1998).

References

Alchian, A. A. (1950). Uncertainty, evolution, and economic theory, *The Journal of Political Economy*, *58*(3), 211–221.

Brown, J. S. & Duguid, P. (1991). Organizational learning and communities-of-practice: toward a unified view of working, learning, and innovation. *Organization Science*, *2*(1), 40–57.

Gersick, C. J. G. (1991). Revolutionary change theories: A multilevel exploration of the punctuated equilibrium paradigm. *Academy of Management Review*, *16*(1), 10–36.

Jarvenpaa, S. L. & Stoddard, D. B. (1998). Business process redesign: Radical and evolutionary change. *Journal of Business Research*, *41*(1), 15–27.

Lewin, K. (1952). Group decision and social change. In T. M. Newcomb & E. E. Hartley (Eds.), *Readings in social psychology* (pp. 459–473). Holt.

Lindberg, P. & Berger, A. (1997). Continuous improvement: Design, organisation and management. *International Journal of Technology Management*, *14*(1), 86–101.

Orlikowski, W. J. (1996). Improvising organizational transformation over time: A situated change perspective. *Information Systems Research*, *7*(1), 63–92.

Robbins, S. P. (1994). *Essentials of organizational behavior* (4th ed.). Prentice-Hall.

14 Digital transformation

Tobias Mettler

14.1 The importance of digitalization for public administration

Over the past few decades, the digital universe has invaded our daily lives from every angle: online shopping, music and video streaming, remote home monitoring and more. Digitalization is conquering our society and overturning our leisure and work habits (for the latter, at least in certain sectors). But what about the digitalization of government services? How does the shift to digital—the digital transformation—affect public administration? Before addressing these issues, we need to distinguish between the confusingly similar terms *digitization* and *digitalization*. They are often used synonymously in practice.

As used in the IDHEAP model, and generally in the English-speaking world, the term *digitization* means the transition (for example, by *scanning*) from analogue information carriers, such as a paper form or deed, to their digital counterparts. This conversion process is usually aimed at dematerializing tangible, archivable objects or documents. This translates into a number of both positive and negative effects that are perceptible in physical reality: for example, a reduced need for storage and archiving systems on the one hand, and increased energy consumption on the other. However, the logic behind day-to-day activities, such as filling in forms or filing paperwork, is practically unaffected.

Digitalization, on the other hand, is a broader term going far beyond the conversion of analogue information carriers to digital media: the word denotes (as the corresponding French term *transformation digitale* makes clear) a radical shift, a huge change in established ways of working. Digitalization requires a complete rethinking, and even redefinition, of daily routines and practices in order to respond to strategic concerns that can only be addressed or facilitated by innovative IT solutions. The term is often used to designate innovations in the field of:

- *communication*, such as asynchronous work or telework, a personalized approach offered to customers, free access to public data and to photographic, cartographic or statistical material;
- *cooperation*, such as participatory thinking and collaboration between public and private organizations or with citizens, at local, national and international levels; and
- *coordination*, such as simplified exchanges of information between different stakeholders with lower information-transmission costs, more global approaches to planning and simulating measures in real time, the organization and automation of specific steps within a process, or complete automation of service provision.

14.2 Key points of digitalization

Digitalization leads to the revamping of services and processes, frequently accompanied by the reshaping of identity that often comes with technological and organizational innovation (► 17 Innovation). Consequently, the adoption of technologies in public administration is always a product of the temporal and cultural context (Mettler 2019). Briefly, starting from *e-government* and arriving at *smart government*, digitalization has gone through five successive phases, the characteristics of which are shown in figure 14.1.

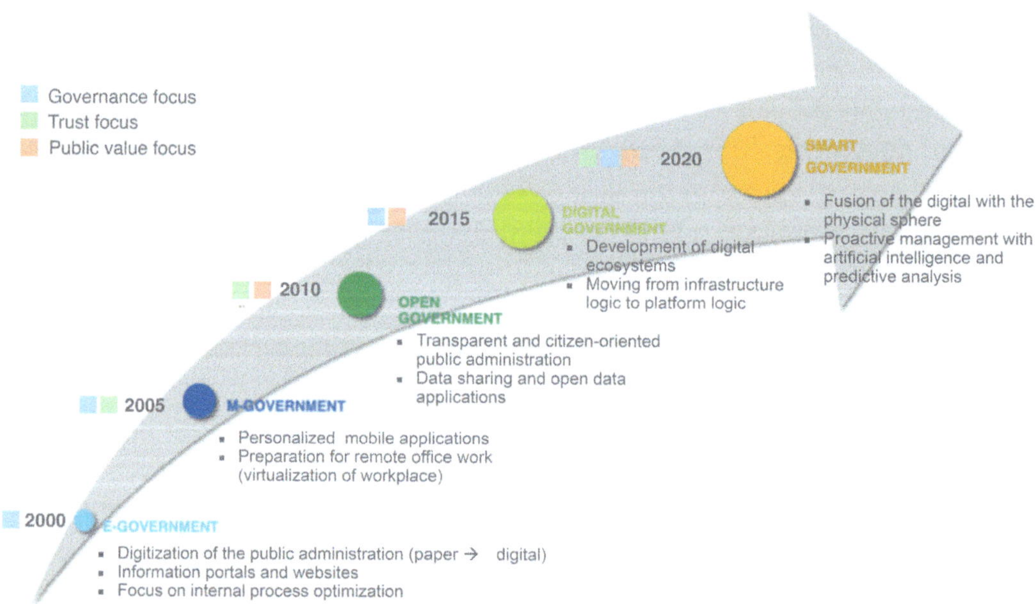

Figure 14.1 Evolution from "e-government" to "smart government"

14.2.1 E-government

The origins of the current debate on digitalization are found in the first wave of government computerization. This phase obviously began well before the 2000s, but only reached its peak with the spread of the internet. Today, e-government is still mistakenly considered to be synonymous with the digitalization of public administration. But the emphasis was more on dematerialization, or *digitization* (as explained above). This manifested itself primarily in the constant development of public organizations' online presence (e.g. through information portals[44] or websites), and in minor process improvements (e.g. changing from paper-based forms to digital forms), mainly geared towards improving internal objectives.

14.2.2 M-government

With the meteoric rise of smartphones and the mobile internet[45], the focus has shifted more towards customized mobile applications ("apps") and solutions enabling administrative staff to work asynchronously or remotely (although telework has only recently, and out of necessity, entered the mainstream). These include, for example, the "tl" app, with which citizens can obtain tickets or information on traffic conditions, or the "Züri wie neu" app, which allows them to report infrastructure damage. The fundamental differences between e-government and m-government are that access to digital administrative services is independent of the user's location, and that greater attention is paid to customer needs and the circumstances in which the application in question is used.

14.2.3 Open government

In the early 2010s, this stronger "customer orientation" or new "proximity to the citizen" gave rise to the so-called open-government movement (McDermott 2010). This axiom presupposes greater transparency in administrative activity, but also free access to data collected by the state and its reuse for both commercial and non-commercial purposes. Digitalization therefore takes on a political dimension. At the start of this third phase, priority was given to setting up data infrastructures for the public sector and digitizing government data sets. From this point on, technical issues were relegated to secondary importance, while organizational and legal issues came to the fore[46], particularly as a result of the shift from an infrastructure logic to a platform logic.

44 See the "citizens' portal" of the Confederation and cantons: https://www.ch.ch/en (accessed 15.01.2024).
45 In international rankings, such as that of the UN e-government Surveys (https://publicadministration.un.org/egovkb/en-us/Reports/UN-E-Government-Survey-2022), Switzerland regularly comes out on top in terms of telecommunications infrastructure, but not in terms of digital government services (accessed 15.01.2024).
46 See "European data strategy": https://commission.europa.eu/strategy-and-policy/priorities-2019-2024/europe-fit-digital-age/european-data-strategy_en (accessed 08.01.2024).

14.2.4 Digital government

This transition marks the fourth phase of digitalization. It is now recognized that the search for solutions requires new ways of establishing a genuine dialogue between the administration and its stakeholders. Digital government therefore focuses on the development and governance of so-called "platform ecosystems". The aim is to strike a balance between the different needs of stakeholders, or between the advantages and disadvantages of digital services. For the most part, today's digital solutions can no longer be developed in a vacuum. They emerge from co-creation, or cooperation between a plurality of actors (e.g. the administration and private companies, or the administration and citizens) who often have multiple interests. For a digital solution to be successful in the long term, all the actors involved in the service it is intended to provide must contribute to and benefit from it. In other words, creating an infrastructure is pointless if nobody uses it or finds it useful. Understandably, then, today's digital government places greater emphasis on economic considerations (such as "value for tax money") than in previous phases. Designing digital business models is not only essential for private companies, but is also becoming a necessity for public administrations, because each new solution generates costs that reduce the budget available to finance innovation in other areas. Advancing the digitalization of public administration therefore means (sooner or later) defining and experimenting with new funding models and innovative forms of collaboration (Brown *et al.* 2014).

14.2.5 "Smart government"

The merging of the digital and physical worlds (e.g. the "internet of things" or "connected objects") is at the heart of the current fifth wave of the digital transformation. This is characterized by information technology moving out of the limelight, leaving the public space to take centre stage. The digital world is no longer limited to the computer screen or the smartphone: it's everywhere. We find it in unsuspected places, such as self-driving buses, sensor-equipped trash containers or QR codes on billboards.

This development, known as intelligent administration, or "smart government" (Guenduez *et al.* 2020a), brings many risks for public organizations (e.g. both digital and physical attacks on public infrastructures). But it also presents them with opportunities and new possibilities for carrying out their mission in an even more efficient and personalized way. Similar to the idea of smart cities, smart government should even be able to transform the way an entire city operates. Coupled with the latest advances in artificial intelligence and predictive analysis, it will enable tomorrow's administration to be more proactive, rather than merely reactive.

For the time being, however, the elements required for smart administration to emerge are the subject of much debate and many studies. The acronym IMPACT is an easy mnemonic for the characteristics of smart digital administrative services (see Table 14.1).

Key aspects	Comments
Integrative	Smart digital administrative services bridge the gap between the digital and physical spheres, using the potential of interaction between them according to the context. Services provided by various administrative bodies and third-party organizations are integrated so that citizens can access them via a "single window".
Multimodal	Interaction with smart services is not only tailored linguistically and visually to the needs of target groups, but is also adapted to take account of space and gestures. Digital content can be communicated without necessarily having to use a computer or smartphone.
Personalized	Smart digital administrative services take into account situational factors (such as events or geographical locations) and/or users' personal characteristics (such as their linguistic or cultural specificities). Unlike digital government, where communication is governed by the "watering-can principle", citizens obtain situation- and context-sensitive information whose content and regularity can be adjusted according to their preferences.
Anticipatory	Smart digital administrative services do not stop at understanding a state of affairs in retrospect. They attempt to draw lessons from historical and current data applicable to future situations. These analyses serve as a basis for devising scenarios and strategies to solve everyday problems (e.g. anticipatory traffic-volume management, early identification of extreme weather conditions).
Collaborative	Smart digital administrative services result from co-creation between public and private organizations, and with citizens. The involvement and participation of various stakeholders not only ensures broader support for the chosen solutions, but also helps solve complex problems (such as meeting climate targets or responding to pandemics).
Transformative	Providing smart digital services requires a significant shift in the mindset of public authorities, away from a "top-down" approach to government towards more collectivist "bottom-up" initiatives. Smart digital services are efficient and effective, both from both an internal (e.g. streamlining of administrative processes) and an external point of view (e.g. an approach better attuned to citizens' needs).

Table 14.1 Characteristics of smart digital services (IMPACT)

14.2.6 Digitalization model

Many specialists are currently preoccupied with the fundamental question of how to anchor the digitalization of public administration and accelerate it so as to achieve the kind of maturity that has been attained in the private sector (Andersen *et al.* 2020). Numerous methods, models and schools of thought—agile management, design thinking, administrative modelling—promise an immediate answer. But from a scientific point of view, and given the multiple facets of digitalization, it is clear that the solution to the problem cannot come from an isolated approach or a universal recipe. On the contrary, putting new technologies to good use and moving public administration into the digital age demands that we rethink the very notion of value creation by the public sector. The necessary structural and cultural changes will result from evolutionary changes in the value chain made by public authorities (see Figure 14.2).

Values and modes of operation such as customer orientation, transparency and a collaborative approach are frequently evoked in connection with digitalization and the evolution of added public value. But merely alluding to them in a strategy document or digital charter is not enough: they have to be translated into concrete measures (▶ 7 Strategy).

The ideal profile for personnel is different now: to support the digital transformation actively, it's now necessary to have a wide range of specialized technical skills (needs analysis, project management, programming, etc.) and cross-functional skills (critical thinking, teamwork, emotional intelligence). Specialized "digital service teams"—working groups dedicated exclusively to digitalization issues—also need to be set up. In this sense, the recruitment, ongoing training and retention of so-called "T-shaped professionals[47]" represent a key factor in the success of digitalization within public administration (▶ 12 Human-resources management). In the context of digitalization projects, thanks to their expertise, these people function as translators, because they are sensitive to problems of both a technical and a human nature. They can act as intermediaries and bridges between two worlds of work and thought that are most often strictly separated from an organizational point of view ("business versus IT").

For digitalization to be understood and put into practice at all levels and in all units, skills relating to digital media and new forms of working must be developed and reinforced throughout the organization. It is not enough to have staff who are more well-versed in technology and its applications. Communication and management styles must also adapt to the demands of the digital age. Technological change is continuous. The process of adaptation must therefore not be seen as an occasional problem, but as an ongoing task, part of an permanent learning process ▶ 15 Organizational learning).

Structural and cultural change of this kind can cause disarray among staff, and discontent among some individuals. Concerns, legitimate or otherwise, can considerably delay or even prevent the implementation of new technologies (Guenduez *et*

47 See Collegiate Employment Research Institute: https://ceri.msu.edu/_assets/pdfs/t-shaped-pdfs/Primer-on-the-T-professional.pdf (accessed 15.01.2024).

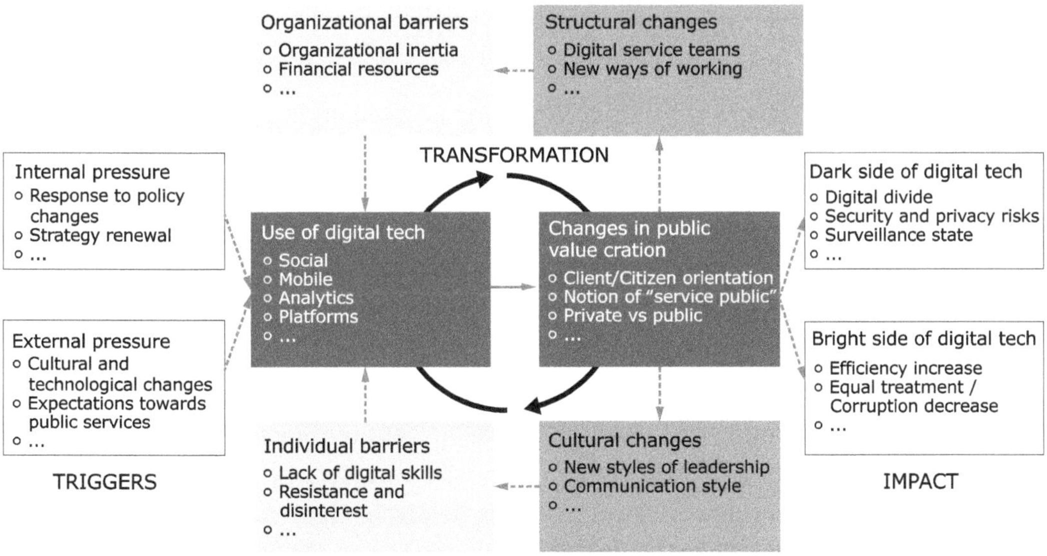

Figure 14.2 Digitalization model

al. 2020b). The key to successful digitalization is therefore to identify and analyze barriers and obstacles early on, and to actively address them: strong resistance to change and lack of enthusiasm for new solutions and forms of work will not disappear on their own. Similarly, from an organizational point of view, it is important to watch out for possible systemic and cultural barriers, such as excessive formalism, technocratic working methods or a strongly hierarchical way of thinking. All this can substantially compromise the success of a digitalization project.

Lastly, the question of usefulness must be addressed. All too often, projects are initiated in response to political pressure or external circumstances. However, while those outside the public sector may have an idea of the technical functionality the solution they recommend will bring, they generally do not formulate concrete objectives in terms of the expected impact on society. As already mentioned, new technology does not have an effect by virtue of its mere existence: it can only have an impact if it is used. Impacts can be positive (more efficient work processes, fair treatment of requests) or negative (exclusion of certain population groups, threats to privacy). Systematic monitoring of actual use and impartial measurement of the ensuing effects (both positive and negative) are a prerequisite for communicating transparently and acting appropriately when problems arise.

14.3 Future prospects and challenges

The gradual digitalization of the public sector is intensifying known areas of tension and generating new ones that will have to be overcome in the future. A specific challenge lies in preserving individual freedoms, which could easily be relegated to second place in the drive to increase the efficiency or effectiveness of government measures. The automation of decision-making or measures designed to maintain the administration's capacity for action—in a chronically overloaded judicial system or in the social sphere, for example—do not relieve the state of its obligation to guarantee the fundamental rights and self-determination of its citizens. Certainly, economic considerations must guide the development of digital infrastructures and platforms, and interests of various kinds must be preserved (such as the protection of intellectual property or third-party copyright in algorithms). However, gains made prior to digitalization must be resolutely protected (Moore 2017).

The same applies to the question of accountability and transparency in administrative activity. Should openness and access to data collected by the state be given priority over preventing a loss of control and a possible increase in workload for the administration? Such questions should not be looked at in only one dimension: they require analysis from several angles (legal, economic, political, technical and social).

Internal public-administration considerations raise another dilemma: does ensuring that digitalization brings the expected benefits require increased centralization? Or greater decentralization? Technically speaking, both options are generally possible (e.g. centralized or decentralized data storage) and their advantages and disadvantages are known (e.g. simplified standardization as opposed to greater agility and flexibility). But the structural and cultural change involved makes either option a perilous exercise for which there can be no universal recipe. Techniques that are available for managing projects (▶ 18 Project management) and change can provide a few points of reference. Yet their focus tends to be specific, often centring on aspects like *designing solutions* within constraints of time, budget and functionality, rather than prioritizing *design for practical use* in specific contexts, for distinct user groups, and within particular situations. Such management techniques have shown their potential in other contexts, but in the digitalization process, they often have to be adapted internally in haste.

Lastly, a fundamental question arises: why do we need digitalization? The axiom that increased automation of repetitive tasks will increase profits (or reduce costs) is leading the private sector down a questionable path (Zuboff 2019). It means fewer jobs, especially for the low-skilled, and exacerbates competition for highly trained labour such as the T-shaped professionals mentioned above. And in the future, businesses will no longer be satisfied with structured data such as addresses and telephone numbers: they will also collect data on non-routine activities, such as media-consumption preferences or eating and exercise habits. This will allow algorithms to use more precise information and provide new answers to more specific questions. Certainly, economic rationality has a role to play: processes must be optimized and customers incentivized ("nudged") to adopt desired behaviours. But it remains to be seen whether this evolution and approach are desirable for the public sector. The administration's goal should not be paternalism towards the population, or maximum profit. Rather, digitalization should be a means of increasing (or at least maintaining) the quality of public services and of overcoming both everyday and unforeseen challenges with the resources available.

Key concepts

- Digitalization (*transformation digitale, digitale Transformation, trasformazione digitale*): the use of information technology to rethink or redefine daily routines and processes, or to devise new solutions to strategic issues.
- Digitization (*digitalisation, Digitalisierung, digitalizzazione*): the transition from analogue media (e.g. paper forms) to digital form (e.g. online forms on a website).
- Smart government (*administration publique intelligente, intelligente Verwaltung, amministrazione digitale e intelligente*): the use of digitalization by the administration to merge the physical and digital worlds, based on collaborative processes, for the purpose of anticipating needs and providing specific solutions to problems rather than confining itself to merely reactive action.

References

Andersen, K. N., Lee, J., Mettler, T. & Moon, M. J. (2020). *Ten Misunderstandings about Maturity Models*. Paper presented at the Proceedings of the 21st Annual International Conference on Digital Government Research, Seoul, Republic of Korea.

Brown, A., Fishenden, J. & Thompson, M. (2014). *Digitizing Government - Understanding and Implementing New Digital Business Models*. Palgrave McMillan.

Guenduez, A. A., Mettler, T. & Schedler, K. (2020a). Citizen Participation in Smart Government: A Conceptual Model and Two IoT Case Studies. In *Beyond Smart and Connected Governments*. Springer: 189–209.

Guenduez, A. A., Mettler, T. & Schedler, K. (2020b). Technological frames in public administration: What do public managers think of big data? *Government Information Quarterly, 37*(1), 101–406.

McDermott, P. (2010). Building open government. *Government Information Quarterly, 27*(4), 401–413.
Mettler, T. (2019). The Road to Digital and Smart Government in Switzerland. In A. Ladner, N. Soguel, Y. Emery, S. Weerts & S. Nahrath (Eds.), *Swiss Public Administration: Making the State Work Successfully* (pp. 175–186). Springer.
Moore, T. (2017). *Trade Secrets and Algorithms as Barriers to Social Justice.* Center for Democracy & Technology.
Zuboff, S. (2019). *The Age of Surveillance Capitalism: The Fight for a Human Future at the New Frontier of Power.* Profile Books.

References for further study

Falk, S., Römmele, A. & Silverman, M. (Eds.). (2017). *Digital Government.* Springer.
Gil-Garcia, J. R., Pardo, T. A. & Gascó-Hernandez, M. (Eds.). (2020). *Beyond Smart and Connected Governments: Sensors and the Internet of Things in the Public Sector.* Springer.
Veit, D. & Huntgeburth, J. (2014). *Foundations of Digital Government: Leading and Managing in the Digital Era.* Springer.

15 Organizational learning

David Giauque and Yves Emery

15.1 The importance of organizational learning for public administration

Over the past few decades, federal, cantonal and municipal administrative services have been actively engaged in a host of organizational transformations and managerial reforms. The objective: to adapt to their changing environment and the demands of their citizen-clients, delivering quality services while sparing the public purse. During this period, they have also faced numerous crises—political, economic and, more recently, healthcare-related. Administrative entities at all three levels of Swiss governance have, it has to be said, managed to cope with these rapid changes with a degree of effectiveness and efficiency, thanks to their staff, who are able to show flexibility, inventiveness and innovation, but also resilience.

The characteristics that have allowed these entities to show such organizational agility and competence are, first, their capacity to learn and, second, their ability to generate, exploit, safeguard and disseminate the knowledge and know-how needed to (re)define, implement and continuously improve public services. From the outset, it is important to realize that every organization learns, if only to continue existing. Organizational learning (OL) is a process through which organizations generate, develop, organize and exploit new knowledge in order to adapt their structures, processes and operations to changes in the economic, political, social and technological context. OL can thus be defined as a change in organizational knowledge achieved by making use of past experience (Argote 2011).

Organizational learning is inextricably tied to an organization's ability to produce, manage, disseminate and exploit the skills, knowledge and know-how of its members. It must be stressed that OL is a process that needs to be activated, steered and regulated, particularly by managers at all levels of the hierarchy. This is both an individual and a collective process involving cognitive, social, behavioural and technical dimensions. It therefore depends on the nature of social interactions, the specifics of the tasks to be carried out, and the particularities of each organization. In other words, the learning process is contingent on the context and environment in which it takes place, and also on the organizational activities that need to be carried out.

OL is a major asset for any administrative entity wishing to engage in a positive dynamic of continuous improvement, and ultimately to become a learning organization[48]. The quality, effectiveness and relevance of structural changes, improvements to processes, quality initiatives and adaptations to environmental contexts are strongly dependent on OL. Neither *single-loop learning* (not making the same mistakes twice) nor *double-loop learning* (questioning the strategies, values and routines on which organizational management is based) (Argyris & Schön 1996) can realistically be achieved unless practices fostering OL are put in place. OL thus enables public administrations to adapt to their environment, to changes in society, to the needs of citizen-clients, and even to sudden crises. It is also an essential ingredient for generating organizational innovations (▶ 17 Innovation). Hence the importance of OL in guaranteeing the viability, quality, efficiency and legitimacy of public-sector organizations in the eyes of various stakeholders (▶ 3 Stakeholders) (politicians, citizens, taxpayers, customers, private organizations and other partners, etc.).

15.2 Key points of organizational learning

Before the OL process can be activated and managed within an organization, certain structural, organizational, cultural and human conditions must be met (▶ Part III. Organization and processes). OL should not be seen as a simplified linear dynamic, starting with employee learning, before consolidating first at group level and finally throughout the whole administrative entity. OL is dependent on the initiatives of individuals, groups and teams, as well as on those of all administrative entities. Which means that it cannot be restricted to developing employees' knowledge and skills. Other means, more collective and structural, must be employed to share individual skills and anchor them permanently in the organization.

Scientific research and many testimonies from actors in the field have identified the levers or "facilitators" of OL. We will begin with structural levers before moving on to other facilitating factors focused on individuals.

15.2.1 The importance of organizational structures

The manner in which organizations are structured is an important factor to consider with regard to OL (▶ 10 Organizational structures). There are four main models,

48 "Learning organization" is a concept frequently encountered in the literature on organizational learning: it could be described as the outcome at which OL aims.

each involving a specific type of work organization (see Table 15.1). It should be noted that, like most organizations, public administration is a hybrid displaying some features of the various models presented below.

As a result, more and more employees are enjoying the benefits of working in learning environments. Given the wide variety of trades and professions represented in administrative entities, several types of organizational structures and work practices coexist. These depend closely on the missions to be accomplished (complex or simple), the procedures to be implemented and the concrete activities to be carried

Structure type	Brief definition
Simple structure	Work divided into simple, repetitive elementary tasks. Little formalization of work procedures, little teamwork and few complex tasks. Very direct hierarchical line. Little autonomy and few learning opportunities for employees. 18% of European employees work in such structures. The sectors most concerned are: shops, hotels, restaurants, recreational activities and personal services. The same type of activities can be found In administrative entities, with very similar organizational and work characteristics.
Taylorized structure	Repetitive, highly specialized and often monotonous tasks, with little autonomy in work methods and content. Strong constraints are imposed on employees, particularly in terms of the pace of work and productivity. This model still affects around 15% of European workers, mainly unskilled and industrial workers. The industrial and manufacturing sectors mainly operate with this type of structure. Some administrative entities have to deal with similar work constraints, particularly in the production of standardized goods based on Taylorian work methods.
"Lean production" structure	High cognitive work content, but reduced autonomy because processes are standardized. Strong constraints in terms of the pace of work, production standards and the importance of quality initiatives. High constraints on workrates are combined with practices such as versatility, teamwork and total quality. Affects 27% of European employees, particularly technicians, skilled workers and sales staff. This model can be found in practically every sector of activity. Public services are also subject to these constraints: the growing number of files to be processed in social services or regional employment offices, productivity targets in hospitals, etc. This type of structure is also found in administrative entities.
Learning structure	High level of learning activity, oriented towards solving complex problems, with a high degree of working autonomy. Monotonous and repetitive tasks are rare, and constraints—productivity standards, workrates—are lighter than in other models. Mainly concerns executives. A model that is mainly found in finance and real estate, and in specialized, scientific and technical activities. 40% of European employees work in such a structure. Some administrative entities are also subject to this type of regime, such as public laboratories, universities, units in charge of complex public policies, etc.

Table 15.1 Main characteristics of organizational structures
Note: percentages are from 2015
Source: Benhamou & Lorenz (2020)

out. Recent research has highlighted the benefits of learning structures. For example, the greater the number of businesses operating with a learning work model in a country or region, the greater the number of world-first innovations in products or services that country or region will produce (Benhamou & Lorenz 2020). There is a proven systemic link between organizations whose structures encourage learning and exploring new knowledge and the ability of these organizations to develop innovative products and services.

15.2.2 Some good organizational practices

Other field studies highlight the importance of specific working conditions in promoting OL. We can summarize them as follows:

- The existence of "close-knit" networks—strong ties between colleagues. Groups that operate within a framework of strong reciprocity and trust, with spontaneous face-to-face interactions, are conducive to the development of OL.
- The type of leadership practised, i.e. participative leadership with a transformational focus (▶ 9 Leadership), oriented towards supporting and encouraging employees, but with collective-development goals in view.
- A culture and climate geared to innovation, risk-taking and the acceptance of failures, where individual initiative is encouraged, diverse viewpoints are respected and the greatest possible number of employees are involved in decision-making.
- Communication practices that are vertical, bottom-up, top-down, cross-functional, transparent and regular, in order to foster the emergence of common values and perspectives, as well as shared language and meaning. OL is also a symbolic issue.
- Organizational support in the form of working conditions based on a few simple principles: give employees autonomy to determine how they carry out their work, make them accountable for their objectives and results, allow for job enrichment and avoid excessively repetitive, monotonous tasks.
- A suitable managerial infrastructure that allows for management of knowledge and skills, with human-resources practices (▶ 12 Human-resources management) that promote the selection, development and retention of staff having career aspirations compatible with the objectives of a learning organization. In other words, the characteristics and expectations of employees must fit with those of the organization (Bright 2007).
- Congruity of the values advocated by the organization, particularly as regards its OL objectives, with employee motivation. It has been shown that individuals with a high level of public service motivation are those most likely to commit to their organization, enabling it to evolve and progress. Public-service mindedness is therefore a powerful driver of OL for administrative entities (Emery & Giauque 2012).

The management principles outlined above are proving effective in fostering the emergence, development and dissemination of OL in administrative entities (Rashman *et al.* 2009). That said, how can one take concrete action? The following table sets out a number of actions aimed at developing OL and managing organizational knowledge for consideration by entity managers.

Concrete measures	Description
Appoint a *chief knowledge officer* (CKO)	A CKO's goal is to create, maintain and develop a knowledge-management infrastructure within the organization. The CKO is at the heart of strategic development in learning and knowledge management.
Introduce coaching and mentoring	Coaching and mentoring disseminate tacit and explicit knowledge specific to each organization to new members. Mentoring, in particular, by pairing an experienced member with a newcomer, helps to disseminate organizational experience and memory.
Organize events to encourage informal interaction	Social events (barbecues, walks, meals, etc.) encourage informal communication and information sharing between members of an organization, and also the development of a common, shared language (building community, forging links).
Rotate positions	This practice is aimed at encouraging members of an organization to switch position, hierarchical rank or area of expertise and responsibility in order to gain new professional experience. This allows knowledge and expertise to circulate, empathy between employees to develop, and organizational creativity to flourish.
Manage skills	A well-known human-resources practice of identifying and tracking employee skills in the form of expertise catalogues or expertise profiles (including in electronic form). These databases can be used to quickly identify experts to solve specific problems within the organization.
Create communities of practice	Groups of employees who meet voluntarily, based on common professional interests or shared expertise, to exchange experiences, identify or develop best practices, and establish new social relationships. These groups are voluntary and self-regulating.
Create cross-functional teams	Teams are created by pooling experts from different parts of the organization to combine varied functional expertise. Members have different identities and missions, and come together to exchange views and solve organizational problems of varying complexity.
Conduct postmortem assessments	Events are held after the completion of organizational projects for project members to exchange views on good and bad experiences or good and bad practices, and to evaluate the running of the project. Minutes are taken to record these so-called ***postmortem*** evaluations.
Set up a Research & Development or Innovation unit	Create an organizational unit specifically tasked with developing new knowledge and expertise. This may involve developing new technologies, quality standards, processes or work procedures. Disseminating this new organizational knowledge is also an important mission for this unit.
Develop ad-hoc training programmes	Create a formalized training programme to allow staff to acquire specific skills or behaviours (both technical and social skills). Training sessions, led by internal or external resources, can be used to disseminate standardized content, practices or behaviours across all the units making up the organization.

Mesures concrètes	Description
Adopt new ways of working	In suitable jobs, new technologies make it possible to work in a much more flexible way, for example, without an assigned workstation. This creates new relationships between staff members, generating interactions that are a source of creative exchange and promote the circulation of knowledge.

Table 15.2 Examples of organizational practices that foster OL

15.3 Future prospects and challenges

15.3.1 OL comes up against classic administrative features

In public-sector organizations, the influence of political orientations, direct (possibly untimely) intervention by elected representatives (▶ 4 Institutions) (members of executives or parliaments) can either thwart or, on the contrary, kick-start learning efforts. It is not uncommon for administrative units to find themselves beset by confusion as to which missions or objectives to pursue (▶ 6 Ethics). Such contradictions, sometimes deftly maintained by political actors, especially when the executive branch is not homogeneous and does not "speak with one voice", are real challenges for OL.

Organizational rigidity and complex administrative processes and procedures are notorious characteristics of administrative entities (Bozeman 2000). So much so that red tape and a procedure-bound climate can sometimes hinder efforts to create a culture conducive to OL. Other organizational features, such as strong departmentalization, segmentation and specialization of administrative units, can also be obstacles to OL, particularly from a cross-functional perspective. Learning from others is key, but it is more difficult when the boundaries between administrative units or departments are difficult to cross.

Public-sector organizations are sometimes described as professional bureaucracies. Some of them, such as hospitals, police forces, prisons and tax authorities, are made up of professionals who are experts in the same field, have attended similar training courses, and share the same beliefs, values and thought patterns, fostering shared conceptions of "quality work". These tacit professional norms, while helping to bind communities of experts together, can stand in the way of new information, knowledge or know-how that does not necessarily fit with the mindsets of these professionals and the routines they have internalized. This homogeneity of views, meanings and conceptions of work is clearly difficult to circumvent, in particular, to allow openness to new approaches (Evetts 2013). It is also crucial to bear in mind that OL takes time, since people's skills and knowledge only evolve over the long term. In other words, investments must be made, and time must be made available for this purpose. Yet most of the reforms of recent decades have been implemented rather abruptly, very often in haste, in a top-down manner (▶ 10 Organizational structures) focused on performance and productivity. The aim was to "do better"—often with fewer financial resources. As a result, these reforms may jeopardize OL, especially if changes are too frequent: people do not have sufficient time to acquire new knowledge and skills before the next organizational transformation is brought in. Successive administrative reforms give rise to feelings of confusion, waste, pointlessness and loss of bearings among members of administrative entities. This can lead to resistance and/or resignation, making the success of OL even more difficult.

15.3.2 OL and crises: a capricious couple

Although times of crisis can sometimes be conducive to OL, because they shake up habits, they generally present a challenge. Crises often lead to more centralized, less participative and cost-cutting organizational responses. These periods coincide with an increase in reporting requirements, based on a battery of short-term quantitative performance indicators. These are therefore less favourable times for OL. The challenge for the manager of an administrative entity is then to maintain spaces for learning and knowledge development, even when times are far than ideal, if only to avoid repeating the same mistakes in future crises.

It is highly likely that in the future, the effectiveness and efficiency of administrative entities will depend even more heavily on their capacity for continuous learning. Particularly so that they can not only continue operating in times of crisis, but also invent new ways of working and innovate in response to the increasing changes in society's needs.

Lastly, another major challenge will lie in the development of management systems, supported by new information and communication technologies, that encourage the activation and sharing of knowledge. The digitalization of public administration (▶ 14 Digital transformation) confronts all administrative actors with substantial challenges that will only increase in the future, placing heavy demands on their learning capabilities. Technological solutions will then be essential to promote OL, alongside structural and organizational changes, and changes in working conditions, as this contribution has attempted to highlight.

But, as ever, cultural change will be the most significant shift, and the most difficult to bring about. OL implies knowledge sharing, greater cross-functionality, and stepping back at a time when the pressure to perform is being felt—concerns that for many people seem far removed from their day-to-day reality. The willingness of entity managers to move forward will prove decisive!

Key concepts

- Competency management (*gestion des compétences, Kompetenzmanagement, gestione delle competenze*): strategic and collective management of the knowledge, know-how, interpersonal skills and development skills of individuals working in an organization.
- Knowledge and skills management (*management des connaissances et des savoirs, Wissen und Wissensmanagement, conoscenze e gestione delle conoscenze*): development, management and sharing of knowledge and know-how within organizations.
- New ways of working (*nouvelles manières de travailler, neue Arbeitsformen, nuove forme di lavoro*): management practices aimed at enabling employees to work independently of a fixed timetable and a fixed place, using new information and communication technologies.
- Organizational learning (*apprentissage organisationnel, organisatorisches Lernen, apprendimento organizzativo*): change in organizational knowledge and skills achieved by making use of past experience.

References

Argote, L. (2011). Organizational learning research: Past, present and future. *Management Learning*. SAGE Publications Ltd., *42*(4), 439–446.

Argyris, C. & Schön, D. (1996). *Organizational learning II: Theory, method and practice.* Addison-Wesley.

Benhamou, S. & Lorenz, E. (2020). Les organisations du travail apprenantes: enjeux et défis pour la France. Document de travail–France Stratégie, (3). https://www.strategie.gouv.fr/publications/organisations-travail-apprenantes-enjeux-defis-france, accessed 09.12.2022. Retrieved from www.strategie.gouv.fr

Bozeman, B. (2000). *Bureaucracy and red tape.* Prentice Hall.

Bright, L. (2007). Does person-organization fit mediate the relationship between public service motivation and the job performance of public employees? *Review of Public Personnel Administration, 27*(4), 361–379.

Emery, Y. & Giauque, D. (2012). *Motivations et valeurs des agents publics à l'épreuve des réformes.* Presses de l'Université Laval.

Evetts, J. (2013). Professionalism: Value and ideology. *Current Sociology, 61* (5–6), 778–796.

Nellen, L. C., Gijselaers, W. H. & Grohnert, T. (2020). A meta-analytic literature review on organization-level drivers of team learning. *Human Resource Development Review, 19*(2), 152–182. Sage Publications Inc.

Rashman, L., Withers, E. & Hartley, J. (2009). Organizational learning and knowledge in public service organizations: A systematic review of the literature. *International Journal of Management Reviews, 11*(4), 463–494.

References for further study

Ingvaldsen, J. A. & Engesbak, V. (2020). Organizational learning and bureaucracy: An alternative view. *The Learning Organization*, 27(5), 403–415. https://doi.org/10.1108/TLO-11-2019-0168 (accessed 28.11.2022).

Sanz-Valle, R., Naranjo-Valencia, J. C., Jiménez-Jiménez, D. & Perez-Caballero, L. (2011). Linking organizational learning with technical innovation and organizational culture. *Journal of Knowledge Management*, *15*(6), 997–1015. https://doi.org/10.1108/13673271111179334 (accessed 28.11.2022).

Schulz, M. (2017). Organizational learning. In: *The Blackwell companion to organizations*. John Wiley & Sons, Ltd., 415–441. https://doi.org/10.1002/9781405164061.ch18 (accessed 28.11.2022).

16 Evaluation

Pirmin Bundi

16.1 The importance of evaluation for public administration

Evaluation has taken on a major role in the modern 21st-century state. When public debt is high, government spending is more closely scrutinized. Evaluations provide policy makers with valuable information for assessing the effectiveness and efficiency of a government intervention. Mirroring the proliferation of evaluation activities internationally, over the past twenty years the practice has developed strongly in Switzerland. From sporadic beginnings, it has today become essential to the functioning of a modern organization.

Its role is particularly important in public administration. Employees of administrative units work in specific areas within their field of activity. They see evaluations as useful, because the results can give them information relevant to their (internal) work. Evaluations can help them in various ways: in implementing a particular measure, developing a new legislative proposal or improving internal processes, for example. Evaluations are therefore mainly commissioned and used by public-administration units, although they have also gained recognition with other bodies, such as Parliament (Bundi 2016).

But what exactly is meant by evaluation? The term is hardly uncommon. In fact, it has become part of our everyday language. Evaluation has become part of our daily lives, whether we are assessing our lunch options or deciding which pair of shoes is best suited to the day's weather. In public administration, evaluation has become a practice and a management tool that is used in a targeted manner. In this context, evaluation refers to a scientific service aimed at making a systematic, transparent assessment of something—a strategy, a law, a programme, a project, a measure or an internal process (Widmer & De Rocchi 2012: 11). There are three aspects to this definition. First, evaluation is based on *scientific principles*, such as intersubjective objectivity or the application of scientific methodologies. This scientific approach is also reflected in the systematic and transparent way in which an evaluation is conducted. Not only do these aspects guarantee clarity and traceability, they also enhance the relevance of the results and impact of an evaluation. Second, evaluation is a *provision of service*. Consequently, the subject of the evaluation is not chosen independently of the evaluator. Unlike basic research, evaluation is always requested by a commissioning organization, which defines its scope. Third, the aim is to make an *assessment*. Evaluation is based on criteria designed to identify the options for action available to the addressee. If possible, these criteria should be predefined, but they can also be added or modified during the evaluation process.

In administrative practice, besides evaluation there are many other instruments used to assess organization, processes or services (monitoring, controlling, auditing, etc.). It is therefore important to distinguish these instruments from evaluation, since these terms are often used interchangeably within administrative units. The main difference lies in the objective: making an assessment of something. An assessment can, of course, also be arrived at using other instruments, although it may not be the main focus in those cases. But evaluation is the only tool capable of showing the causal links between a public policy and its consequences. Demonstrating these causal links is imperative in any evaluation, whereas other instruments only provide hints at best.

Despite the relevance of evaluations for administrative units, their results are still being used to only a limited extent. This is surprising, given that evaluations help administrative units to assess the impact of an intervention and legitimize government action. Every year public bodies devote considerable financial resources to evaluations only to make restricted use of the results. This paradox is the starting point for this chapter, which focuses on evaluation within public administrative units. After describing how an evaluation is conducted, we look at the different ways in which it can be used. In the final section, we discuss perspectives for the role of evaluation, and present approaches for making better use of its results.

16.2 Key points of evaluation

This section describes the conduct of an evaluation, as developed by Horber-Papazian & Baud-Lavigne (2021). It is important to note, however, that here we limit ourselves to outlining the main stages in the process.

Evaluation is always a service, and the first step is to define who is to provide it. Here, an organization commissioning an evaluation is faced with a dilemma. Evaluators need to have two areas of expertise that are generally difficult to combine. On the one hand, they need to be very familiar with the subject of the evaluation and its context. This is necessary in order to carry out the evaluation correctly and to be able to make an assessment of its findings. On the other hand, a certain detachment from the subject under evaluation is desirable to ensure the most objective analysis possible. For this reason, a distinction is made between *internal evaluations*, conducted by those responsible for implementing the subject of evaluation or working in the same organization, and *external evaluations*, conducted by third parties.

Both variants have their advantages and disadvantages, and the choice should be based on the situation. Bussmann (1995) considers that internal evaluators are characterized not only by their special knowledge of the subject of the evaluation, but also by their contacts with stakeholders (▶ 3 Stakeholders) and by facilitated learning processes (▶ 15 Organizational learning). However, personal interests may influence the analysis. This is why internal evaluations are generally considered less credible than their external equivalents. The opposite is true for external evaluations. Their conclusions are often better accepted because of greater independence from the subject of the evaluation and higher evaluation skills. However, those in charge of the evaluation need to devote more time and resources to familiarizing themselves with the subject under scrutiny. Moreover, they have only limited knowledge and information about internal processes. As a result, a hybrid form, the "critical friend" model, is gaining in importance. This follows the usual conception of an external evaluation, but at the same time involves the commissioning organization more closely in the process (Balthasar 2011).

It is important to bear in mind that when an external player is commissioned to conduct an evaluation, the process can take longer. The first step is precisely to put together a competent evaluation team using a selection procedure. At this point, a distinction should be drawn between, on the one hand, invitations and mandates awarded by mutual agreement, and on the other, public calls for tenders, where selection does not depend solely on internal rules. Selection must also comply with the provisions laid down by the World Trade Organization (WTO). In any case, it is advisable to draw up a specifications document. The commissioning organization will define the scope of the evaluation (e.g. by defining the subject of the evaluation), the questions to be answered, the financial and time requirements in addition to the services expected and the requirements placed on the evaluation team.

Although an evaluation may be carried out by various actors, the steps involved are often similar. In principle, the approach is based on the eight distinct steps outlined in Figure 16.1 (Horber-Papazian & Baud-Lavigne 2021).

Step 1) Identify the context and objectives of the evaluation

The first step is to determine the context and purpose of the evaluation. The scope of the analysis can then be defined and the next steps planned. In addition to the scope of analysis, it is advisable to identify the key actors (▶ 3 Stakeholders) and gather information on the purpose of the evaluation. Before even starting the process, an interview with those responsible for the subject of the evaluation can provide a great

Step 1)	Identify the context and objectives of the evaluation
Step 2)	Formulate evaluation questions
Step 3)	Develop an impact model
Step 4)	Select one or more comparison methods
Step 5)	Collect and analyse data
Step 6)	Construct an assessment
Step 7)	Formulate recommendations
Step 8)	Promote evaluation results

Figure 16.1 The eight stages of an evaluation
Source: Horber-Papazian & Baud-Lavigne (2021)

deal of contextual information and valuable indications as to the evaluation method to be used.

At this stage, it is also important to ensure that the necessary data is available and accessible. Lastly, it is absolutely essential to define the objectives of the evaluation. Sager & Hinterleitner (2014: 444) report that most evaluations focus on one particular aspect of the subject of evaluation, mainly due to time and resource constraints. This largely determines the orientation of the evaluation, depending on whether it is intended to be *formative* or *summative*. In a formative evaluation, there is a conscious effort to initiate learning processes to help improve the subject of the evaluation. The aim of a summative evaluation, on the other hand, is to produce a final report on a government intervention, thus providing third parties with evidence of the performance and/or effectiveness of the subject of evaluation. That said, orientation is also dependent on institutional considerations. Evaluations are very often commissioned by public-administration bodies that are primarily interested in learning more about a specific intervention, and therefore favour formative evaluations. In recent years, however, some political actors, including parliaments, have increasingly initiated evaluations of a summative nature (Bundi 2016).

Step 2) Formulate evaluation questions

Evaluation questions should be formulated in line with the objectives of the evaluation. They will determine the next steps. While these questions are often already included in the terms of reference, it is advisable for the commissioning body and the evaluation provider to discuss them together. This will help to build a shared understanding of the purpose of the evaluation. This step is especially important because the evaluation questions are crucial for making an assessment on the subject of the evaluation. Questions can be of three types: first, descriptive questions, which are aimed at building a picture of a state of affairs; second, normative questions, which seek to compare a planned situation with the actual situation; and third, causal questions, which set out to determine the causes of a state of affairs. It is wise to use questions of these different types during the evaluation process.

Step 3) Develop an impact model

An impact model is often used to represent the interrelations and consequences of a government intervention. The model is based on a theoretical perspective and seeks to outline the rationale underlying the intervention concerned (Rossi *et al.* 2018). This rationale is often referred to as intervention theory. It explains why the intervention was initiated, its content and the expected consequences. An impact model generally takes the form of a graphical representation of the intervention's activities and their repercussions. It comprises five phases: input, process, output, outcome and impact. Figure 16.2 shows a simplified impact model.

Input: this involves defining the objective of the public intervention and all the types of resources needed to achieve it. This phase also encompasses the various legal bases and a political concept. Lederman & Sager (2009: 10) consider that the political concept covers four different aspects. The *problem definition* looks at the problem to be solved, its possible causes and the way in which it manifests itself in society. In an ideal case, the concept establishes causal hypotheses describing how a public intervention could solve the problem concerned. The *objective* states the

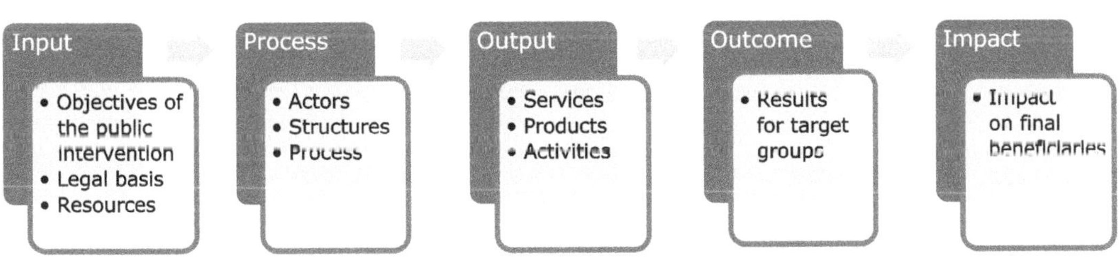

Figure 16.2 Evaluation impact model
Source: representation according to Weiss (1972), Sager & Hinterleitner (2014) and Balthasar & Fässler (2012)

concrete intentions of the intervention, making a distinction between substantive goals (effects of the public intervention) and operational goals (process of implementing the public intervention). If possible, the objective should also include a time frame, as well as primary and secondary objectives. It can also cover any unintended side-effects of the public intervention. The political concept sets out *operational requirements*. These specify the policy instruments to be implemented, describe possible activities and define areas of intervention. Lastly, the political concept contains *organizational prescriptions*, which define the necessary skill set and resource endowments (Sager & Hinterleitner 2014: 445).

Process: this involves implementing the political concept to deliver the benefits and products linked to public intervention. In this phase, the areas of action and activities required to provide the services are defined. Here, the structures and processes of the administrative units or organization providing the public service must be taken into account. The process thus covers the entire organization that governs progress and cooperation between the players involved in implementation. Often, these are not only actors from within the public sector, but also private organizations or administrations from other levels of government entrusted with the provision of the service.

Output: output encompasses all the products and services that are provided through the public intervention concerned and are aimed at the target group concerned. These include not only concrete products and offers, but also output that is processed by other actors before it reaches the addressees. Output will vary according to the target group, and is often predefined in laws and ordinances. As mentioned above, output from the subject of the evaluation can be made available by various actors and encompass various activities. The important point is that output should help to change the target groups' behaviour. Ideally, this interrelationship will have already been defined in the intervention hypothesis of the political concept.

Outcome: outcome is the first level of the results of a public intervention: the changes that the intervention brings about in the direct target group (the groups of actors or the organization directly responsible for the societal problem). This level concerns the short- and medium-term effects of output, those that can be observed fairly quickly. Depending on the intervention, the target group is reached directly or through intermediaries. Intermediaries are generally actors who maintain close links with a specific target group, such as public-administration specialists who interact directly with the target group in the course of their work. In such cases, a distinction is drawn by referring to the results as Outcome I (intermediate) and Outcome II (target group). The output of a public intervention can modify the knowledge, approach and behaviour of intermediaries and of the target group. It is also important to address behavioural changes that may influence the public intervention, or even have negative consequences in other areas.

Impact: impact is the second level of results of a public intervention. It covers changes to individuals, groups, organizations or other things beyond the direct target group. These are often deemed to be the final beneficiaries of an intervention, in that they benefit from the changes in the behaviour of the target group. The impact is often a long-term change that can be observed only after a number of years. It covers all the changes that affect the societal issue in question and can be attributed to the public intervention. Ideally, the situation of the final beneficiaries should have improved in line with the policy concept, to the point where the societal problem can be considered solved. This phase also encompasses the other social, political and economic repercussions of the intervention.

Step 4) Select one or more comparison methods

Evaluation always involves comparison. Once the evaluation objectives and questions have been formulated, and the impact model has been defined, the subject of evaluation must be analysed empirically. Analysis of the concept and impact of the subject of evaluation requires comparative approaches. There are four possible approaches: 1) a normative approach comparing the observed state—whether in terms of services or consequences—with the expected state, in order to determine whether the expected repercussions have actually occurred; 2) a cross-sectional approach comparing the situation between different geographical areas, for example different regions of a country; 3) a longitudinal approach comparing the subject of evaluation over a given period, for example before and after the introduction of a specific activity; 4) an approach comparing the situation with and without the subject of evaluation. All these comparison methods can be used simultaneously during an evaluation.

Step 5) Collect and analyse data

In order to make comparisons and answer evaluation questions, information must be gathered. A whole series of empirical procedures exist; we summarize them here, without claiming to be exhaustive. A common approach is to gather documents, compile statistics, and conduct interviews or organize surveys. It is wise to collect information from all available sources, combine both qualitative and quantitative data and then carry out a form of triangulation. This allows a question to be examined from different approaches and points of view. The next step is to develop designs for analysing the information gathered. Here, it is important to implement techniques. The evaluation must follow a systematic and transparent methodology, so that the reasoning is perfectly understandable for future users. Attention should also be paid to ensuring that the text is clear and accessible to all stakeholders.

Step 6) Construct an assessment

Once the analysis phase has been completed, the time has come to evaluate the policy, programme, project or internal process under review. The evaluation must be based on the data collected and the analysis made of that data in order to ensure complete consistency. Users of the evaluation should be able to reconstruct the reasoning presented, which can be based on the evaluation criteria that emerge from the various phases of the impact model (Sager & Hinterleitner 2014: 444). Obviously, the criteria we present below must be adapted to suit the needs of the situation. Where appropriate, other elements may be considered, depending on the purpose of the evaluation.

Input: one of the evaluation criteria can be whether the policy concept has been established on the basis of empirical evidence. This involves assessing the extent to which the input is based on the latest scientific knowledge as regards the definition of the problem and intervention hypotheses. It is also possible to use the *intra-policy* criterion (consistency of different interventions within the same area of intervention) or the *inter-policy* criterion (consistency with other public interventions). The main aim of both these criteria is to ensure that full use is made of synergies within the various administrative units and with other actors involved.

Process: the main criterion for evaluating a process is its *relevance for implementation*. It is crucial to determine whether the structure put in place to deliver services is optimal, and whether the right implementing agencies have been mobilized. The latter should have sufficient knowledge, experience and resources to take charge of the intervention. Another important criterion is the sustainability of the process. The aim is to ensure that the implementation structure is institutionally anchored and that the necessary budget is available to guarantee the provision of services in the longer term.

Output: this being a matter of services and products, there is a need to distinguish between the *relevance* and the *efficiency* of output. The criterion of relevance is used to assess the extent to which the various services comply with the requirements set out in the intervention concept. Efficiency, on the other hand, is examined in order to determine whether the services provided justify the resources committed.

Outcome: the criteria for this step are designed to assess the repercussions of the benefits and products of the public intervention. The *effectiveness* criterion seeks to determine the extent to which the intended results have been achieved with the target groups, and have therefore led to changes in their behaviour. *Efficiency* provides information on the relationship between the resources committed and the results achieved with target groups.

Impact: the criteria to be used concern the effects of the public intervention. *Effectiveness* here indicates the degree of concordance between the planned impacts and the effects actually observable among the final beneficiaries. *Efficiency* indicates the relationship between resources committed and impacts obtained with the beneficiaries of the public intervention.

Step 7) Formulate recommendations

An evaluation is only useful if it is accompanied by recommendations. The evaluation providers may propose adaptations, the feasibility and acceptability of which should be verified and discussed in advance with the commissioning body. Recommendations should always be based on the results of the evaluation, have a necessary degree of concretization and designate the actors responsible.

Step 8) Promote evaluation results

It's not unusual for an evaluation report to end up in a drawer somewhere. This is obviously contrary to the purpose of an evaluation. Evaluations should initiate learning processes not only among managers, who can critically examine their own decisions and the way they are implemented, but also among the actors involved in the evaluation. Disseminating the results of evaluations and planned adjustment measures also helps to strengthen the relationship of trust between the political authorities and the public, and to promote democratic debate based on facts. This is only possible if the results of evaluations and recommendations are properly taken into account and made public. This is why an evaluation report is normally published and made widely available to the public, either via the website of the commissioning organization or by the evaluators.

16.3 Future prospects and challenges

Once the final report has been written, the question arises of how to use the results of the evaluation. While the evidence suggests that they are mostly ignored, there are in principle two ways of using the results (Eberli 2019: 51-52). An *analytical use* involves actors taking a stand on the results of the evaluation—to position themselves, or pronounce themselves. In this case, members of the public bodies concerned can first obtain information from the evaluation. This enables them to better understand the situation (conceptual use) or to make a decision directly on the basis of the evaluation results (instrumental use). In any event, this type of use is highly dependent on the organization's willingness to accept the results of the evaluation and therefore to examine itself critically. Where this willingness is absent, one often sees a *political use* of evaluations. In contrast with analytical use, the entity concerned does not regard the evaluation as an opportunity to make changes, but rather to support or confirm the status quo. It can thus use the results of the evaluation to condone the existing situation (legitimizing use) or to convince third parties of its validity (persuasive use). In both cases (legitimization and persuasion), the will to solve problems is lacking. In addition to these two types of use (analytical and political), Patton (2008) indicates that an evaluation also generates explicit usefulness. This usefulness derives from the evaluation process (not to be confused with the public-intervention process) and not from the results of the evaluation. Thus the evaluation process itself leads the actors involved in the evaluation to modify their way of thinking and acting through what they have learned throughout the process. Figure 16.3 gives an overview of the various ways evaluations can be used.

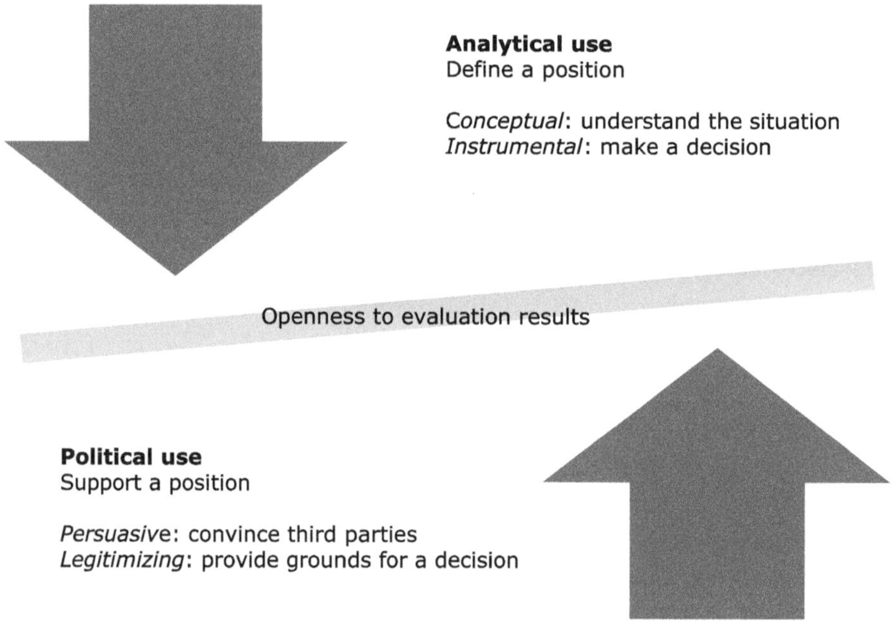

Figure 16.3 Types of evaluation use and differences
Source: representation according to Eberli (2019)

Although the second use is described as political, this does not mean that it is only used by the political class. Evaluations may be commissioned by administrative units in order to persuade political actors of the legitimacy of an existing measure. The results of evaluations are also used to convince politicians of the merits of a measure, especially one that has not yet been implemented or is still under discussion. Conversely, the political class can also make analytical use of evaluations to obtain information about a given subject or to make a decision, although current research shows that this occurs only rarely at present (Eberli 2019). Use of an evaluation for political purposes often irritates those who conducted it, particularly when they claim to have based it on facts. From a democratic point of view, however, this type of use poses no problem. Fact-based information—which evaluations help to bring to light—is just one of the elements on which a decision is based. Institutions, interests and ideologies also play an important role (Weiss 1999).

Today, it is no longer possible to imagine public administration without evaluation. As a tool for analysing public interventions, it makes an essential contribution to the accountability of administrative units, their improvement and the expansion of knowledge. It is hardly surprising, then, that evaluation—and the movement that promotes it—has made so much progress in Switzerland over the past three decades. It has become "good form" to evaluate.

In addition, evaluation plays an important role in the transformations that administrative units are undergoing (▶ Part IV. Managing change), since it allows actors to empirically highlight the changes that have taken place and make decisions on an objective basis.

Key concepts

- Causality (*causalité, Kausalität, causalità*): the effect of an explanatory variable on a given outcome: the causal effect measures the difference in value of the dependent variable that occurs when the value of the independent variable changes state.
- Evaluation (*évaluation, Evaluation, valutazione*): a scientific process that seeks to systematically and transparently assess a subject (a strategy, law, programme, project, measure, etc.).

References

Balthasar, A. (2011). Critical friend approach: Policy evaluation between methodological soundness, practical relevance, and transparency of the evaluation process. *German Policy Studies, 7*(3), 187–231.

Balthasar, A. & Fässler, S. (2012). Wirkungsmodelle: Ursprung, Erarbeitungsprozess, Möglichkeiten und Grenzen. *LeGes – Gesetzgebung und Evaluation, 28*(2), 301–325.

Bundi, P. (2016). What do we know about the demand for evaluation? Insights from the parliamentary arena. *American Journal of Evaluation, 37*(4), 522–541.

Bussmann, W. (1995). *Instrumente der Erfolgskontrolle*. VOP. Bd. 6.

Eberli, D. (2019). *Die Nutzung von Evaluationen in den Schweizer Parlamenten.* Seismo.

Horber-Papazian, K. & Baud-Lavigne, M. (2021). *Guide de l'évaluation des politiques publiques destiné aux acteurs politiques et aux magistrats de Madagascar.* IDHEAP, Université de Lausanne.

Ledermann, S. & Sager, F. (2009). Problem erkannt, aber nicht gebannt. Der Nutzen einer Verknüpfung von Konzept- und Umsetzungsevaluation am Beispiel der schweizerischen Strategie «Migration und Gesundheit», *Zeitschrift für Evaluation, 1*(1), 7–25.

Patton, M. Q. (2008). *Utilization-focused evaluation: The new century text.* Sage.

Sager, F. & Hinterleitner, M. (2014). Evaluation, In K. Schubert& N. Bandelow (Eds.). *Lehrbuch der Politikfeldanalyse* (pp. 437–462). Oldenbourg.

Weiss, C. H. (1972). *Evaluation research. Methods for assessing program effectiveness.* Prentice-Hall, Inc.

Weiss, C. H. (1999). The interface between evaluation and public policy. *Evaluation, 5*(4), 468–486.

Widmer, T. & De Rocchi, T. (2012). *Evaluation: Grundlagen, Ansätze und Anwendungen.* Rüegger Verlag.

References for further study

Bundi, P., Frey, K. & Widmer, T. (2020). Does evaluation quality enhance evaluation use? *Evidence & Policy, 17*(4), 661–687.

Bussmann, W., Klöti, U. & Knoepfel, P. (1997). *Einführung in die Politikevaluation.* Helbing und Lichtenhahn.

Horber-Papazian, K. & Balthasar, A. (2015). *Regards croisés sur l'évaluation en Suisse.* Presses polytechniques et universitaires romandes.

Knoepfel, P., Larrue, C. & Varone, F. (2005). *Analyse et pilotage des politiques publiques.* Rüegger Verlag.

Rossi, P. H., Lipsey, M. W. & Henry, G. T. (2018). *Evaluation: A systematic approach.* Sage.

Sager, F., Widmer, T. & Balthasar, A. (2017). *Evaluation im politischen System der Schweiz: Entwicklung, Bedeutung und Wechselwirkungen.* NZZ Libro.

Scriven, M. (1991): *Evaluation Thesaurus.* Sage.

Société suisse d'évaluation (SEVAL). (2016). *Standards d'évaluation de la Société suisse d'évaluation.* Adoptés par l'assemblée générale au 9 septembre 2016. SEVAL.

17 Innovation

Oliver Neumann and Tobias Mettler

17.1 The importance of innovation for public administration

Public entities are often seen as less innovative than private companies. This point of view cannot be ignored, even if, historically, a host of major visionary innovations originated in the public sector (such as the first postal services or the beginnings of the aerospace industry). But in the age of digitalization, in which innovation is an essential feature, big technology companies, startups and other private actors are overtaking the public sector in terms of innovation capacity. Very often, the state does no more than promote innovation in the private sector, missing the opportunity to play a leading role in the process. Yet in view of the challenges facing society today, and from a citizen's point of view, it is regrettable that many public bodies are not making the most of their potential for innovation.

Of course, innovation serves a different function in the public sector than in the private sector, which can make comparison more difficult. In the private sector, innovation is almost always aimed at increasing market share and maximizing profits. In the public sector, its purpose is to contribute to the common good, improve the functioning of the administration or bring other benefits for a country's society and economy. While this makes innovation in administration more difficult to perceive and measure, it is certainly no less important.

Citizens' trust in politics, administration and public organizations is dependent on innovation in the public sector. If government services do not evolve quickly enough while the world changes, other actors will fill the gaps created by the state's lack of dynamism, confronting it with a problem of legitimacy.

Three examples illustrate missions or areas of regulation that were formerly the domain of the state but are now taken on by private actors or civil society thanks to innovative approaches. European cross-border rail traffic provides a first case. Historically organized by national public railways, it suffered from a fragmented service offering and a lack of ergonomic booking platforms. In the wake of a wave of liberalization, private operators offering platforms for bus travel and carpooling have rapidly been able to acquire large market shares. The secret of their success lies in the simplicity of their digital channels, reasonable fares and the fact that they offer cross-border service seamlessly. In short, these operators have succeeded in taking customer needs into account where state-owned railways failed to do so for decades (▶ 14 Digital transformation). The second example is food waste. According to the Swiss Foundation for Consumer Protection, nearly a third of food produced in the world is thrown away. Retailers are responsible for a large proportion of this waste, either because they discard products whose best-before date has passed or that look less than perfect, or because they divert such products to energy generation instead of making them available to those in need. In Switzerland, politics and public authorities have so far failed to limit this problem through innovative legislation, unlike countries, such as France, who have. As a result, many citizens' initiatives have sprung up to collect food that has been thrown out by retailers but is still edible, so that it can be eaten or redistributed. Our third example is the controversy surrounding digital identity (e-ID) in Switzerland, one of the main pillars of the digitalization of public administration. So far, public authorities have not succeeded in coming up with a solution to the problem of securely identifying citizens (or have not dared to try). As a result, the possibility of this basic government task being entrusted to a consortium of private companies is still being debated. The outcome is uncertain.

Given citizens' growing expectations, the complexity of social problems and the scarcity of resources, the public sector would do well to substantially increase its capacity for innovation, without sacrificing its principles and values. Some time ago, Borins (2001: 311) aptly summed up the emerging dilemma in the following terms: "In all likelihood, we as a society do not want the public sector to be as innovative as the private sector, nor to display the volatility of internet startups. Yet it is equally likely that we want the public sector to be more innovative than it traditionally has been."

In the following section, we explore key aspects of innovation in order to define it in the public-sector context, describe various types of innovation and shed light on the phenomenon from various angles. We also present areas where friction can arise in various phases of the innovation process, before discussing typical barriers to the emergence of innovation in public organizations—and some principles for overcoming them. The final section is devoted to future developments and challenges, placing particular emphasis on the involvement of external actors, notably from civil society, who can provide vital impetus and resources. This is why we look at concrete possibilities for participative innovation, such as innovation competitions, collaborative innovation with other organizations, and the role of startups in the public sector.

17.2 Key points of innovation

What exactly is innovation? How does one go about "creating" it? Countless myths and success stories surround the notion of innovation and how it is supposed to happen. In reality, there is no magic recipe. In fact, opinions differ widely regarding the very essence of innovation. From a managerial point of view, innovation can be understood as a solution that provides a more effective, productive, sustainable or equitable response to a problem than existing processes, services or products. It generates measurable added value that can be highlighted at the end of an innovation project. In a systemic view of innovation, on the other hand, the term is primarily understood as a process of radical change involving the restructuring of daily routines and resource flows. In this sense, innovation sooner or later leads to a transformation of an organization and its culture, structures and processes (▶ Part III. Organization and processes). The changes can be so drastic that they can not only cause upheaval in certain organizations, but also overturn the logic of entire business sectors (Yoo *et al.* 2010). Lastly, from a social-criticism perspective, innovation can also be seen as a force for political mobilization and empowerment. It can reshape the way in which a social construct, such as public administration, operates, as well as its power relations. Accordingly, innovation can be mobilized as a political tool.

These different views suggest that innovation rarely progresses smoothly or without conflict. As shown in figure 17.1, there are several areas of friction that need to be taken into account. One example is the question of the implementation speed. Should the organization be gradually adapted over the long term, or would a radical transition with a "big bang" be preferred? Controversies can also arise regarding the direction in which action flows. Public administration generally operates on

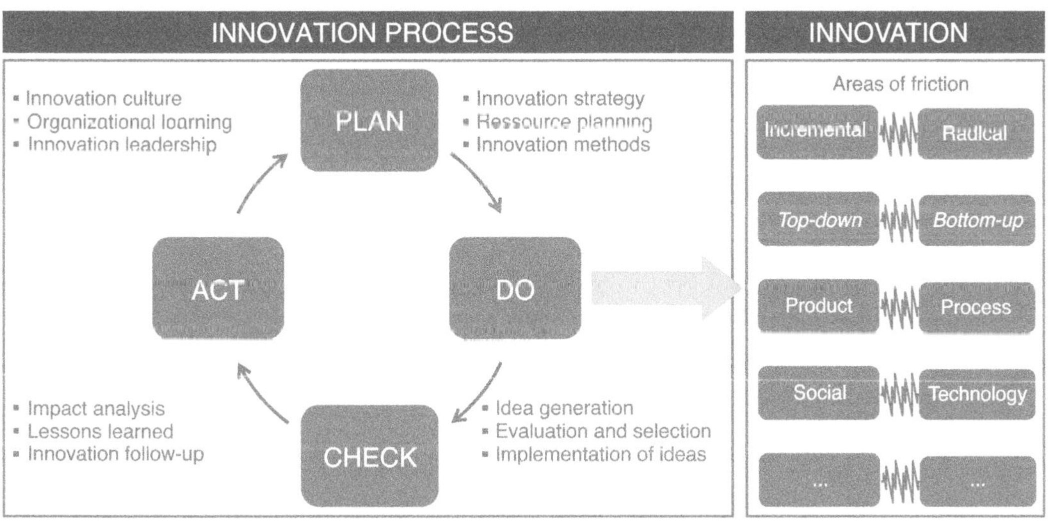

Figure 17.1 The innovation processes and areas of friction

a top-down basis. However, this can be ineffectual, because innovation is not something that simply happens "on command". On the other hand, practical experience with bottom-up, participative forms of working is still lacking, and this can jeopardize the success of a project. Defining the scope of innovation can also generate tensions. What exactly should it cover? Is it primarily a question of improving an existing process, or one of totally rethinking a service or product? Is the main goal technological innovation or social innovation?

17.2.1 The innovation process

All these questions must be clarified during the planning phase ("Plan") of an innovation process. At the same stage, an appropriate innovation strategy and method has to be determined. Stock should be taken of the resources available for innovation. Innovation has a cost: it takes time. It should not therefore be considered as a project of secondary importance, ancillary to main activities. Taking part in an innovation project can be an inspiring experience for the staff of a public body. But when, as often happens, no structures or organizational hubs dedicated to innovation are planned, such a project can result in an excessive workload. Indeed, the work of innovation (the "Do" phase) usually takes place in the context of projects, outside the usual activities. Normal procedures need to be adapted to some extent, or make way for novel approaches that encourage the emergence, evaluation and implementation of innovative ideas (▶ 18 Project management). Clearly, the bulk of the effort is devoted to this phase. But in the euphoria of the creative process, people often forget that the launch of an innovation should be systematically followed by an assessment ("lessons learned"), as well as an ongoing examination and analysis of the effects of the solution developed (the "Check" phase). This is the only way to ensure that mistakes are not repeated and to identify the success factors for the organization in the context concerned (▶ 16 Evaluation). Finally, on the basis of experience gained and—hopefully— systematically documented, appropriate measures (the "Act" phase) need to be taken so that a broad-based innovation culture can be established in public administration. These measures include, on the one hand, people-related initiatives such as raising awareness and developing "innovative-leadership" skills. On the other hand, they include technical measures, such as the introduction of an innovation-monitoring system, and the development of innovative methods to be incorporated into the existing catalogue of organizational methods.

17.2.2 Barriers to innovation

In practice, innovation is often seen as incompatible with long-established mindsets and ways of working in public administration. This overlooks the fact that the public sector has been and remains significantly involved in the development, funding and widespread adoption of revolutionary innovations such as telecommunications and electronic data processing. However, it is fair to say that public administration faces many barriers in its quest for innovation (De Vries *et al.* 2016).

Figure 17.2 shows four different factors that can be identified as barriers to innovation in public administration. The age-old "private versus public" dichotomy reveals a number of organizational aspects that are particularly detrimental to innovation in the public sector. The public sector is characterized by relatively bureaucratic processes and a strongly parochial mindset, elements that often have a crippling effect on the potential for innovative collaborative managerial culture. Moreover, many places lack the resources and appropriate structures needed to actively promote innovative projects (▶ Part III. Organization and processes). But individual factors also play a role. The traditional profile of administrative staff is characterized by a precise, efficient working attitude. This comes with high risk aversion and a low propensity for experimentation. Creativity—an essential prerequisite for innovation—is generally undervalued. In addition, the typical top-down working approach often hampers autonomy and the potential for encouraging innovation. Public employees are often simply not used to taking the initiative, and the resulting feeling of powerlessness or lethargy is aggravated by external factors. Public administration is subject to explicit rules and directives that result in a reactive rather than a proactive working style. Also, unlike the private sector, it is exposed to relatively little competitive pressure. This explains why practices in public administration are

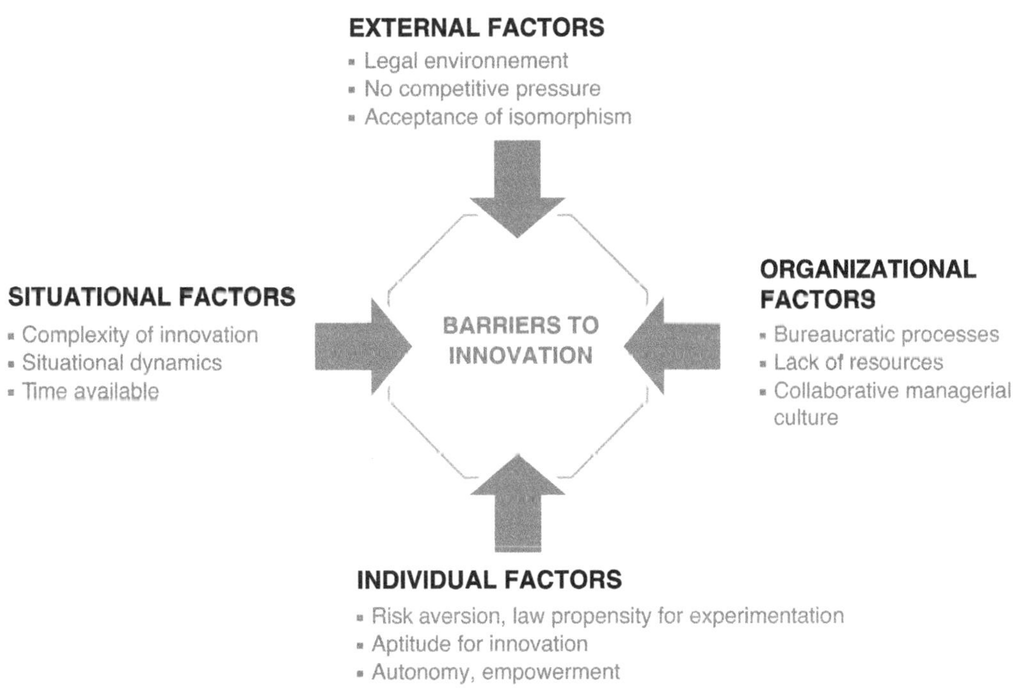

Figure 17.2 Barriers to innovation

largely harmonized (known as "isomorphism", as opposed to differentiation driven by innovation), and thus fall in with a policy of "blame avoidance" (Weaver 1986). Lastly, situational factors can also present major obstacles for public administration. Many of the innovative projects undertaken by public authorities are complex and highly dynamic. Multiple interactions with internal and external actors are involved, and the initiatives launched have no basis for comparison. This is particularly true of crisis management, which calls for the handling of often unprecedented problems, and where innovation must fit into a meticulously calculated timetable. Faced with these parameters, conventional public administration is soon out of its depth. The solutions we set out below for implementing an effective innovation process are therefore all the more useful.

17.2.3 Organizational principles to foster internal innovation

How can administrative bodies sidestep the dilemma regarding innovation described by Borins, quoted above, and strengthen their capacity for innovation?

As regards internal organization, it is vitally important to create dedicated cross-functional innovation hubs, or teams—in the form of new organizational units, for example. These hubs need to be provided with adequate resources, particularly a core group of people in charge of innovation with a dedicated budget. In addition, they must have the necessary autonomy and appropriate decision-making skills. As far as possible, they should also be decoupled from day-to-day activities and bureaucratic processes (▶ 12 Human-resource management). Ideally, these teams will also formulate an innovation strategy in collaboration with management. This approach makes it possible to define the development prospects desired by the hierarchy, making use of cross-functional thinking. In this way, the risk of encouraging innovations that are too small in scale or of no great importance can be avoided. One of the main tasks of an innovation unit should therefore be to triage innovative ideas, separating those that are worth encouraging from those that should be stopped (the "fail fast" principle in the implementation phase). Otherwise, there is a risk of launching numerous innovations, but bringing few to fruition. With this in mind, another important task of an innovation hub is to promote innovations and ensure that they are incorporated into core activities. Experience has shown that innovations that demonstrate their added value at the pilot or prototype stage often fail on attempted deployment in the administrative system and in the world of existing managerial processes. Another potentially useful device for supervision and steering is a differentiated portfolio of innovation projects. In this portfolio, distinctions can be made between top-down and bottom-up projects, between disruptive and incremental projects, and between short- and long-term projects. In summary, here are a few principles that may be useful from the point of view of internal organization:

- Create a dedicated, cross-functional innovation hub, for example in the form of a permanent core team with its own budget and appropriate decision-making powers.
- Create free spaces for employees to contribute concrete ideas for innovation.
- Instil a culture of error within the innovation hub and, to a lesser extent, when integrating innovations into core activities.
- Encourage regular intensive exchanges between innovation-hub members and those who will be deploying and using the innovations in the future.
- Develop (non-financial) incentives and a sense of "being in competition" among administrative units (including outside their own service, department, canton or even country) with the aim of encouraging emulation in order to spark innovation.

17.2.4 Organizational principles to foster external innovation

In organizational terms, it makes very good sense to cooperate with external actors of various types: innovation can thus be generated not only to suit the needs of the administrative entity, but also in the interests of the common good in general. The creativity and additional resources of external actors can drive innovation within the entity concerned. One of the simplest ways of generating innovative ideas is to set up an idea-management platform where anyone can make suggestions for innovation (▶ 15 Organizational learning). However, the ideas submitted will need to be systematically evaluated and, where appropriate, developed or implemented in-house. In addition, everyone who makes a suggestion should receive constructive feedback. This open-access platform should be publicized, and internal contacts should be available to respond to requests for information and clarification. Additional information materials could also be provided, for example outlining the challenges facing the administration or giving free access to data available from the organization. In Switzerland, the Swiss Federal Railways (SBB) are using this type of open-access idea-management system with their "Customer Voice" programme.

An approach that goes beyond simply collecting ideas is to set up innovation competitions—"hackathons", "makeathons" or online contests. The aim is to tackle internal organizational challenges. Volunteers from civil society attempt to provide an answer through creative and sometimes unusual approaches, within a relatively short timeframe (48 hours, for example), while aiming for a prize (which is not necessarily monetary). In these competitions, the contribution of external participants is not limited to putting forward ideas: it can go as far as the first experimental solutions or prototypes. Usually, however, contributions are not operational immediately, needing to be perfected in-house, then integrated when they prove to be useful. In Switzerland, a growing number of federal administrative bodies, cantons and even some municipalities are using this type of competition, particularly hackathons, with quite convincing results.

In summary, here are a few principles for organizing the external innovation process:

- Create an open-access idea-management platform, at a fairly high level in the administrative hierarchy, or even straddling several administrations.
- Encourage serious, professional participation in creative competitions such as hackathons, makeathons, etc.
- As regards concrete innovative projects, develop a collaborative innovation process (rather than outsourcing) involving close cooperation, for example with a university, startups or parapublic organizations.
- Initiate a cultural shift towards open government: transparently present internal challenges and open data and abandon the penchant for secrecy that arises from excessive caution.
- Introduce instruments to identify the "winners" and "losers" of innovation and, if necessary, bring in compensation (e.g. making sure no one can be denied access to a service following the introduction of a purely digital solution).

17.3 Future developments and challenges

Innovation is a continuous process that touches on all areas of administration. A dedicated innovation hub may prove useful in implementing the principles outlined above. However, it may lack the specialized knowledge to innovate in all sectors of an administration or administrative unit. Hence the importance of setting up mechanisms that also allow experts an opportunity to contribute innovative ideas in their own (or other) disciplines. For this purpose, it may be wise to (partly) release such people from their main tasks for a while. Swisscom's Kickbox programme for "intrapreneurs" is a case in point. It allows employees to obtain a physical "box" containing various resources, including a budget, to innovate. This gives them the means to devote themselves to developing their own idea, in conjunction with experts (or coaches) within the innovation hub. To make this possible, direct line managers should not be able to veto a person's desire to work on an innovative idea. The decision of whether to validate the innovative nature of an idea should therefore be taken later by the innovation hub. It is important to trust staff members, encourage them to contribute their innovative ideas and offer them incentives to do so. Every innovation must be assigned a permanent resource charged with supporting it and moving it forward through all its phases. This person must take ownership of the idea and have sufficient expertise in the field concerned. Delegating matters to another person or unit frequently hampers the development of an innovation. Even though the innovation hub is meant to carry out its work as independently as possible from core activities, it must never lose sight of technical requirements. It therefore needs to keep up regular exchanges with the users of an innovation in order to ensure that it is useful and will remain accepted. The innovation hub also has to develop its own culture, with a high tolerance for error. Only rarely does an innovation result in a perfect plan that simply has to be implemented. In the vast majority of cases, an iterative approach with a multitude of test phases, satisfaction surveys, error corrections and improvements must be followed before an innovation develops sufficient maturity for deployment in a production environment. Despite all these precautions, new errors may still occur, and will have to be rectified as quickly as possible, without seeking to unduly assign blame. Errors are an integral part of innovation. By proceeding in this way, many barriers to innovation in public administration can be overcome, whether they are organizational, situational or individual in nature (external obstacles remain, however). The chances of becoming distinctly more innovative will improve.

Collaboration, both internal and external, is essential to the success of innovation projects. In the view of Sørensen & Torfing (2012: 1), mobilizing relevant innovation resources from public and private actors is a prerequisite for the exchange of knowledge and for transformation-oriented learning. This is the only way to "foster innovation by [...] building joint ownership [of] new innovative visions and practices". This, then, is real cooperation, not the outsourcing of innovation. Working in this way, strengths can be pooled and the shortfall of innovative resources within public organizations can be made good by external resources. External partners are often subject to fewer regulatory and bureaucratic constraints and more competitive pressure than public entities. What is important is close cooperation beyond the organization's borders and a constructive shared vision. Partnerships between public authorities and other parapublic actors are often a success. An illustration is provided by the city of St. Gallen's innovative "smart city" project, where cooperation between the municipal administration proper and its industrial departments enabled the latter to contribute their technical know how to the project. Collaborative innovation between public authorities and universities can also prove highly fruitful for both parties. The administration benefits from additional innovation resources and allows universities to transfer the knowledge acquired through research and teaching. In contrast with collaborations with private-sector partners, specific funding—a factor that often prevents partners from devoting all their energy to the project, obliging them instead to seek additional mandates—is not even necessarily required. An example of this approach can be found at the State Secretariat for Migration which, in conjunction with researchers at ETH Zurich, is developing an algorithm to better allocate asylum seekers to the cantons and improve their chances of finding a job. Cooperating with startups is also an interesting avenue. This is shown by a series of projects being conducted by Swiss Post studying the use of drones in logistics. Clearly, then, approaches that involve external actors help to overcome the barriers to innovation, and the organizational, situational and individual obstacles. When choosing instruments, administrative bodies should select or combine the approaches best suited to their own organization and its specific challenges.

In summary, there are a host of structural reasons why public organizations have, in the past, paid less attention to innovation and given more importance to values such as stability and continuity. These reasons have provided excuses for not tackling the question of innovation seriously. All too often, however, innovation has been rejected out of hand, either on the basis of debatable claims such as "our administration is different and that's why it cannot embark on this process", or out of fear of unfortunate consequences in the event of failure. And yet public organizations have a whole range of internal and external options for overcoming barriers to innovation. Naturally, each administrative entity has intrinsically motivated and innovation-minded members of its staff. But the organization's context and culture do not always allow them to innovate or to do so in cooperation with external actors. Laying the foundations for innovation, both inside and outside the administration, is the major challenge that management has to take up.

Key concepts

- Barriers to innovation (*obstacles à l'innovation, Innovationshürden, barriere all'innovazione*): situational, external, organizational or individual factors that complicate the launch or progress of innovative projects for an organization.
- Collaborative innovation (*innovation collaborative, kollaborative Innovation, innovazione collaborativa*): collaboration between several actors to foster innovation, bringing together public and private actors with appropriate resources for the purpose of innovating. This simplifies knowledge exchange and transformation-focused learning and fosters joint ownership of new innovative visions and practices.
- Innovation (*innovation, Innovation, innovazione*): a solution that provides a more effective, efficient, sustainable or equitable response to a problem than existing processes, products or services, and generates measurable added value. The term also refers to a process of change that transforms an organization and its culture, structures and processes. It also designates a force for political mobilization and empowerment.
- Innovation process (*processus d'innovation, Innovationsprozess, processo di innovazione*): a succession of phases typical of an innovation (to be considered as a cycle where appropriate), from planning (Plan) to innovation work (Do), impact analysis (Check), to a transformation of the organization's culture (Act).

References

Borins, S. (2001). Encouraging innovation in the public sector. *Journal of Intellectual Capital, 2*(3), 310–319.

De Vries, H., Bekkers, V. & Tummers, L. (2016). Innovations in the Public Sector: A Systematic Review and Future Research Agenda. *Public Administration, 94*(1), 146–166.

Sørensen, E. & Torfing, J. (2012). Introduction: Collaborative innovation in the public sector. *The Innovation Journal, 17*(1), 1–14.

Weaver, R. K. (1986). The Politics of Blame Avoidance. *Journal of Public Policy, 6*(4), 371–398.

Yoo, Y., Henfridsson, O. & Lyytinen, K. (2010). Research Commentary—The New Organizing Logic of Digital Innovation: An Agenda for Information Systems Research. *Information Systems Research, 21*(4), 724–735.

References for further study

Rønning, R., Enquist, B., & Fuglsang, L. (2014). *Framing Innovation in Public Service Sectors.* Routledge.

Torfing, J. (2013). *Collaborative Innovation in the Public Sector. Handbook of Innovation in Public Services.* Georgetown University Press.

18 Project management

Olivier Glassey

18.1 The importance of project management for public administration

The concept of project management originated in the world of architects and engineers before gradually entering the business world during the 20th century. Aïm (2018) traces the formal separation of the design and execution phases of a project back to Italian Renaissance architecture, using the construction of the Santa Maria del Fiore cathedral in Florence as an example: architect Filippo Brunelleschi spent much of his life laying the theoretical foundations of the laws of perspective and solving the daunting technical challenges involved in building the cathedral's massive dome.

Leaping forward in time, the methodological approach to project management has considerably expanded in order to solve other technical challenges, notably those of the conquest of space. Many tools have been developed by NASA and the European Space Agency. While the service sector is not concerned with the manufacture of tangible products (cathedrals or space shuttles), it faces the same cost, time and quality constraints in the delivery of intangible services, which can be highly complex. In a similar vein, public-sector entities are managing numerous transformation projects. These are projects in which a structured approach makes it easier to mobilize available resources and do everything possible to prevent failure.

Project management differs from operational management. The latter is in fact recurrent and repetitive, and is aimed at maintaining stable operations for as long as possible (Knuston & Webster 2018). In contrast, project management is time-bound and is aimed at delivering all the work needed, but only the work needed, to complete a project (PMI 2017). The notion of life cycle must therefore be incorporated into project management, with projects' beginning and end being clearly defined. Specific planning and progress monitoring tools must be used. Due to the very nature of projects, with short-lived teams being formed to achieve a goal, project management must pay particular attention to stakeholder management. The approach has to be significantly different from that of traditional human-resources management.

A project must produce results. Four types of generic tangible or intangible outcomes can be distinguished (PMI 2017):

- a product or component, for example, the construction of a school building;
- a service or the ability to provide a service, such as a public-health prevention campaign;
- an improvement in a product or service, e.g. optimization of a building permit procedure; and
- a deliverable or document, such as a financial inspectorate audit report.

In more targeted fashion, the HERMES project-management method (Swiss Confederation 2015) incorporates the idea of "scenarios" leading to expected outcomes, for example:

- development or supply of a service, staging of an event;
- development of an IT system;
- purchase and integration of a standard IT solution; and
- changes to an organization at both structural (organization chart) and functional (process) levels.

Without emphasizing the technical aspects of project management, this contribution presents three methods (PMI/PMBOK, PRINCE2 and HERMES). We explore these methods in the next section, illustrating the main challenges of project management in the process. Aimed primarily at administrative managers in Switzerland, the text refers primarily to the HERMES[49] method. This has become a *de facto* standard in Swiss public bodies, with most cantons and major cities having adopted it. There is a training and certification system, both internal to the Confederation and outside it. This system involves strategic partners such as the Swiss Conference of Higher Education Institutions in German-speaking Switzerland and the Association Suisse d'Organisation et de Management (ASO) in French-speaking Switzerland.

18.2 Key points of project management

ISO 9000 defines a project as "a unique process consisting of a set of coordinated and controlled activities with start and finish dates, undertaken to achieve an

49 Some notions taken from PMI/PMBOK are used, however, since these methods are in some cases complementary to, and even more detailed than, HERMES.

objective conforming to specific requirements, including constraints of time, cost and resources[50]". This norm defines project management as follows: "planning, organizing, monitoring, controlling and reporting of all aspects of a project and the motivation of all those involved in it to achieve the project objectives".

Many theoretical and methodological works cover all aspects of project planning, organization, control and reporting, as well as aspects relating to the quality of project results. The book by Lock (2013) is still a standard reference, even though its first edition was published in 1968.

The most widespread method of project management is based on PMBOK, an acronym for *Project Management Body of Knowledge*. A guide to this method published by the Project Management Institute (PMI 2017) is a benchmark in the field. PMI is also a training and certification organization. By 2015, 700,000 people worldwide had been certified as PMI project managers (Linke 2019). The certification exam is based on PMBOK concepts.

The other major project-management method is PRINCE2 (Turley 2010). It was originally developed by the Office of Government Commerce (OGC), a body set up by the UK Cabinet Office. In 2013 the Cabinet Office created a joint venture to manage PRINCE2 training courses. Over 250,000 people have obtained certification (Linke 2019).

It is no coincidence that this method was developed by a government. Public bodies are responsible for a wide range of complex projects (social, economic, environmental, organizational, IT, etc.). This means they must be able to define the requirements of projects in terms of deadlines, costs and resources. Switzerland also set itself to the task, resulting in the Confederation's creation of its HERMES project-management method.

While each of these three methods has its own specific features, they are based on a number of common concepts. We present here a few key points of these methods, without going into the details of the differences between them[51].

18.2.1 The project-management triangle

The goal of project management is to strike a balance between three potentially contradictory constraints. These constraints form the three apexes of the project-management triangle:

- *cost* management;
- *deadline* management; and
- *quality* management.

50 https://www.iso.org/obp/ui/#iso:std:iso:9000:ed-4:v1:en (accessed 02.04.2024).

51 Linke (2019) provides a comparison of these three methods and also puts them into perspective in relation to so-called "agile" approaches.

According to Lock (2013), project managers must rank these three constraints in order of priority. They have to find the right compromise between deadlines and costs, costs and quality, and deadlines and quality. Projects that fail to achieve the sought-after balance fall into a number of categories (Aïm 2018). These cases have been illustrated many times in practice and are briefly discussed below.

Cost overruns. The project was delivered on time, with a satisfactory level of quality. But additional technical and human resources had to be allocated beyond what was initially planned.

Cost overruns and missed deadlines. The project was delayed and cost more than expected. Teams had to be committed for longer and/or financial penalties were incurred due to the delay.

Failure to meet quality requirements. The notion of quality is of course linked to the type of project being carried out. This aspect is dealt with in section 18.2.5. For the moment, suffice it to say that failure in this area can be the result of construction defects, IT faults or organizational dysfunction. Beyond quality in the strict sense of the term, quality non-compliance may also be due to a reduction in functional scope as a project progresses. For example, some functionalities of an information system were defined in the initial specifications, but were abandoned along the way for cost reasons.

Project managers must be vigilant to ensure that balance between these three constraints is maintained throughout the project. This requires adjustments: re-estimating costs, re-assigning tasks and resources, revising the schedule, and so on. Reductions in quality or functional scope are also possible, but this should only be a last resort, for example, when a deadline takes precedence over everything else.

18.2.2 Project life cycle

There are various ways of dividing a project into phases. A relatively simple and classic approach is described in Verzuh (2015):

- *Define* the project;
- *Plan* the project;
- *Execute* the project;
- *Close out* the project.

The HERMES method is also based on four phases, but the breakdown and vocabulary are different: *initiation, concept, implementation, deployment*.

This sequential view of a project represents the traditional project-management approach (Knuston & Webster 2018). Other approaches have been developed in various sectors of activity.

One example is the *iterative approach*. This makes it possible to go back and rework the elements defined in a previous phase. The scrum software development method is based on "sprints". A sprint is a period of a few hours to a few weeks (Linke 2019). Every sprint begins with an estimate, followed by operational planning, and ends with a demonstration of what has been achieved. This approach helps to avoid errors in initial planning, and to adjust expectations regarding the quality of results as the project progresses.

Evolutionary and *agile* approaches both seek to involve the project's addressee—its customer—as much as possible. The aim is to offer a high level of responsiveness to developments and requests for changes. The central role is thus given to the "product owner" (addressee, or customer) rather than to the project manager.

HERMES integrates this approach, proposing scenarios for developing an agile product:

- Each phase comprises a series of tasks to be carried out under the responsibility of a "role". The method offers some sixty standard tasks and, for each task, a list of activities to be carried out with the expected outcomes. HERMES standardizes certain roles, distinguishing between those of the core organization and those of the project organization (project manager, test manager, project sponsor, steering committee, user, etc.).
- Each phase closes with a "milestone", or quality gate, covering project progress, quality and costs. In this way, verification criteria can be used to report on the progress of a project. If criteria are not met, project management may decide not to "release" the current phase (therefore not moving on to the next one). A decision not to release a phase means that management must ask for corrective measures to ensure that the project will meet requirements. It can also mean the total, definitive shutdown of the project.

18.2.3 Managing project stakeholders

As indicated in section 18.2.1, the aim of project management is to strike a balance between time, cost and quality constraints. However, as Lock (2013: 12) points out, "it is easy but dangerous to forget that no objective can be achieved without people". Identifying stakeholders is thus a crucial step in starting a project. Although they may be quite different, depending on the type of project, several key roles are always present: the project addressee, his or her agent, the supplier, the end-user person or entity, the project team, the project sponsor (the person representing the organization's management who is formally responsible for the project), etc. Verzuh (2015) proposes a list of questions for identifying the various stakeholders in a project.

Defining stakeholders is not enough: they must be supported throughout the project. This support can take various forms. One important point is to set up rules for communication between and with stakeholders (e.g. an e-mail usage policy, archiving rules, meeting management). It is also a matter of defining who contributes, and to what extent, at different stages of the project, who decides what, etc. Communication media also need to be decided upon: meeting minutes, periodic progress reports, electronic project-management platform, etc. The PMBOK contains an entire chapter devoted to managing project communications (PMI 2015).

Beyond the formal aspects of communication management, a project manager spends a good deal of time motivating teams, solving problems, managing conflicts and negotiating compromises. Verzuh (2015) presents various techniques for team management and collaboration between stakeholders.

18.2.4 Planning and estimating costs

While project management must cover many more aspects than planning and resource allocation (Knuston & Webster 2018), these two are always the most fundamental tasks in the process.

The first step in planning and estimating costs is to break down the project's scope into smaller, more manageable components and batches of components. One well-known technique is the *Work Breakdown Structure* (WBS) advocated by PMBOK (PMI 2015). It involves a hierarchical breakdown of the activities to be carried out, based on "work packages". The PRINCE2 method uses the *Product-Based Planning* (PBP) technique, in which the product or deliverable is broken down into sub-products, with a workflow logic between the various deliverables. Lastly, HERMES has opted for a thematic breakdown, with reusable "modules" that make it easy to create scenarios. They contain tasks designed to produce outcomes on a given theme. The "Procurement" module, for example, includes the tasks *Prepare a call for tenders*, *Evaluate tenders* and *Decide on contract award*.

Depending on the type of project and their own experience, project managers will choose the most appropriate technique. They can use structural (WBS), dynamic (PBP) or thematic (HERMES) breakdowns, or even combine different techniques.

The next step is to establish logical links between tasks (what task must precede a given task, what tasks can be carried out simultaneously, etc.). These links can be represented graphically in the form of a network diagram, which will show only the logical sequence. A Gantt chart allows the time dimension to be incorporated (Verzuh 2015). Various software tools make it very easy to create and update these types of diagrams. The PERT method (*Program Evaluation and Review Technique*) was developed by the US Navy in the 1950s precisely for this purpose. It uses a chart—a dependency chart—to represent the task sequence. This makes it possible to calculate the critical path in terms of time and the critical path in terms of cost. The notion of "critical path" refers to an ordered list of all the activities required to achieve the desired outcome. This notion also underpins the *Critical Path Method* (CPM), an algorithm used to plan the Manhattan Project and the construction of New York's Twin Towers, among other projects. This algorithm is still used in some project-management software, albeit in a somewhat improved version that can be used to simulate alternative critical paths when time or cost constraints are changed, or to reallocate resources.

These applications are now capable of graphically representing task sequences or calculating critical paths. But the project manager's experience and judgment are essential requirements in establishing optimistic, pessimistic or most-likely scenarios for the sequence of these tasks. This means that for every task (or at least, for all critical tasks), a human must define realistic start and end dates, as well as advanced or delayed start/end dates. The PERT method mentioned above offers a decision-making aid, using the following formula, for example, to estimate anticipated duration: [optimistic duration + pessimistic duration + (4 × most likely duration)]/6.

The next step is to determine the direct costs of carrying out a task (i.e. duration multiplied by labour costs), indirect costs, fixed costs, etc. Costing is closely linked to the project's field of activity. In fact, in some fields, such as construction, "estimator" is a profession in its own right, given the complexity of the tasks involved. A simple example of costing (based on a real case) is presented below, to illustrate the logic.

The example is taken from the field of IT application development. One of the most frequently used costing methods is based on requirements management[52]. Requirements in terms of screens, data interfaces and data processing are described and assessed.

Screens. This means an interface on the user's computer screen. A login screen with two input fields is considered simple for costing purposes; a screen for entering a tax return is considered complex.

Data interface. A direct database query is considered simple. Combining data from multiple external repositories is complex.

Data processing. If the only data entered on a form are an e-mail address and a telephone number, checking that the form is correct is a simple matter. On the other hand, applying advanced management rules will be considered complex.

Requirement	Screen	Data interface	Data processing
Identify the user	Simple	Simple	Simple
Open an administrative file	Moderate	Moderate	Simple
Request additional information	Simple	Moderate	Moderate
Apply entry criteria	Moderate	Simple	Complex
Provide grounds for non-consideration	Moderate	Simple	Simple

Table 18.1 Example of breakdown for a computer application

52 A requirement is the formal expression of a user need, for example printing a proof of residence.

Project managers then apply metrics based on their experience or on current scales, for example:

- Single screen by experienced developer = 0.5 day;
- Complex screen by experienced developer = 1.5 days; and
- Moderate data interface by junior developer = 1 day.

After that, they use the daily rates generally charged by contractors (e.g. CHF 1000 for an experienced developer and CHF 750 for a junior), plus a 20% margin on total development costs for project management and contingencies. This yields a total amount for the completion of an IT project of this nature.

To conclude this section, it is worth mentioning the distinction made by Lock (2013) between *planning* and *scheduling*. Planning is the logical and temporal breakdown of the sequence of activities explained above. It calculates the theoretical time required to complete a task to be calculated. Scheduling requires additional thought to take into account the availability of resources (e.g. people employed part-time or assigned to several projects simultaneously, vacation periods, etc.). These considerations are necessary to set target dates for the completion of a task.

18.2.5 Project progress monitoring

Sophisticated IT tools—such as Basecamp and Asana, to name two current market leaders—are available for measuring task progress. These tools, which can be used to count hours worked and monitor budgets, or to reallocate resources on a project, make a project manager's job much easier. They allow project-team members to visualize the tasks assigned to them, as well as the allocated time and the deadline for completion. Team members then enter the progress of their tasks on a daily or weekly basis. Verzuh (2015) recommends that the recording of task progress should be kept simple, using only three levels: 0%, task not started; 50%, task in progress; 100%, task completed. A word of clarification is in order here: recording the progress of tasks serves to gauge whether deadlines have been met, whereas recording the hours worked by project-team members serves to calculate costs. As always, IT tools make it easier to aggregate data, measure lead times and costs by task, by person, by work package, and so on.

While deadlines and costs are relatively easy to track and quantify, the same cannot always be said for the third apex of the project-management triangle: quality. In some business areas, there are standards to measure product quality and resolve problems in the event of a defect[53]. This is particularly the case when the deliverables are tangible, but less so for projects with intangible deliverables (such as a

53 Standard SIA 118, for example, sets out the general conditions for carrying out construction work in Switzerland.

reorganization project). In the latter case, one way to guarantee a project's success is to focus on risk management. This approach seeks to develop strategies that take into account both factual elements and the integration of the project's potentially unpredictable environment (Huf 2016). In concrete terms, this means identifying positive or negative events that could affect the success of a project. The next step is to assess the likelihood of these events, and then to implement measures to reduce the probability of glitches occurring. Finally, response protocols are prepared, in case a risk should materialize. This approach is not discussed here, but both Lock (2013) and PMI (2017) devote detailed chapters to it.

18.3 Future prospects and challenges

It is not necessary for managers of public bodies to be experienced or certified project managers. But it is very important that they understand the notion of balancing cost, deadline and quality constraints. This is because public administration is increasingly organizing itself in "project mode[54]". A major resulting challenge is that of bringing project logic into administrative units that function along operational-management lines. Then again, some project managers focus primarily on the outcomes they have committed to delivering, ignoring how these outcomes are subsequently used in operational management.

In the future, the challenge for administrative managers will be threefold. First, they will of course be responsible for ensuring the stability of day-to-day operations. Second, they will have to take steps to ensure that projects actually come to fruition. Third and last, they will have to ensure that project outcomes are implemented: that the transition from project logic to utilization logic is smooth and sustainable. This challenge is reflected in the semantics of the HERMES method. It calls the final phase of a project the "deployment" phase rather than the "closing out" phase. Another pitfall frequently arises when initiating projects. This is the temptation to assign responsibility for a project to specialists in the field concerned, without giving them time for project-management activities, without training them and without providing them with adequate methods and tools.

54 See, for example, the French government's *Action Publique 2022* transformation plans https://www.modernisation.gouv.fr/actualites/action-publique-2022-accelerer-la-transformation-du-service-public (accessed 02.04.2024).

Key concepts

- Deliverable (*livrable, Ergebnis, prodotto finale*): a tangible, measurable, specific outcome of a project stage. This could be a document such as specifications or a report, a software component, or any other intermediate product.
- Estimating or costing (*chiffrage, Einschätzung, quantificazione*): quantitative evaluation of the costs and time required to complete a task, based on explicit assumptions, e.g. labour costs, human-resource skill levels, external constraints, etc.
- Planning (*planification, Planung, pianificazione*): a process that sets the objectives to be achieved, the resources needed to achieve them, and the stages in the process, and incorporates the time dimension.
- Project life cycle (*cycle de vie projet, Projektlebenszyklus, ciclo di vita del progetto*): a breakdown into phases of the path that takes a project from start to finish.
- Project scope (*perimètre project, Projektumfang, ambito del progetto*): clear delimitation of the boundaries of a project, based on needs to be met, work packages, and tasks to be carried out to achieve project objectives.

References

Aïm, R. (2018). *La gestion de projets* (6th ed.). Gualino Editeur.

Huf, A. S. (2016). Project Innovation: Evidence-Informed, Open, Effectual, and Subjective. *Project Management Journal*, 47(2), 8–25. DOI: 10.1002/pmj.21576 (accessed 30.11.2022).

Knuston, J. & Webster, F. M (2018). What Is Project Management? Project Management Concepts and Methodologies. In P.C Dinsmore & J. Cabanis-Brewin (Eds.) *The AMA Handbook of Project Management*, 1–10.

Linke, K. (2019). Traditional and Agile Management Approaches. *12th ILERA European Congress*, Heinrich-Heine-Universität, Düsseldorf, Deutschland.

Lock, D. (2013). *Project Management* (10th ed.). Routledge.

PMI (2017). *A Guide to the Project Management Body of Knowledge (PMBOK Guide)* (6th ed.). Project Management Institute.

Schweizerische Eidgenossenschaft (2015). *Hermes – Projektmanagementmethode für alle Projekte – Referenzhandbuch.* https://www.hermes.admin.ch/ (accessed 30.11.2022).

Turley, F. (2010). *The PRINCE2® Training Manual - A common sense approach to learning and understanding PRINCE2.* MgmtPlaza.

Verzuh, E. (2015). *The Fast Forward MBA in Project Management* (5th ed.). Wiley.

PARTIE V
Implementing the IDHEAP model

Introduction

Nils Soguel

1 The goal of implementation as illustrated by five cases

As we wrote in our introductory contribution: "The IDHEAP model seeks to understand public administration as a process of action, movement and transformation." It describes a complex reality in a simplified, illustrative, pragmatic way. It seeks to provide a better understanding of the issues involved, and to give public-sector managers the keys they need to analyse the situation, so that they can take action within their organization, thus designing and shaping public administration. The model and its various dimensions and components highlight the key elements to consider, the resources to activate and ways to use them, thus giving the model a dynamic dimension. The model must therefore enable the actors involved to conceive of and deploy public intervention.

But does it? This question echoes the one posed by Varenne (2012): "Should we believe the models?" To provide an initial answer to this question, we wanted to put the IDHEAP model of public administration into action. That is the purpose of this fifth part, in which the model is put to the test in the face of very real issues.

We have chosen five very different issues, all of them topical: welfare-to-work policies; elite sport; integrating refugees and asylum seekers; managing an educational institution; and wind-power generation.

These issues call for government intervention for a variety of reasons, sometimes cumulative. The grounds for intervention may be the values (▶ 1 Values) of our society, or the needs or interests of stakeholders (▶ 3 Stakeholders). Public administration thus always develops in interaction with the environment. Either the environment and its components envelop and condition public administration, or public administration influences and shapes its environment. The relationship is bidirectional and dialectical, as shown in figure V.1.

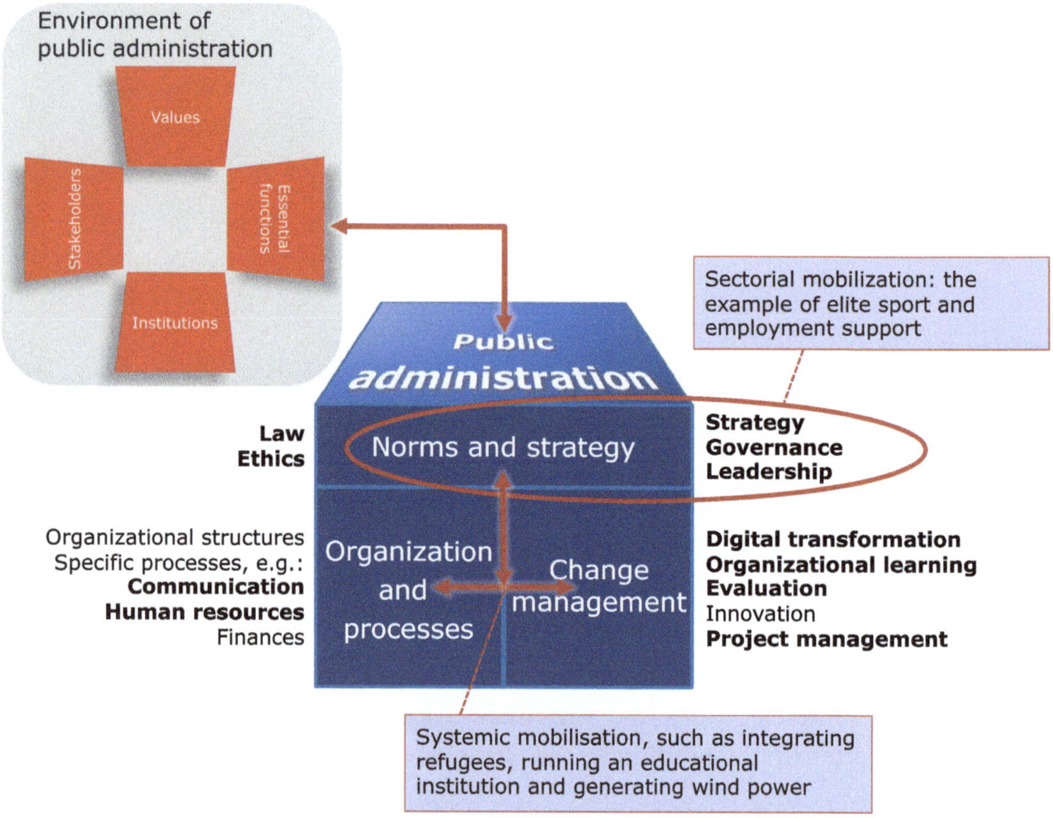

Figure V.1 Dimensions and components of the IDHEAP model mobilized in the context of the selected issues

2 Dimensions and components mobilized by the five selected cases

The model, its dimensions and its components can be used in two ways.

The first is to mobilize the model in a *sectorial* way. This involves analyzing the deployment of public administration and responding to the problems encountered in a single dimension of the model (environment; norms and strategy; organization and processes; change management). It is even possible to focus on a single component of the model. This is demonstrated by two of the issues addressed in this section (indicated by the elliptical line on Figure V.1):

- The issue of *welfare-to-work policies* serves to illustrate how to mobilize the "norms and strategy" dimension alone and focus on the "governance" component (▶ 8 Governance).

- The issue of *elite sport* shows how to mobilize the "norms and strategy" dimension alone and two of its components: "strategy" and "governance" (▶ 7 Strategy and ▶ 8 Governance).

The second way of mobilizing the model is *more systemic*. It consists in analyzing public administration and seeking solutions through the interaction of several dimensions and several components of the model. This is demonstrated by three of the issues discussed here (shown by the arrows in the centre of Figure V.1):

- The issue of *integrating refugees and asylum seekers* illustrates how to mobilize the three dimensions that make up the cube of public administration and six components: ▶ 5 Law, ▶ 6 Ethics, ▶ 11 Communication management, ▶ 14 Digital transformation, ▶ 15 Organizational learning and ▶ 16 Evaluation.
- The issue of *educational-institution management* illustrates a way of mobilizing two complementary dimensions: the "norms and strategy" dimension with its ▶ 9 Leadership component and the "organization and processes" dimension with, in particular, its ▶ 11 Communication management and ▶ 12 Human-resources management components.
- The issue of *wind-power generation* shows how to mobilize two dimensions and four components ▶ 5 Law, ▶ 7 Strategy, ▶ 8 Governance and ▶ 18 Project management.

We focus on the dimensions and components we consider most relevant to the issue at hand. To some extent, each issue is approached as a case study. We describe how to design an appropriate public-administration response within the framework of the model's dimensions and components. Problems encountered are also described.

Reference

Varenne, F. (2012). *Théorie, réalité, modèle*. Éditions Matériologiques.

19 Welfare-to-work policies

Giuliano Bonoli

19.1 Introduction to the social-policy challenges of welfare-to-work issues

In recent decades, social policy has shifted towards supporting access to employment. This development is part of a strategy to combat social problems. Traditionally, the main role of the welfare state was to guarantee a replacement income for people who, for various reasons, were unable to work. But since the 1990s the main social programmes have undergone a transformation, focusing on employment-support and welfare-to-work policies.

While this reorientation, which to some extent is still ongoing, has not been without its critics (Bonoli 2013; Hemerijck 2017), it seems to have taken hold in Switzerland and in the rest of Europe. Various terms are used to describe the new welfare state. Examples include "social investment", "active welfare state", "activation" and "flexicurity". In Switzerland, the greatest effect of this movement has been on federal unemployment- and disability-insurance programmes, and on cantonal and municipal social assistance.

In this contribution, we mobilize one of the components of the "norms and strategy" dimension of the IDHEAP model of public administration: governance (Figure 19.1). Implementing a comprehensive strategy for employment-support and welfare-to-work policies raises a fair number of problems, both in Switzerland and elsewhere (van Berkel *et al.* 2011). The challenges in terms of governance are at least threefold: access to the necessary skills, cost shifting, and contractualization of social actors.

Access to the necessary skills. Welfare-to-work policies fall under what Athias and Pasquier call "public services produced within a network" in their contribution (► 8 Governance). Obstacles to employment arise from different and sometimes multiple issues. For example, some unemployed people simply need to improve their knowledge of job-search techniques. Others have skills that have become

Figure 19.1 Example of the "governance" component that can be mobilized to promote access to employment (in bold in the figure)

obsolete and need additional training. Access to employment can be made difficult by health problems. Obstacles can also come in the form of practical difficulties, such as obtaining childcare.

Generally, we can assert that the competencies needed to help unemployed people to reenter the job market are available within the Swiss welfare state. However, they are not all available in every social-security scheme. For example, the unemployment-insurance system, and regional job centres (ORPs) in particular, have specialized competencies in job-search support and employer-recognized training courses in a given sector or region. But ORPs do not specialize in medical or occupational-health matters. These competencies do exist, however, in the disability-insurance system. Nor are ORPs supposed to find a childcare solution for a parent in need of one. But this problem could easily be solved in a municipal or regional social service.

Cost shifting. The institutions called on to work jointly on implementing an employment-support policy belong to different levels of the federal government. Social insurance is a federal responsibility, with implementation delegated to the cantons under the principle of federalism of execution (▶ 4 Institutions). Social assistance, on the other hand, is a cantonal or municipal responsibility, or shared between the two lower levels of the federal state, with different forms depending on the canton.

This institutional architecture raises financial issues that can give rise to a system of perverse incentives. This is because each institution involved in implementing employment-support policy has two options when faced with each individual situation of unemployment: either, as envisaged by the legislator, do everything possible to help the jobless person back into employment; or attempt to transfer them to another institution. Sometimes, especially in the case of people facing serious obstacles to employment, the second option can be the most attractive. This perverse incentive, which represents an "institutional moral hazard", is a recurring problem in multi-level welfare states (Luigjes & Vandenbroucke 2020). The problem has probably been exacerbated by the adoption of techniques inspired by the New Public Management movement (NPM) which, by emphasizing the achievement of measurable objectives, makes institutions more "selfish" (Øverbye *et al.* 2010).

To give a concrete example, a municipality can take on a person on welfare as an employee for a period of twelve months so that thereafter the person will be entitled to federal unemployment insurance and no longer dependent on municipal or cantonal social assistance. The same municipality can also help welfare recipients to prepare an application for a disability pension. In the event of refusal, the municipality can pay legal fees to have an appeal heard. Changes to federal legislation over the years have attempted to limit these possibilities, and have probably also led to a shifting of costs onto the cantons and municipalities, for example by making access to federal social insurance more difficult. All these practices at federal, cantonal and municipal levels have been well documented for Switzerland as well as for other federal countries such as Germany (Bonoli & Trein 2016).

Contractualizing social actors. When it comes to welfare-to-work policies, as with other public administration tasks, the question arises of whether government should produce the necessary services itself or outsource the task to non-governmental actors (to *do* or to *get done*? ▶ 3 Stakeholders and ▶ 8 Governance). In this specific case, the interest in using non-governmental agents is partly due to the need to involve private actors such as employers, who are key actors for success in meeting the welfare-to-work challenge. In addition, having a number of non-governmental actors involved makes the system more agile, helping it to adapt to the frequent changes in labour-market conditions.

While the involvement of non-state actors in the production of welfare-to-work services is a generally accepted principle, managing their relationship with the state can be a complex matter. The basic challenge lies in aligning the interests of the state, in terms of effectiveness, efficiency and fairness, with the interests of non-state actors who provide employment-support services.

Implementing an employment-support strategy in Switzerland therefore raises serious governance issues that are due partly to our country's federal structure and partly to the nature of the task in hand. The remainder of this contribution aims to show how the IDHEAP model of public administration can contribute to discussing the various solutions that have been considered and implemented in Switzerland and in some foreign countries. As we shall see, some of the problems are still with us.

19.2 Key points of governance

In Switzerland, since the early 2000s the main response to the governance issues outlined above has been to encourage collaboration between the various actors. This is an easy strategy to advocate, but its impact is limited, because its success depends very much on the goodwill of the actors and institutions concerned.

Collaboration between institutions is not generally conducive to transparency and accountability. For example, if two agencies work together in an attempt to place an unemployed person in a job, but fail to do so, who will be held responsible for the failure? "Simple" collaboration, i.e. collaboration not structured by a clarification of roles and lines of accountability, is not a very promising mode of governance. In fact, in the typology proposed by Athias and Pasquier for the governance of public-service delivery, simple collaboration is not even mentioned.

19.2.1 Promoting inter-institutional collaboration

The problem of access to the necessary competencies touched on above can be solved in various ways. One could imagine each institution equipping itself with all the competencies required for welfare-to-work services for "its" beneficiaries. This would probably be the most expensive solution, and would result in duplication. Switzerland has not considered it. Contracting between entities within the state would be another avenue. If an unemployment-insurance recipient developed a health problem, the unemployment-insurance department could mandate the disability-insurance department to try to solve the problem. However, this avenue has not been pursued in Switzerland.

The option chosen in Switzerland is inter-institutional collaboration. This represents a kind of public-public partnership, relying largely on the willingness of the actors involved to collaborate. All the cantons have in fact developed inter-institutional collaboration platforms or processes designed to handle the cases of unemployed people affected by multiple problems, and therefore requiring the help of several institutions. The form of these collaborations varies, but in general they are based on a joint assessment of the unemployed person's situation, and an agreement on a plan that may involve provision of services by several institutions.

Institutional collaboration only covers the provision of certain assessments or welfare-to-work measures available to beneficiaries covered by other schemes. It is therefore a very limited mechanism, first because the institutions concerned do not make available to beneficiaries of other schemes the full range of measures at their disposal and second, because the collaboration only concerns employment-support measures. Moreover, it does not address the matter of bearing the (much higher) costs of the financial assistance paid to beneficiaries month after month.

19.2.2 Minimizing institutional moral hazard

As we saw above, the problem of institutional moral hazard is common to every multi-level welfare state. It refers to the incentive for an institution to transfer beneficiaries to another institution at a different level of government.

In Switzerland, measures have been taken to limit the scope for the lower levels of the federal state (cantons and municipalities) to transfer beneficiaries to federal social insurance. As far back as 1996, the Unemployment Insurance Act (LACI, 2nd revision) was amended to prevent participation in subsidized temporary employment from conferring new entitlements to federal unemployment-insurance benefits. In 2011, this rule was extended to cantonal programmes.

Access to disability insurance has also been made more difficult over the years. Here, the aim of the reforms has not been simply to limit cost-shifting practices, but also to achieve a more general objective of consolidating the disability-insurance budget. However, the measures also restrict access to disability insurance for recipients of social-assistance or unemployment-insurance. The main measures are the establishment of Regional Medical Services in 2004 (which led to stricter application of medical criteria for access to benefits) and the introduction in 2008 of tighter supervision of cantonal disability-insurance offices (Bonoli & Trein 2016). These measures contributed to a 35% drop in the number of new disability pensions between 2003 and 2008 (Wayland-Bigler 2009).

These various measures have undoubtedly reduced the severity of the institutional-moral-hazard problem. However, their scope is limited. As regards unemployment insurance, a municipality retains the right to offer a fixed-term employment contract to a person on welfare, who will then be entitled to compensation under the federal unemployment-insurance scheme. Also, social services still assist welfare recipients with health problems in preparing applications for a disability pension. In the event of a refusal by a disability-insurance office, some welfare departments also go so far as to instruct a lawyer (obviously at the taxpayer's expense) to lodge an appeal against the decision. These practices seem light years away from the positivity- and goodwill-infused rhetoric that underpins the official discourse on inter-institutional collaboration.

19.2.3 Subcontracting the welfare-to-work mission to private actors

In Switzerland, as in most European countries, the welfare-to-work mission is shared between institutional actors (regional job centres, disability-insurance offices, social services) and social actors (NGOs, foundations, more rarely private companies) (▶ 3 Stakeholders). This solution solves some of the governance problems mentioned above. For example, rather than relying on the goodwill of another actor in the framework of a collaboration, an institution can simply purchase the employment-support services it needs in a competitive market. Although this solution is used, it also comes up against a number of problems. In particular, it is difficult to set up a system of incentives for welfare-to-work service providers that is in line with public-policy objectives. For example, traditional solutions such as pay-for-performance will cause service providers to indulge in the selection or "skimming off" of certain beneficiaries. This results in the weakest beneficiaries being excluded from the reintegration effort, which generally runs counter to public-policy objectives and the principles of equity in access to government services.

The case of Australia provides a good illustration of this problem. To counter these practices, the Australian Department of Employment introduced highly sophisticated contracts to encourage providers to align themselves with public-policy objectives (OECD 2012). However, success has been limited, probably because a segment of the unemployed population is not well served by welfare-to-work policies capable of producing rapid, measurable results.

19.3 Future prospects and challenges

The governance of welfare-to-work policies in Switzerland presents a number of problems that have been addressed in this contribution. These problems are well understood by specialists and professionals, which has led to various initiatives and attempted solutions. Generally, these initiatives focus on collaboration. This approach and the various measures that have been adopted have their limits, however. So why do the authorities not try to embark on a more ambitious reform process? Why not review the entire governance of the social-security system? In the face of similar difficulties, Germany adopted a fundamental reform in 2005 (known as Hartz-IV) which, according to a number of observers, has at least partly contributed to the spectacular drop in unemployment in the country (Hassel & Schiller 2010).

Although thought has been given to the matter in the circles concerned and in the Swiss Federal Parliament, fundamental reform of the social-security system is not on the agenda. The main reason is that, despite its inconsistencies, the Swiss social-security system produces results that appear reasonably satisfactory. Most social indicators (unemployment, long-term unemployment, poverty) are quite favourable by international comparison. And while a complete overhaul of the system might result in a more appropriate institutional architecture, it would not necessarily lead to better indicators. In the case of people far removed from the job market, welfare-to-work policies come up against objective difficulties that even the best possible social-security system would have trouble overcoming. As a result, there seems to be a consensus among decision-makers that the status quo, despite the shortcomings, is preferable to fundamental reform, which would undoubtedly be very difficult to carry out and whose final outcome would be uncertain (Bonoli & Champion 2014).

This conclusion, while persuasive, is dangerous. Dangerous in the sense that the current relatively favourable social situation is probably more fragile than we think. Although Switzerland's social indicators are good, this is partly due to its healthy labour market. A deep, lasting crisis could quickly change the game.

The main challenge in the governance of welfare-to-work policies therefore lies in developing a system capable of operating in different labour-market contexts. A system that works only in periods of fair weather does not seem adequate. True, Switzerland's economic situation is generally enviable. But the country has to reckon with the possibility that profound crises could occur. Should that happen, the risk would be to witness the emergence of all the tensions and contradictions arising from the inconsistencies in our social-security system.

Key concepts

- Institutional moral hazard (*aléa moral institutionnel, institutionnelle moralische Risiko, rischio morale istituzionale*): an incentive for an institution to pass the case of a person in need on to another institution or scheme rather than take care of them.
- Social investment (*investissement social, soziale Investition, investimento sociale*): a social-policy perspective that emphasizes human-capital development and labour-market participation to combat social problems.

References

Bonoli, G. (2013). *The origins of active social policy. Active labour market policy and childcare in a comparative perspective.* Oxford University Press.

Bonoli, G. & Champion, C. (2014). Federalism and welfare to work in Switzerland - The development of active social policies in a fragmented welfare state. *Publius the Journal of Federalism, 45*(1), 77–98.

Bonoli, G. & Trein, P. (2016). Cost-shifting in multitiered welfare states: responding to rising welfare caseloads in Germany and Switzerland. *Publius: The Journal of Federalism,* 4(46), 596–622.

Hassel, A. & Schiller, C. (2010). *Der Fall Hartz IV. Wie es zur Agenda 2010 kam und wie es weitergeht.* Campus Verlag.

Hemerijck, A. (2017). Social investment and its critics. In A. Hemerijck (Ed.), *The uses of social investment* (pp. 3–42). Oxford University Press.

Luigjes, C. & Vandenbroucke, F. (2020). Unemployment benefits and activation on federal welfare states: An institutional moral hazard perspective. *Regional & Federal Studies, 31*(5), 647–669.

OECD. (2012). *Activating jobseekers. How Australia does it*. OECD.

Øverbye, E., Strohmeier Navarro Smith, R., Karjalainen, V. & Stremlow, J. (2010). The coordination challenge. In Y. Kazepov (Ed.), *Rescaling social policies towards multilevel governance* (pp. 389–428). Ashgate.

Van Berkel, R., de Graaf, W. & Sirovátka, T. (2011). The governance of active welfare states in Europe in a comparative perspective. In R. V. Berkel, W. d. Graaf & T. Sirovátka (Eds.), *The Governance of Active Welfare States in Europe* (pp. 237–263). Palgrave Macmillan.

Wayland-Bigler, Nancy (2009). Gemeinsam zum Ziel. *Soziale Sicherheit-CHSS, 2009*(1). 33–35.

20 Elite sport

Mickaël Terrien

20.1 Introduction to the challenges of elite sport for sport policies

Since 1970, sport policies have had a legal basis in article 68 of the Federal Constitution of the Swiss Confederation. The Federal Council cited several reasons for adopting this article: public health, national defence, general education, the judicious organization of leisure activities, and honourable representation of Switzerland in international competitions (Chappelet 2006). The last of these reasons targets the performance of elite athletes. Three decades later, it became one of the five strategic objectives set by the Confederation in its concept for a Swiss sport policy. It should be noted that two of the five reasons given by the Federal Council in 1970 have since disappeared (national defence and judicious organization of leisure activities).

While public investment in health and education through sport is easily understandable, the lasting importance of the elite-sport objective raises issues for public administration. These issues are heightened by the "arms race" that many nations are engaged in to improve their athletes' performance (see De Bosscher *et al.* 2015). There are therefore a number of reasons justifying the public sector's involvement in elite sport. Analysis of political discourse reveals several of them (Grix & Carmichael 2012).

The first reason is geopolitical. Although not officially recognized by the International Olympic Committee, the medals table attracts a great deal of media attention at the conclusion of every Olympiad. In the 1970s, it was used as a tool of "cold-war macroeconomics". Comparisons of the athletic performance of the blocs sought to establish the superiority of one politico-economic system over another (Andreff *et al.* 2008). The collapse of the Soviet Union has not diminished the importance attached to rankings. A more recent example is the dispute between China and the United States over the Olympic-medal counting system[55].

The prestige conferred by national athletes' strong performances is more than a diplomatic tool. It can also spread a sense of wellbeing throughout society (quantified by various studies in the economics of wellbeing). The fact that this sensation can be experienced by everyone, with no rivalry, makes the performance of national athletes a public good (▶ 2 Essential functions). This aspect legitimizes public intervention in favour of elite sport. In the same vein, the sense of belonging to the country and national cohesion can be strengthened by an international sport competition. Media praise for Switzerland's strongly multicultural youth soccer team, which won the U-17 World Cup in 2009, provides eloquent evidence of this. These externalities of sport are recognized by the European Commission.

The European Commission has identified another external effect: spectator sport as a tool for the development of grassroots sport. This trickle-down effect is also the third lever of political discourse legitimizing public intervention for elite sport (Grix & Carmichael 2012). It is assumed that results from the top of the pyramid will be passed on to its base. With elite athletes providing role models for the next generation, young people are thought to be more likely to get involved in sport, which would in turn help to achieve the other strategic objectives of public sport policies[56].

Given elite sport's importance for the community, this contribution addresses the way public administration operates in this field. In particular, we mobilize two components of the IDHEAP model of public administration's "norms and strategy" dimension: first strategy, and then governance (figure 20.1).

These two components are essential to enable public authorities to help Swiss athletes to shine at international competitions. First, regarding strategy, an analysis of Switzerland's socio-demographic constraints shows that specialization in sport is essential. Specialization promotes efficient resource allocation. Second, regarding governance, successful government intervention in elite sport requires close collaboration between the public-administration system and its environment (market and third sector).

A description of these key components is followed by a discussion of future challenges for public administration in elite sport. In particular, we look at the concept of the trickle-down effect from elite sport to grassroot levels.

55 The controversy concerns whether Olympic medal counts should reflect podium placing. At the 2008 Olympic Games, the United States finished ahead of China in terms of medals won (110 versus 100), but the positions were reversed when gold medals alone were considered (36 versus 51).

56 Regarding the health objective, the cost of physical inactivity in Switzerland has been estimated at CHF 2.4 billion (Kempf & Lichtsteiner 2017).

Figure 20.1 Examples of components that can be mobilized in elite sport (in bold in the figure)

20.2 Key points of strategy and governance

20.2.1 Strategy

Numerous studies have examined the deciding factors of sporting success (e.g. Andreff *et al.* 2008). The chief explanatory factors are socio-economic. Population size and wealth are two key success factors that enable a nation to shine on the international sport stage. As a result, specialization in certain sporting disciplines becomes the only solution for a country like Switzerland with its reduced demographic weight (Kempf *et al.* 2021).

This strategy in the medals market stems from a dual analysis (Weber *et al.* 2018): an internal study of resources (resource-based view) and an external examination of the competition (market-based view). This tells a nation which sports and/or disciplines offer the greatest chances for success. 28% of the medals won by Switzerland at the Summer Olympics between 1988 and 2016 were in cycling (Kempf *et al.* 2021).

Specialization means devoting resources mainly to the federations best able to excel. The strategy adopted by public entities sets a common direction, thus allowing a concentration of resources and strengths. For the 2016 Olympics in Rio, Swiss Olympic allocated the majority of its financial support to just eight disciplines. Five of the seven medals won by the Swiss delegation were in these disciplines (Kempf *et al.* 2021). Efficient allocation of resources is one way of staying competitive in the sporting arms race. Between 2001 and 2011 spending on elite sport exploded in many countries, making the dream of Olympic medals ever more costly (De Bosscher *et al.* 2015)[57].

57 Between 2001 and 2011, spending rose by 210% in Brazil, 143% in South Korea and 101% in France.

In elite sport, money is the primary tool in the competition for success, and public spending[58] is a necessary condition for international success. Sport financing is one of the ten factors of international sporting success (Sport Policy factors Leading to International Sporting Success [SPLISS hereafter]; De Bosscher *et al.*). 2015).

20.2.2 Governance and SPLISS pillars

Ten pillars of SPLISS are identified in the literature (De Bosscher *et al.* 2015.) A detailed description of these pillars goes far beyond the scope of this contribution, especially since they are linked with over a hundred key success factors. Our aims here are more modest: to present the diversity of stakeholders (▶ 3 Stakeholders) associated with each of these pillars in order to demonstrate the need for a systemic analytical approach, and then to list all the measures that can favour elite sport. Of course, this wide diversity of stakeholders requires solid governance if government intervention is to be successful.

	Sectors	State		
		Confederation (OFSPO and other bodies)	**Cantons**	**Municipalities**
SPLISS pillars	**1 Financial support**	CHF 185.1 million (OFSPO)	CHF 232 million	CHF 1350 million
	2 Governance, organization and structure	Youth+Sport	Funding for sport infrastructure and grassroots sports, physical education for students	Promoting sport in Switzerland
	3 Participation in sport			
	4 Talent identification and development			
	5 Career and post-career management	Swiss Army athlete support systems	"Sport-études"	
	6 Training centre	Design of national sport facilities		
		Magglingen and Tenero national centres		
	7 Training and development for coaches	*Training (Youth+Sport, federal diploma)*	Bachelor's and master's in sport science	
	8 (Inter)national competitions	Subsidies for major sporting events		
		Days of service provided by the Swiss Army		
	9 Scientific research and innovation	*Swiss Federal Institute of Sport Magglingen, Innosuisse, Swiss National Science Foundation*		
	10 Media and sponsorship			

Table 20.1 Systemic approach to the SPLISS pillars
Note: financial data are from 2018 and were collected in Kempf *et al.* (2021); italicized cells indicate the predominant stakeholder in each SPLISS pillar

58 Mostly in the form of current expenditure (▶ 13 Financial management).

For example, Swiss Olympic is responsible for allocating resources for sport specialization. This third-sector organization serves as the National Olympic Committee, the "confederation of national federations". It is the national body responsible for associative sport (Kempf & Lichtsteiner 2017). It also acts as a subsidiary steering body for funds sourced mainly from the private sector via Sport-Toto (thanks to the cantonal monopoly granted to Swisslos and Loterie romande) and the state (Federal Office of Sport, FOSPO). This tangle of actors testifies to the complexity of the Swiss sport ecosystem. It also shows the ultimately limited role played by the Confederation.

Table 20.1 illustrates that the sport-funding SPLISS pillar (financial support) is not the only one to depend on a constellation of stakeholders. It also shows the different forms of governance (▶ 8 Governance) needed to implement effective measures for elite sport. The "do it" (internally) logic predominates within certain pillars: classic administration in the "governance, organization and structure" pillar; transfer to autonomous entities in the "scientific research and innovation" pillar. On the

Third parties				
Swiss Olympic	**Federations**	**Clubs**	**Others**	**Market**
				CHF 167.7 million (lotteries)
Service-level agreement	81 listed by Swiss Olympic	*18,824 clubs, 1.99 million members*		Private commercial sport (e.g. fitness centres)
Swiss Olympic Cards	Scouting work			
wiss Olympic Sport School			Swiss Sports Aid	
Swiss Olympic Training Bases/Medical Center	National performance centres (NPCs)			
	Federal training			
	Employers of elite coaches			Athletes
Financial support for the ganization of international competitions "	*Organization of competitions*		International sports federations, SwissTopSport	Professional clubs, Sport event organizers
Sport Science" scheme				
				TV channels, Businesses

other hand, the "get it done" (externally) approach may be favoured in other areas: delegation to the third sector for the "participation in sport" and "talent identification and development" pillars.

Note that several forms of governance may be chosen for a single SPLISS pillar. For example, the national training centres are under the supervision of public bodies (FOSPO), while some infrastructures have been provided through public-private partnerships (e.g. the Tissot Arena in Biel).

Given this complex ecosystem, in which the interests of the various stakeholders may diverge, how can a sport policy enabling the country's athletes to excel at major international competitions be implemented? The question is all the more problematic given that there is a political will to guarantee the autonomy of sport organizations and shield them from too much public interference.

20.3 Future prospects and challenges

The success of public policy aimed at elite sport requires an alignment of interests between third-party and commercial actors. This is necessary to guarantee a minimum level of performance within each of the SPLISS pillars. To achieve this alignment, it is not enough to understand the complexity of the Swiss sport ecosystem. Autonomous organizations also need to be dealt with. Autonomy is an important concept in sport. Introduced into the Olympic Charter in 1949, then accepted by the Council of Europe in 1979, it was reinforced by the European Union through the Nice Declaration in 2001. It guarantees sports organizations a degree of freedom of action in relation to public authorities (Chappelet 2019). The autonomy enjoyed by Swiss Olympic and the national federations, which are key actors in many SPLISS pillars, can therefore be a problem when it comes to implementing a coherent elite-sport policy.

One leveraging tool that the public sphere can make use of is the resource dependency of sports organizations (Terrien *et al.* 2021). Conditional payment of subsidies is a tactic for changing the behaviour of third-sector actors. Many programmes require the implementation of sport-health measures for target populations (e.g. the elderly, the disabled). There may also be obligations relating to the SPLISS pillars, such as requirements for the qualifications of coaches, particularly with the Youth+Sport programme introduced in Switzerland in 1972. In addition to training activities (see Table 20.1), this programme also subsidizes centres that organize sports courses and camps, on the condition that they meet the necessary requirements. The strategy of (threatened) withdrawal of resources is a governance measure that can bring the interests of the various actors into alignment.

This measure can also benefit from unilateral intervention by the public actor in setting rules for service providers, whatever the mode of governance chosen. This occurred in the wake of physical and psychological abuse of underage female gymnasts reported in 2021[59]: in 2023, the Federal Council amended the Sports Promotion Ordinance, making adherence to ethical principles obligatory, with payment of funding to federations being conditional on compliance.

Beyond the tactics of implementation, an elite-sport policy's impact must be assessed (▶ 16 Evaluation). At the Tokyo 2020+1 Olympic Games, the Swiss delegation won thirteen medals, including three golds. This was well above Swiss Olympic's expectations (seven medals, the score from the previous Olympiad). Note that from the 1988 to the 2016 Summer Olympics, Switzerland's objective was not to win medals, but to finish in the top 25 of nations. In terms of both total medals and gold medals alone, Switzerland never attained this ambition during that period (Kempf *et al.* 2021), but finally succeeded at the Tokyo 2020+1 Games (24th and 19th nation respectively). That performance was the reward for the substantial expenditure that the Swiss Confederation, cantons and municipalities had devoted to an ambitious public policy on elite sport.

The output, or public good, was undeniably the expected one. But what about the outcomes, the public-policy objectives indirectly targeted by intervention in favour of elite sport? The trickle-down theory has it that these Olympic results should trigger a virtuous circle: state support for sport should be stepped up because it is a pillar of future elite performance. However, empirical findings on the subject are controversial (Frick & Wicker 2016). Future investigations should be made to determine whether the theory proves true in practice.

Political discourse also claims that public spending on Switzerland's honourable representation in sporting competitions is justified by spin-off benefits on other strategic objectives (Grix & Carmichael 2012). In fact the positive impact of top-level sporting results on sport policies, and even on other public policies, remains to be demonstrated, and measured. Do sport-health or education-through-sport indicators really progress when Swiss athletes accomplish exceptional performances, as was the case at Tokyo 2020+1? Conclusive evidence would provide an assurance that the resources devoted to elite sport, particularly by public authorities, could not be put to other uses to achieve these objectives more efficiently.

59 The link to the external investigation report is available at https://www.newsd.admin.ch/newsd/message/attachments/68967.pdf (accessed 30.11.2022).

Key concepts

- Resource dependency (*dépendance en ressources, Ressourcenabhängigkeitsansatz, dipendenza dalle risorse*): the theory that organizations sustain themselves by managing the demands of the interest groups on whose resources they depend.
- SPLISS pillars (*piliers SPLISS, SPLISS-Säulen, pilastri SPLISS*): pillars of the "Sport Policy factors Leading to International Sporting Success" model.
- Sport specialization (*spécialisation sportive, sportliche Spezialisierung, specializzazione sportiva*): allocation of resources in favour of sporting disciplines offering the highest probability of success in the medal market.
- Sports autonomy (*autonomie sportive, sportliche Autonomie, autonomia sportiva*): the ability of nonprofit, non-governmental sports organizations to operate with limited interference from third parties.

References

Andreff, M., Andreff, W. & Poupaux, S. (2008). Les déterminants économiques de la performance olympiques : Prévision des médailles qui seront gagnées aux Jeux de Pékin. *Revue d'Economie Politique, 118*(2), 135–169.

Chappelet, J.-L. (2006). La lente maturation des politiques publiques du sport suisse. Chappelet (Eds.), *Beiträge zum öffentlichen Handeln* (pp. 29–46). Presses polytechniques et universitaires romandes.

Chappelet, J.-L. (2019). L'autonomie du sport d'hier à demain. In: J.-L. Chappelet, E. Bayle, J. Donzel, F. Latty, D. Poracchia, D. & S. Robert-Cuendet (Eds), *L'autonomie des organisations sportives* (pp. 1–19). Observatoire international des politiques publiques sportives.

De Bosscher, V., Shibli, S., Westerbeek, H. & Van Bottenburg, M. (2015). *Successful elite sport policies: an international comparison of the sports policy factors leading to international sporting success (SPLISS 2.0) in 15 nations*. Meyer & Meyer Sport.

Frick, B. & Wicker, P. (2016). The trickle-down effect: how elite sporting success affects amateur participation in German football. *Applied Economics Letters, 23*(4), 259–263. https://doi.org/10.1080/13504851.2015.1068916 (accessed 30.11.2022).

Grix, J. & Carmichael, F. (2012). Why do governments invest in elite sport? A polemic. *International Journal of Sport Policy and Politics, 4*(1), 73–90. https://doi.org/10.1080/19406940.2011.627358 (accessed 30.11.2022).

Kempf, H., Lichtsteiner, H., Güntensperger, A., Neuenschwander, M., Renaud, A., Stopper, M., & Weber, A. (2015). *"Das" System Sport-in der Schweiz und international*. Bundesamt für Sport BASPO; Verbandsmanagement Institut Universität Freiburg.

Kempf, H., Weber, A., Zurmühle, C., Mrkonjic, M., Weber, A., Pillet, F. & Sutter, S. (2021). *Leistungssport Schweiz*. Momentaufnahme SPLISS-CH 2019 https://www.baspo.admin.ch/de/dokumentation/publikationen/studie-leistungssport-schweiz.html (accessed 30.11.2022).

Terrien, M., Feuillet, A. & Bayle, E. (2021). A taxonomy of national sport federations based on their financial profiles: the case of France's state-subsidized model. *Managing Sport and Leisure, 28*(5), 1–18. https://doi.org/10.1080/23750472.2021.1936615 (accessed 30.11.2022).
Weber, A. Ch., De Bosscher, V. & Kempf, H. (2018). Positioning in Olympic Winter sports: analysing national prioritisation of funding and success in eight nations. *European Sport Management Quarterly 18*(1), 8–24. https://doi.org/10.1080/16184742.2017.1336782 (accessed 30.11.2022).

References for further study

Bayle, E. (2017). Switzerland: The organisation of sport and policy towards sport federations. In Scheerder, Willem & Claes (Eds.), *Sport Policy Systems and Sport Federations: A cross-national perspective* (pp. 263–282). Palgrave Macmillan.
Henry, I., Dowling, M., Ko, L. M. & Brown, P. (2020). Challenging the new orthodoxy: a critique of SPLISS and variable-oriented approaches to comparing sporting nations. *European Sport Management Quarterly, 20*(4), 520–536. doi.org/10.1080/16184742.2020.1719428
Suykens, B., George, B., De Rynck, F. & Verschuere, B. (2021). Determinants of non-profit commercialism. Resource deficits, institutional pressures or organizational contingencies? *Public Management Review, 23*(10), 1456–1478. https://doi.org/10.1080/16184742.2020.1719428

21 Social and economic integration

Flavia Fossati

21.1 Introduction to the challenges of integrating asylum seekers and refugees

Social and economic integration of asylum seekers and refugees has always been a major challenge for public administration in Switzerland, just as in other developed countries. Scientific studies show that the probability of this category of migrants taking up gainful employment remains below average, even after several years in the host country (Konle-Seidl & Bolits 2016).

The difficulty asylum seekers and refugees have in finding work depends on a variety of factors. In times of crisis (war, natural disasters, etc.), migrants have less time to prepare their departure than in other situations. This entails a whole series of disadvantages, for example the absence of identification documents or academic and professional qualifications. Other obstacles to entering the job market include a lack of resources, skills or specific competencies. Additional factors may be insufficient or unrecognized qualifications, the absence of a social network to help in the job search, language barriers and health problems possibly linked to trauma experienced during migration. Moreover, asylum seekers and refugees—perhaps to an even greater degree than other categories of migrants—face discrimination from employers, who see them as less productive and are therefore less inclined to hire them (Auer *et al.* 2019; Fossati & Liechti 2020).

Social and economic integration of asylum seekers and refugees is thus proving difficult, not only because they may require above-average government support, but also because integration is especially important for maintaining good relations between communities in the destination society. Public administration should therefore take appropriate measures to facilitate integration.

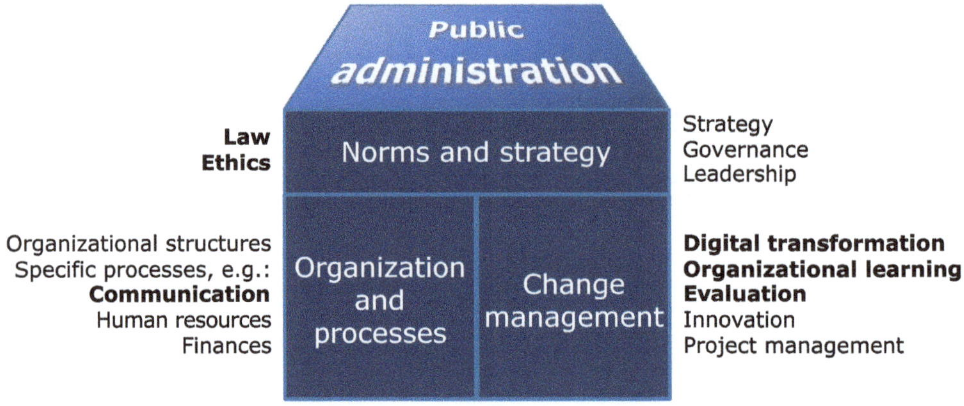

Figure 21.1 Examples of components that can be mobilized to integrate asylum seekers and refugees (in bold in the figure)

This contribution is based on the "Digitalization" component of the "Change management" dimension of the IDHEAP model of public administration (figure 21.1). Research shows that the use of artificial intelligence in the distribution of asylum seekers and refugees[60] across the country may help their chances of integration. The focus of this contribution is on labour-market prospects. In short, public administration strives to optimize refugees' allocation to the various cantons, so that as many as possible have a good chance of finding a job. This reduces their risk of having to depend on the welfare state and facilitates the integration process (Hangartner 2018; Bansak *et al.* 2018).

This contribution also illustrates that a successful implementation of artificial-intelligence tools in public administration may require the mobilization of other components of the IDHEAP model. These components may be part of the same dimension: "Evaluation" and "Organizational learning" are both found in the "Change management" dimension. But such a major change also affects legal and ethical aspects, that is, the fundamental components of public action grouped together in the "Norms and strategy" dimension. And naturally this approach inevitably requires activating the "Communication" component (► Part III. Organization and processes) and involving the stakeholders of public administration, as well as the general public.

60 For simplicity's sake, in the remainder of this contribution the term "refugees" will also include asylum seekers.

21.2 Key concepts of digitalization

21.2.1 The traditional system

In Switzerland, asylum seekers can apply for a residence permit. Applications are processed within 140 days, the period during which asylum seekers stay in the Confederation's reception centres. If no decision is made, or if the application for asylum is accepted, the applicant is assigned to a canton.

As mentioned above, assignment to a particular canton is an important decision regarding a person's potential social and professional integration. For example, a French-speaking person has a lower chance of rapid integration if they are assigned to a canton in German-speaking Switzerland rather than to one in French-speaking Switzerland (Auer 2018). Similarly, when in a canton many job vacancies suitable for a particular refugee's profile are available, integration into the labour market is likely to prove easier than in a canton with a high unemployment rate.

Traditionally, allocation of refugees to the various Swiss cantons has been based on a random allocation process that primarily considers the cantons' population as a proportion of the country's total population. Refugees are then allocated randomly, additionally considering the status of their application or of the procedure. Other factors such as the presence of family members in a canton are also considered. In this system, however, the decision-making process for allocation does not take into account the applicant's (labour-market) integration potential. This method of allocation is therefore based above all on an approach of "burden sharing" between Swiss cantons, in which refugees' chances of integration are barely considered (SEM 2020).

21.2.2 Using artificial intelligence to improve allocation

Studies have shown that improving the allocation system by taking each applicant's integration potential into account would bring social and economic benefits, both for the cantons (higher tax revenues thanks to job growth, lower social spending, etc.) and for the refugees (economic independence, better social integration, etc.). Another advantage—at least in theory—of an allocation system based on an artificial-intelligence tool lies in economic efficiency and simplified organizational implementation, since many time-consuming decisions could be delegated to an automated process. It is also expected to guarantee equal treatment for all concerned persons.

A group of Swiss and American scientists has proposed optimizing the traditional allocation system using artificial intelligence, that is, by developing an algorithm to increase the efficiency of refugees' assignment to individual cantons (see Hangartner 2018; Bansak *et al.* 2018). Two factors are particularly important here.

First, the new algorithm could take into account refugees' personal characteristics, such as language skills, academic qualifications, occupational training and experience. In addition, a canton's integration potential is quantified using various indicators. In a final step, the match between personal characteristics and the canton's potential for economic integration would be calculated. In theory, the algorithm could maximize applicants' integration potential by assigning them to the canton that best matches their professional profile.

Switzerland is not the only country interested in developing digital systems to implement political and social interventions. Similar tools have been tested and used for some time in Sweden, Denmark and Austria (OECD 2018). Austria tested an algorithm specifically designed to sort job seekers into groups based on their employability. The aim of this categorization was to achieve a better match between labour-market measures and the profiles of the various job seekers, and thus to better allocate limited financial resources to the groups of job seekers most in need of support. People in the first group—those with a good chance of finding a job on their own—would, for example, be less closely monitored by job centres, saving valuable resources. The second group consisted of people who were a little further away from the job market and therefore require more intensive support. These people would benefit from specific measures, such as training or subsidies, to improve their chances of entering the job market. Lastly, the third group consisted of people experiencing great difficulty in finding a job, who would need specific support or alternative solutions such as a disability pension (OECD 2018).

Here again, the use of an algorithm focused on assessing people's labour-market-integration potential and possible vulnerabilities in order to allocate and invest government resources and measures in the most efficient way possible (Badertscher & Kayser 2018). Pilot projects such as the two mentioned above also allow us to better understand political priorities. In our case, the aim is not only to improve outcomes for the people concerned, but also to reduce the (social) costs of integration. This trend towards more consistent, adapted, efficient and cost-effective implementation of administrative decisions can be observed in many OECD countries.

21.2.3 Advantages and disadvantages of automated decision-making

The goal of automated decision-making is to ensure the absence of any potential bias or prejudice, which should be conducive to fairer decisions. Achieving this objective, however, depends entirely on the fairness that such a system is capable of generating. The literature shows that administrative staff can act—consciously or unconsciously—in a discriminatory way, putting certain people at a disadvantage. The idea is that, especially where complex decisions are involved, the use of algorithms would lead to better outcomes, because a computer is better able to compare a multitude of alternatives than the human brain.

In the specific case of assigning refugees to cantons, the main advantage lies in the fact that an algorithm would use more diverse criteria in its decision-making than a random process. It seems undeniable that such a system could—on average—provide better outcomes than those based on purely random assignment. However, this does not apply to all automated decision-making processes. The fairness of a system always depends on the underlying mathematical models and their (implicit) assumptions. Any form of programming bias (deliberate or unintentional) therefore carries the risk of (possibly) discriminatory results (e.g. Committee of Experts on Internet Intermediaries 2017).

21.2.4 Possible ethical and legal reservations about allocation algorithms

The use of algorithms in public administration for allocating state benefits (▶ 14 Digital transformation) raises a whole series of ethical and practical questions. When administrative decisions are made by algorithms, the ethical dilemmas that arise from decisions made by individual public servants are less present (▶ 6 Ethics). However, this does not mean that ethical issues disappear altogether. The first question concerns the quality of the mathematical model and of the data that is used to determine a person's integration potential. In particular, the question arises of whether it is possible to correctly assess refugees' integration potential based on a limited number of indicators (SRF 2018). Or, to put it another way: does the mathematical model really have access to all the data required to make a satisfactory decision and guarantee fairer allocation? It seems plausible that at least some important variables could be missing, for the simple reason that they are difficult to measure. One example is a person's "motivation to integrate", which seems very difficult to assess correctly. Other characteristics may be overlooked by the system because they were mistakenly deemed unimportant, or because they involve highly personal information that would be likely to raise data-protection issues.

Furthermore, the question is whether it ethically acceptable to "reduce" a human being to a handful of characteristics, albeit important ones (▶ 1 Values). Some of their strengths or weaknesses, or aspects of their specific situation, might be overlooked in the process. It is also possible that some of an algorithm's decisions may be discriminatory. One might be tempted to assume that people sharing the same specific characteristics have the same integration potential, but this is not necessarily the case. The theory of statistical discrimination shows that when the integration potential of a group of people sharing a specific characteristic is calculated, the potential does not apply to each individual equally. We know, for example, that the employment rate for women is on average lower than that for men. However, it is not accurate to conclude that a particular woman would have greater difficulty entering the job market unless other characteristics, such as possible family-care obligations, had been considered.

Another ethical question is whether an automatic categorization system could disadvantage certain (groups of) people. This is a recurring issue in social policy, since research has shown that many measures inevitably generate losers as well as winners (Bonoli *et al.* 2017). The ideal of developing an algorithm or policy measure that benefits the entire population concerned often proves difficult. Consequently, when piloting an algorithm, it is essential to determine—by means of an evaluation procedure, for example—whether it brings advantages and disadvantages, and if so, for whom (▶ 16 Evaluation).

Another difficulty in the development of automated allocation systems is that the database used for calculations must be as precise, accurate and up-to-date as possible (▶ 6 Law). An algorithm can only be as effective as the mathematical model and empirical data on which it is based (OECD 2018). Regarding this Swiss pilot study, the challenge is to obtain reliable information on the characteristics, aptitudes and skills of refugees, to be able to assess their integration potential correctly. In parallel, it is important to have good cantonal indicators that reveal the possibilities for integration. Furthermore, the uncertainty of a statistical model must not be overlooked. Every mathematical model has a margin of error. It is essential to determine the uncertainty associated with the algorithm's prediction, for which groups it is particularly large. Political actors, and society as a whole, can then discuss its acceptability in an informed public debate.

Another point to bear in mind is that technologies are not "neutral" (▶ 1 Values). They are always based on certain values and societal conceptions of a subject or problem. The algorithm proposed by Bansak *et al.* (2018) for instance bases the allocation to different cantons on existing administrative databases. While certainly pragmatic, this approach carries the risk of existing structures of inequality being "reproduced". This is because an administrative database is built on a pre-existing consensus—for example, as regards "useful" variables for measuring integration potential—and on societal definitions of the issue (one question that we could ask is: what is the underlying definition of "successful integration"?). In practice, this means that the use of existing data can indeed improve allocation, but also that it will doubtless be difficult to identify and correct hidden or little-known inequalities. A review of existing biases and distortions, for example as part of an evaluation, should therefore be considered.

In addition, it seems essential to determine by whom, under what circumstances and on what basis an appeal can be filed against a decision made by an algorithm. This is also important to ensure that the process remains as transparent and fair as possible (Heinrich 2003).

21.3 Future prospects and challenges

21.3.1 Ongoing evaluation of an algorithm

As with any other policy measure, and pilot projects especially, systematic evaluation to measure effectiveness, identify difficulties and make adjustments is of crucial importance. At the same time, maintaining a public debate on the advantages and disadvantages is also important.

Initial changes have already been made to the mechanism for allocating refugees among Swiss cantons. One aspect that attracted criticism in the national media was that this allocation mechanism could result in a concentration of certain nationalities in the cantons of French-speaking Switzerland. This would bring a risk of "ghettoization" (Bär 2018) and hence reduced chances of integration for the people concerned, plus create discontent among the local population. In response to this criticism, the programmers made changes to take this possible scenario into account and ensure even distribution of different nationalities across the territory. This adaptation increased political acceptance of the measure, while slightly reducing the algorithm's effectiveness, but of course also helped to alleviate public fears and concerns. When evaluating an instrument, it is important to consider the opinions of the various actors involved: the institutions responsible for migration policy; the bodies that host refugees, such as cantons and municipalities; and other stakeholders and interest groups who advocate for these populations (▶ 3 Stakeholders and ▶ 16 Evaluation).

Moreover, steps need to be taken to ensure that the commitment to continuous improvement is maintained over time. Societal or economic changes could make it necessary to adapt or modify the criteria used to assess the employability of refugees for the purposes of allocation. For example, economic aspects are very important in assessing a canton's integration capacity. When a canton is hit by a recession in the construction sector, it makes little sense for it to be allocated people with masonry training. More fundamental changes should also periodically be taken into account when adapting the programming of the algorithm, such as changes in the employment landscape, technological progress or demographic developments in the cantons.

Observations in other countries have shown that, in times of economic crisis or labour shortages, these periodic adjustment measures often fall victim to cost-cutting measures, which can then lead to an obsolete allocation key being used. The consequences would be both economically and socially damaging, with possible negative repercussions on the lives of refugees.

21.3.2 Informing the public

Communicating on a new policy measure to the public can be a challenge. Clear, transparent, comprehensive institutional communication is crucial so that misgivings among the population can be forestalled (▶ 11 Communication management). Even more so in the case of sensitive or highly politicized issues, migration being a good example in our country.

On a positive note, the main news programmes have described the discussions surrounding the new allocation method accurately and in an easily understandable way (SRF 2018; Badertscher & Kayser 2018; Badertscher 2018; Hangartner 2018).

In political (and social) science, it is well known that widespread public acceptance of a measure improves its implementation and increases its effectiveness. This makes efficient communication particularly important on such a sensitive issue as the distribution of refugees among cantons. The native population can sometimes react to the arrival of migrants with a degree of scepticism. Fears and concerns may arise, for example about the prospect of ghettoization (see above), possible competition for jobs or soaring (social) costs in the cantons concerned. To ensure a successful implementation of the algorithm, it is thus important to demonstrate the positive impacts that the measure will have on both the economic and social dimensions of cantons.

Another element that should not be overlooked is the publication of details of the method and data on which the algorithm bases its calculations (OECD 2018). On this point, the example of Austria is instructive: failure to publish the algorithm used led to a particularly lively public debate (Cech *et al.* 2019). Communication is essential, not only to inform the general public and target groups about how the algorithm works, but also to allow scientific debate on the subject.

21.3.3 Communication with employees

Much talk is heard in the public sphere of the digital revolution and its impact on employment in Switzerland and abroad. Worries about human work being taken by machines, computers and algorithms arise repeatedly, reflecting fears of job losses in public administration and other sectors.

Here again, the issue of effective communication arises, since the algorithm will take over at least part of the work done by the administrative staff responsible for making decisions on the allocation of refugees. The framework and scope of the measure play a major role here. Employees may fear a kind of devaluation of their expertise (▶ 14 Digital transformation). They may also be afraid of finding themselves unemployed, their work now being done by the algorithm.

Experience from other fields has shown that acceptance of an algorithm by employees plays a crucial role. In order to be able to make any changes that may prove necessary, it is important to give them the right to speak, especially when they discover errors or criticize certain aspects of the programme. Agents working in refugees' integration are well trained and have many years of experience, and are therefore able to identify possible problems (OECD 2018).

Implementing an automated system will require significant institutional change in public policy in this area (▶ 15 Organizational learning). It is important that employees trust the allocation proposals produced by the algorithm, and also that they apply them. This was not the case in some countries, where administrative staff refused to implement the project, for instance categorically refusing to use the newly developed systems (OECD 2018). One possible approach to motivating employees to trust the algorithm is to explain that it will free up capacity to take on more extensive support functions, and that they will therefore continue to perform their functions—perhaps simply with different priorities.

In summary, we can be sure that the use of algorithms will continue to increase, including in the public sector. It is therefore wise to provide the public with transparent information on the objectives, and the data on which algorithms and mathematical decision models are based, in order to allow informed public debate on their advantages and disadvantages. The aim is not only to make administrative processes more efficient and cost-effective, but especially to make them fairer, without sacrificing political acceptance of the measures concerned. This can only succeed if a continuous evaluation process is followed to prevent dichotomy between an algorithm and reality.

Key concepts

- Algorithm (*algorithme, Algorithmus, algoritmo*): figuratively, a recipe for computers to follow. A sequence of mathematical commands and operations defined by a programmer, which a computer executes in a defined order.
- Artificial intelligence (*intelligence artificielle, künstliche Intelligenz, intelligenza artificiale*): a process that enables machines to replicate human behaviour using statistical models. The aim is to program computers and other machines to learn autonomously using existing databases.
- Asylum seeker (*demandeur·euse/requérant·e d'asile, Asylbewerber·in, richiedente asilo*): a person of foreign nationality (or no nationality) seeking protection from persecution and/or torture in a destination country. A person remains an asylum seeker for as long as the administrative procedure to determine whether they will be granted the right to stay in the country of destination lasts. In Switzerland, asylum seekers are granted an N permit.
- Integration (of immigrants) (*intégration [des immigré·es] Integration von [Migrant·innen], integrazione [di immigranti]*): the process whereby a person

from a foreign country is incorporated into the society of the destination country. On the one hand, this calls for immigrants to make an effort to understand the language and customs of the destination country, and to try to participate in economic and social life. On the other hand, the population of the destination country is called upon to try to accept newcomers and help them to become part of the community. This can be done, for example, by hiring immigrants and introducing them to social networks and/or other day-to-day activities. In other words, integration is not a one-sided concept. Both immigrants and the population of the destination country must collaborate in order to live together harmoniously.

- Random allocation (*allocation aléatoire, Zufallszuweisung, distribuzione casuale*): distribution of people based on the principle of chance. This means that any person should, in theory, have the same chance as any other person of being placed in a given location (town, village, etc.).
- Refugee (*réfugié·e, Geflüchtete/Geflüchteter, refugiato-a*): a person of foreign nationality (or no nationality at all) who has suffered persecution and/or torture in their country of origin and who has been granted protection in a country of destination (e.g. on the basis of the Geneva Convention). Refugees must demonstrate to the authorities that the persecution they suffered was individualized and targeted. In general, such persecution is based on a characteristic such as ethnic origin, nationality, religion, sexual orientation, social group or political opinion. In Switzerland, recognized refugees are granted a B permit.

References

Auer, D. (2018). Language roulette – the effect of random placement on refugees' labour market integration, *Journal of Ethnic and Migration Studies*, *44*(3), 341–362.

Auer, D., G., Bonoli, F., Fossati & Liechti, F. (2019). The matching hierarchies model: evidence from a survey experiment on employers' hiring intent regarding immigrant applicants, *International Migration Review*, *53*(1), 90–121.

Badertscher, C. (2018). Algorithmus verteilt neu Asylbewerber auf Kantone. *SRF.* https://www.srf.ch/news/schweiz/jobs-fuer-fluechtlinge-algorithmus-verteilt-neu-asylbewerber-auf-kantone (accessed 05.12.2022).

Badertscher, C. & Kayser, R. (2018). Computer sollen Asylsuchende auf Kantone verteilen. *SRF.* https://www.srf.ch/news/schweiz/asyl-algorithmus-computer-sollen-asylsuchende-auf-kantone-verteilen (accessed 05.12.2022).

Bansak, K., Ferwerda, J., Hainmueller, J., Dillon, A., Hangartner, D., Lawrence, D. & Weinstein, J. (2018). Improving refugee integration through data-driven algorithmic assignment, *Science*, *359*(6373), 325–329.

Bär, T. (2018). Algorithmus verteilt Asylsuchende – Sprache spielt weiterhin keine Rolle, *Aargauer Zeitung.* https://www.aargauerzeitung.ch/schweiz/algorithmus-verteilt-asylsuchende-sprache-spielt-weiterhin-keine-rolle-132558528 (accessed 05.12.2022).

Bonoli, G., Cantillon, B. & van Lancker, W., (2017). Social investment and the Matthew effect: limits to a strategy. In A. Hemerijck (Ed.), *The uses of social investment* (pp. 66–76), Oxford University Press.

Committee of Experts on Internet Intermediaries (MSI-NET) (2017). *Algorithms and Human Rights.* Study on the human rights dimensions of automated data processing techniques and possible regulatory implications, Strasbourg: Council of Europe Study, DGI, 12.

Cech, F., Fischer, F., Human, Soheil, Lopez, P. & Wagner, B. (2019). Dem Algorithmus fehlt der Beipackzettel, *Futurezone, Technology News.* https://futurezone.at/meinung/dem-ams-algorithmus-fehlt-der-beipackzettel/400636022 (accessed 05.12.2022).

Fossati, F. & Liechti, F. (2020), Integrating refugees through active labour market policy: A comparative survey experiment, *Journal of European Social Policy, 30*(5), 601–615.

Konle-Seidl, R. & Bolits, G. (2016). *Labour market integration of refugees: strategies and good practice.* European Union.

Hangartner, D. (2018). *Medienmitteilung: Algorithmus verbessert Erwerbs-chancen von Flüchtlingen.* Zurich: ETH Zürich. https://ethz.ch/de/news-und-veranstaltungen/eth-news/news/2018/01/algorithmus-verbessert-erwerbschancen-von-fluechtlingen.html (accessed 05.12.2022).

Heinrich, C.J. (2003). Measuring public sector performance and effectiveness. In B. G. Peters. & J. Pierre (Eds), *The SAGE handbook of public administration* (pp. 24–38). Sage.

OECD (2018), *Profiling tools for early identification of jobseekers who need extra support*, Policy brief on activation policies, OECD Publishing.

Staatssekretariat für Migration (SEM) (2020) Verteilung der Asylsuchenden auf die Kantone. Confédération suisse. https://www.sem.admin.ch/sem/de/home/asyl/asylverfahren/nationale-verfahren/verteilung-kantone.html (accessed 05.12.2022).

Schweizer Radio & Fernsehen (SRF) (2018) Ein Mensch, der in unser Land kommt, ist kein Datensatz. *SRF.* https://www.srf.ch/news/schweiz/asyl-algorithmus-der-eth-ein-mensch-der-in-unser-land-kommt-ist-kein-datensatz (accessed 05.12.2022).

22 Educational-institution management

Olivier Glassey

22.1 Introduction to the challenges of managing an educational institution

In Switzerland, almost 90% of employees of businesses deemed to be "commercial" work in organizations with fewer than ten people: that adds up to more than 500,000 micro-businesses for a total of almost 1.2 million jobs. In addition, over 99% of Swiss businesses are SMEs, that is, companies with fewer than 250 employees (SECO 2023[61]). There are over 10,000 public educational institutions in Switzerland, with a total of 152,841 teachers (FSO 2021). Although they fall into the domain of public action and education policy, in terms of size and autonomy they can be considered as SMEs. While there are small primary schools with four or five teachers, a city primary school generally has between 20 and 50 teachers, and an upper secondary school with 1,000 students employs over a hundred staff. Table 22.1 shows the number of teachers in Switzerland, by educational institution and level.

The directors of these approximately 10,000 educational institutions are tasked with overseeing the implementation of public education and training policies in the field. Although they generally report to the cantonal departments, they do have some room for manoeuvre. This varies according to level and region, and between general education and vocational training. Huguenin *et al.* (2019) define growing school autonomy as an important trend in public education policy. Moreover, according to the Swiss Conference of Cantonal Ministers of Education (EDK), "important features [of the education system] are cantonal autonomy [...] and the decentralized organization of schools[62]". In contrast, in a survey of 219 school managers in

61 https://www.kmu.admin.ch/kmu/en/home/concrete-know-how/facts-and-figures/figures-smes/companies-and-jobs.html (accessed 02.04.2024)
62 https://www.cdip.ch/en/education-system/basics (accessed 05.12.2022).

2019 figures	Number of teachers	Total number of public institutions	Average number of teachers
Compulsory school: primary 1-8 and secondary I, excluding special education	94,288	10,572	9
Secondary level II: general/transitional schools and initial vocational training	29,402	483	61
Tertiary level: higher professional education, universities, universities of applied sciences and teacher training colleges	29,151[62]	171	170
Total	152,841	11,387	80

Table 22.1 Data compiled on the basis of FSO *Education and Science* statistical tables. Source: FSO (2021)

French-speaking Switzerland, Soguel *et al.* (2013) showed that, in all areas of management, school managers wanted more autonomy than they felt they had. This was true across all cantons, all levels of the education system and all functions.

The Swiss education system reflects the country's federal structure, with compulsory education, which is mainly the responsibility of the 26 cantons, and public post-compulsory education (general education, vocational training and higher education), where responsibility is shared between the Confederation and the cantons. The cantons and municipalities together finance 90% of public spending on education, totalling CHF 38.9 billion in 2018 (17.6% of total public spending). Lastly, the Constitution stipulates that the Confederation and the cantons must "jointly ensure the high quality and accessibility of the Swiss education area", which has led to the introduction of "education monitoring" (CSRE 2018).

However, this contribution does not focus on education policies or their evaluation. Rather, it aims to show how the IDHEAP model of public administration can contribute to action in educational institutions. Ultimately, these institutions are similar to administrative units. Admittedly, the room for manoeuvre available to the directors of educational institutions varies greatly from one canton or level to another. But many managerial activities are common to all.

63 Including assistants, scientific staff, administrative and management personnel, tertiary-level institutions employ 95,709 people, or an average of 560 per institution.

Here, we mobilize two dimensions of the IDHEAP model of public administration (Figure 22.1) that can generally be exploited by educational-institution managers within their room for manoeuvre:

- the "Norms and strategy" dimension and its "Leadership" component—participative leadership with a transformational focus—to foster strong bonds between work colleagues in particular; and
- the "Organization and processes" dimension and two of its components: the "Communication" component, to encourage the development of shared values and perspectives, as well as a shared language and meaning; and the "Human resources" component, because human-resources-management (HRM) practices must be conducive to the selection, development and retention of personnel.

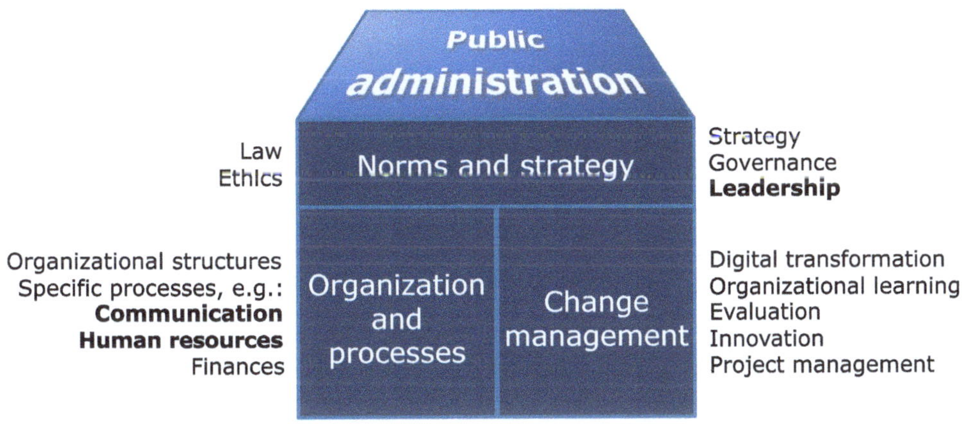

Figure 22.1 Examples of components that can be mobilized to manage an educational institution (in bold)

22.2 Key points of leadership, communication and human-resources management

22.2.1 Leadership

The field of education and training has undergone a number of transformations in recent decades:

- the harmonization of compulsory schooling between Swiss cantons (the HarmOS concordat came into force in 2009);
- the gradual introduction of standard curricula (the "plan d'étude" in French-speaking Switzerland since 2010, and the "Lehrplan 21" in German-speaking Switzerland from 2014);

- the creation of universities of applied sciences and the rapid growth in student numbers (as an illustration, the University of Applied Sciences and Arts Western Switzerland has seen enrolment rise from 4200 at its opening in 1998 to 21,000 at the start of the 2022-2023 academic year[64]);
- the 2009 overhaul of the Federal Vocational Baccalaureate and the introduction of the Specialized Baccalaureate; and
- the impact of digitalization on professions and teaching methods.

These transformations must be backed up by leadership that contributes to an organization's ability to achieve its objectives. As Giauque and Emery point out in their contribution on the subject, "an interest in leadership thus calls for a better understanding of the organizational, structural and individual levers that politicians and senior administrative staff use to steer public action" (▶ 9 Leadership). Leithworth *et al.* (2020) assert that leadership has a significant effect on the organizational characteristics of an institution, positively influencing the quality of teaching and learning. They go even further, stating that leadership can have a particularly positive influence on students' results when it is *distributed*. In her review of the literature on changes in school leadership policy in OECD countries over the last thirty years, Pont (2020) examines the factors that foster the adoption of reforms. She notes a shift from a bureaucratic function to an approach that involves teachers in the process of change. She also notes that leadership practices and their impact are greatly influenced by specific contexts, and need to be adapted to them.

In an implicitly critical manner, Giauque and Emery note, again in their contribution to this book, that *administrative leadership* in Switzerland is "sober leadership", in which "'heads that rise above' are disliked (the 'tall poppy syndrome')". This seems particularly true in the field of education, where the vast majority of principals or directors come from the ranks of teachers: suddenly, their former colleagues become their subordinates. Giauque and Emery point out that, generally speaking, technical expertise is important to legitimize this administrative leadership role. This approach seems difficult to apply in a school, since being a very good teacher gives little indication of human-management, motivation or communication skills. Since this kind of "instrumental" leadership, in which technical expertise helps in coaching people by showing them how to do their job, seems ill-suited to the world of education, other approaches need to be considered.

This is why Giauque and Emery also discuss *transactional leadership*, which is based on steering by objectives, using explicit performance-measurement criteria. This approach is highly appreciated by participants in the Diploma of Advanced Studies (DAS) programme of the Formation en direction d'institutions de formation

64 https://www.hes-so.ch/la-hes-so/a-propos/la-hes-so-en-chiffres (accessed 05.12.2022).

(FORDIF)[65], a certification course in the field of educational-institution management, when the theme of balanced scorecards is addressed. While these tools certainly make it possible to identify trends (increasing absenteeism, falling success rates, deteriorating learning conditions, etc.) and to steer an institution, they are more a matter of management and a rational, quantifiable vision. To go further than measuring steering indicators, Giauque and Emery recommend the use of *transformational leadership*, in which the aim is to provide meaning (the "why" rather than the "what") and to develop motivation, trust and values. They conclude that "few executives are able to juggle with all three registers of leadership" and that "contemporary public leadership must be seen as primarily collective". This applies particularly to the world of education. We can thus see that transformational leadership permeates the ideas of *collective or distributed leadership*, which are based on participation and empowerment.

As mentioned above, leadership calls for an interest in the organizational, structural and individual levers that can be used to steer public action. Beyond the organization of teaching, a key lever for educational-institution directors is communication, which is presented in Pasquier and Mabillard's contribution to this book (▶ 11 Communication management). Communication tools are used "to present public-policy issues, explain the decisions made by governments and administrations, promote values or behaviours, facilitate access to public services, highlight the activities of organizations, or reinforce recruitment."

22.2.2 Communication

Pasquier and Mabillard address various types of communication specific to the public sector. While government or political communication does not emanate from an educational institution, other types of communication do happen directly at this administrative level:

- *institutional communication* to promote a school and its missions to parents, students or future students, etc.;
- *communication on services provided*: days or sessions presenting courses or orientations, explanations of how activities are organized, etc.;
- *internal communication*, from classic teachers' meetings to digital channels such as e-mail or collaborative platforms; and
- *crisis communication*, in the event of issues affecting the institution (conflicts, harassment, etc.).

Pasquier and Mabillard go on to point out that, while the instruments used in business communication and public communication are the same, communication

65 https://www.fordif.ch/structure-et-organisation/presentation-de-la-fordif/ (accessed 05.12.2022).

activities are different because of public organizations' legal (and sometimes moral) obligation to communicate. In addition, there is stronger pressure and higher expectations from the public. Anyone who has attended an information session with parents worried about their offspring's future educational path can testify to this difference!

On the whole, "traditional" communication is well mastered in educational institutions: information days or brochures present a school or its training activities effectively, teachers' meetings remain a tried-and-tested means of coordinating work, and so on. But Pasquier and Mabillard implicitly point out that efforts still need to be made in the face of growing citizen expectations, the shift to the principle of transparency, increased media pressure, etc. In addition, the omnipresent new media and online platforms (digital communication) are having a strong impact on modern communication. There has been widespread discussion in the media about the use of mobile phones and WhatsApp in schools: news of bans, recommendations from data-protection officers in favour of applications that are virtually unused by young people, or undue enthusiasm for tools seen as having strong educational potential[66]. Directors and principals also have to deal with conflicts on social networks or cases of cyberbullying that go far beyond their usual communication-management activities. Finally, with regard to internal communication, the introduction of distance or hybrid learning has seen many school managements struggle with the technical problems of making collaborative platforms available. These new channels have presented school managers with new challenges in terms of their ability to communicate and control the messages they send out.

In its June 2018 strategy[67], the EDK stipulates that schools should "exploit the possibilities offered by digital services to simplify exchanges with their various interlocutors (parents, government offices, specialized services, etc.)". This approach works very well for disseminating simple, factual information, and is certainly to be preferred wherever possible. But school administrators inevitably spend time collaborating with social workers or specialized interveners, reassuring parents or defusing conflicts, or trying to ensure the physical and psychological wellbeing of teachers. These activities, commonly grouped under the banner of interpersonal communication (Table 22.2), are an integral part of distributed leadership, presented in the previous section.

These interpersonal communication skills can be put to good use in exchanges with parents, or with businesses in the case of vocational training. They are also frequently applied in the management of teachers or human resources, which is the third lever identified in this contribution for the implementation of public action in education.

66 Without going into too much detail, the following fact sheet provides a good summary of the issues at stake: https://www.educa.ch/fr/themes/securite-informationnelle-et-juridique/services-de-messagerie-dans-le-contexte-scolaire
67 https://www.cdip.ch/fr/themes/transversaux/numerisation (accessed 05.12.2022)

Communication	Verbal and nonverbal communication skills, listening ability
Collaboration	Ability to build relationships and develop trust
Conflict resolution	Problem solving, negotiation, conflict management
Tolerance	Understanding of other points of view and cultures, empathy

Table 22.2 Classification of interpersonal communication skills
Source: table adapted from Hardjati & Febrianita (2019)

22.2.3 Human-resources management

Emery and Giauque differentiate between several aspects that are generally grouped together under the HRM label:

- administrative personnel-management processes—management of salaries, schedules, leave and absences;
- candidate selection and recruitment, forward-looking HRM;
- management of staff performance through the setting of objectives, interviews or reviews, appraisal and feedback, skills acquisition, etc.; and
- management of HR issues such as conflict, toxic behaviour or poor performance.

The HRM panorama in Swiss educational institutions is highly heterogeneous. In some cantons, personnel management and recruitment is carried out at department level, while management of working hours and absences is handled by the institutions themselves. Some principals or directors can select teachers directly, while in other contexts this is done at a centralized level. Primary-school teachers are sometimes even hired by municipalities, or circles of municipalities. The only constant noted in all these different contexts is the difficulty of managing substitute teachers, but this is a somewhat separate issue.

In any case, the world of teaching is no different from the rest of the public sector, or from the private sector. It is "a subject that gets people talking", because "HRM is not only about big strategies, 'HR policies', and 'employer marketing' to present an attractive prospect on the job market and on social networks. It's also about the little everyday things: a muddle within the team, the feeling of not being recognized, work that is poorly defined or not at all, an inflexible timetable, and colleagues who always keep the most interesting work for themselves" (Emery *et al.* 2019: 4). In connection with aspects of transformational leadership and communication, and the fact that administrative aspects are often dealt with at cantonal level, we will focus here on two concepts: *staff appraisal* and *motivation*..

In a chapter whose evocative title translates to "Personnel appraisal: managerial disaster or indispensable practice?", Emery *et al.* (2019) discuss the challenges of staff appraisal. At the outset the authors note that, in a system where employees have no objectives with regard to the quality of work delivered, and never receive feedback, "the chances are that things will not go well!" (*ibid*: 24). They also ask whether it is possible to set up an appraisal system that is free from distortion, particularly that caused by the quality (good or less good) of human relations between the people involved. Without providing a definitive answer, they describe the phases of the HRM process for which the hierarchy is responsible:

- job description or specifications;
- staff supervision and leadership;
- introduction of an annual appraisal cycle; and
- adjustment of responsibilities and objectives based on the appraisal.

Emery *et al.* (2019) point out that most appraisal systems combine elements of the *summative* approach (aimed at "sanctioning" work done) and the formative approach (aimed at developing the skills of the person being evaluated). The difficulty of implementing a coherent appraisal system lies in the fact that these two approaches are contradictory and difficult to reconcile. Despite this issue, Emery *et al.* (*ibid.*: 26) assert that the primary benefit of appraisal "is unquestionably that of clarifying expectations". They also stress the importance of giving positive, supportive feedback that allows the person being evaluated to understand how their action fits within the context of the organization. Lastly, they recommend dropping the bureaucratic and routine aspects of appraisal, which can be demotivating.

This brings us to the final lever discussed here: motivation. Emery *et al.* (*ibid.*: 34) define it as "the internal and/or external forces that produce the onset, direction, intensity and persistence of behaviour that prompts a person to achieve specific goals". They then distinguish between intrinsic motivation (linked to job content) and extrinsic motivation (working conditions and professional context). Public-sector teachers in Switzerland generally benefit from favourable working conditions (job security, salary, holidays, etc.). These conditions are not levers on which a school principal can act directly, so we will leave them aside and concentrate on intrinsic motivation.

Emery *et al.* (*op. cit.*) propose tools and practices for nurturing motivation, which we discuss here in general terms. Broadly speaking, we can assume that young teachers are generally highly motivated at the start of their careers, responding to the calling of teaching. But this motivation can wane with time spent in the classroom. Teachers have few vertical or horizontal career-development opportunities—generally considered by HRM specialists to be a decisive factor in maintaining and boosting employee motivation. Performance-related pay is another lever used to motivate staff, but it does not apply (or only exceptionally) in the world of teaching. That leaves *skills management*, which has been gaining in importance in schools over the past few decades. Gone are the days when teachers could give the same maths or geography lesson for years without questioning their educational approach.

To conclude this contribution, we draw attention to two types of situations that can lead to demotivation in the view of Emery *et al.* (2019). A lack of the skills required for particular activities is a situation that teachers may find themselves facing when the social or psychological dimensions of their task take precedence over pedagogical work. Among the problems they have to deal with are learners with behavioural problems, and difficult relationships with some parents. The second factor is boredom. While there is no magic formula to enable school principals to remedy these situations, an important step for them to take is to examine their professional practices in the area of motivation management. Stress prevention and occupational-health management are also increasingly important concerns for school managers, but these matters go beyond the scope of this contribution.

22.3 Future prospects and challenges

Educational institutions are subject to many external changes—political, sociocultural and technological—and the implementation of education and training policies provides a fine illustration of Swiss federalism. Because of the EDK's express desire for autonomization and decentralization, educational institutions and their management enjoy considerable room for manoeuvre in their handling of these changes.

The leeway varies between cantons, levels or systems of compulsory education or vocational training. School managers must adapt to their organizational environment, but it is clear that questions of leadership, communication, appraisal and staff motivation are all part of their remit. This means that is important for them to have the tools and practices needed to apply these concepts in their own field of public administration. However, and this is where the challenge lies, they must *guard against multiplying bureaucratic rules and procedures*, because many teachers feel that their profession is becoming increasingly "technocratic".

The academic literature recommends shifting from administrative leadership to *transformational leadership*, but the transition can be complex for overburdened school managers. Without even going into the details of the complexity, the *time resources* this transition requires are significant. According to Emery *et al.* (2019), it takes between two and four hours to prepare and follow up on an individual appraisal interview. Since schools often have several dozen teachers, the workload is considerable. Faced with the urgency of other situations requiring their attention, school managers may be tempted to neglect these tasks. In addition, they often have to devote much of their time to meetings with various stakeholders (parents, employers, social workers or specialized interveners). They may therefore find themselves in "passive communication" mode (simply responding to requests), rather than an active—planned, organized—communication mode. Digital tools seem to be an appropriate solution for conducting more active communication, with channels providing direct access to recipients. But this does not obviate the need to plan and organize communications.

Lastly, while HRM practices in large organizations (private companies or cantonal departments) have undergone far-reaching changes over the last 25 years, small and medium-sized structures such as educational institutions have some catching up to do. Centralized HR departments are responsible for recruitment policies, technical aspects or specialized tools. However, in their contribution on HRM, Emery and Giauque clearly state that unit managers are key actors in contemporary public HRM. This empowerment in HRM matters is seen as a decisive point, as is the fact that these people have the requisite HR skills, time and motivation. Organizations that employ school managers therefore need to create favourable conditions, particularly in terms of HR skills development. They must also give due recognition to the time and energy that managers of educational institutions devote to HRM, communication and leadership-development activities.

Key concepts

- Appraisal (or evaluation) of teaching staff (évaluation du corps enseignant, Beurteilung der Lehrkräfte, valutazione del personale docente): identifying, measuring and developing the key competencies of teaching staff (knowledge, know-how and interpersonal skills) is a major challenge for the management of educational institutions.
- Digital communication (*communications numérique, digitale Kommunikation, comunicazione digitale*): educational institutions are increasingly sending messages to students, parents or employing organizations via digital media, and must therefore become proficient in their use and stay abreast of their technological development.
- Empowerment (or autonomization) of educational institutions (*autonomisation des établissements de formation, Autonomisierung der Bildungseinrichtungen, potenziamento degli istituti di formazione*): the Swiss education system is based on strong cantonal autonomy and decentralized organization, which means that educational institutions must manage their own affairs.
- Harmonization of cantonal school systems (*harmonisation des systèmes scolaires cantonaux, Harmonisierung der kantonalen Schulsysteme, armonizzazione dei sistemi scolastici cantonali*): the Swiss Confederation sets out general principles for the Swiss education system and provides for checks to ensure that the cantonal systems comply with them.

References

BFS (2021). *Wissenschaft und Bildung - Panorama*. Neuenburg: Bundesamt für Statistik. März 2021.

Emery Y., Giauque D. & Gonin F. (2019). *Gestion des ressources humaines : pour le meilleur et pour le pire*. Collection Savoir Suisse, EPFL Press.

Hardjati S. & Febrianita R. (2019). The Power of Interpersonal Communication Skill in Enhancing Service Provision. *Journal of Social Science Research, 14*, 3192–3199.

Huguenin, JM., Yvon, F., & Perrenoud, D. (2019). *Relever les défis contemporains dans la gestion des établissements scolaires*. L'Harmattan.

Leithworth, K., Harris A. & Hopkins D. (2020). Seven strong claims about successful school leadership revisited. *School Leadership & Management*, 40(1), 5–22. https://doi.org/10.1080/13632434.2019.1596077 (accessed 05.12.2022).

Pont B. (2020). A literature review of school leadership policy reforms. *European Journal of Education, 55*, 154–168. https://doi.org/10.1111/ejed.12398 (accessed 05.12.2022).

SKBF (2018). *Bildungsbericht Schweiz 2018*. Schweizerische Koordinationsstelle für Bildungsforschung, Aarau.

Soguel N., Huguenin JM. & Ecabert C. (2013). *Les cadres scolaires souhaitent plus d'autonomie qu'ils pensent en avoir : une analyse de la situation en Suisse romande*. IDHEAP Working Paper 6/2013.

23 Wind-power generation

Stéphane Nahrath

23.1 Introduction to the challenges of wind-power generation

As part of its "Energy Strategy 2050" developed beginning in 2007[68], the Federal Council has progressively established four fundamental principles of action for its energy policy. These principles are (1) *rapid, simultaneous withdrawal* from fossil and nuclear energy, (2) improved *energy efficiency* in a number of areas (buildings, mobility, industry and electrical appliances), (3) *lower per-capita energy consumption* and (4) *development of renewable energies* (RE). These objectives stand at the crossroads of the energy transition, the ecological transition and the fight against climate change.

Regarding the fourth principle, relatively precise production targets for the various RE sources have been set in the new Federal Energy Act, which came into force in 2017[69]. As far as wind power is concerned, a target of around 15% to 17% of domestic electricity production by 2050 has been set, which is an extremely ambitious goal given its current contribution (0.2% in 2022). The number of wind turbines needed to meet the targets set for wind-power generation is estimated at between 400 and 600 nationwide by 2050.

To achieve these targets, the Confederation launched a wind-energy support programme in the 2000s (SFOE, SAEFL, ARE 2004). The main instrument of this programme is the *feed-in remuneration* (KEV). This instrument, first introduced in 2009 under the name "retribution at cost", guarantees that the state will buy kilowatt-hours (kWh) from producers at a price equivalent to production cost, thus transferring the economic risks of producing this type of energy to the state.

68 The development of this strategy is dynamic and evolving, and is not contained in a single document. For a chronological overview of this strategy (as of June 2022), see: https://www.bfe.admin.ch/bfe/en/home/policy/energy-strategy-2050.html (accessed 05.12.2022).
69 Energy Act (EnA) of 30 September 2016 (RS 730.0).

Implementation of the programme follows the basic principles of federalism of execution as regards the division of competencies. The Confederation is responsible for formulating the framework conditions and providing financial support through KEV. The cantons and municipalities are responsible for overseeing the construction and operation of wind farms: planning, granting of permits (including supervision of environmental impact assessments—EIAs), operating permits, monitoring, etc.

Thanks to KEV, the federal wind-power funding programme has been a resounding success, with a large number of wind-farm projects emerging in the 2010s, particularly in regions identified as suitable for this type of installation in the 2004 "wind-power concept for Switzerland"[70]. However, the proliferation of projects, combined with the weakness of wind-power regulation (at both federal and cantonal level), has created a relatively chaotic situation. In the absence of appropriate legal instruments, cantonal and communal energy and planning departments have to handle a very large number of building-permit applications. To deal with the most pressing issues, these departments have resorted to land-use planning instruments (negative structural plans[71] and zoning plans), but these have not proved sufficient to control the geographical distribution of these projects, or to balance the interests of RE development against the protection of biotopes and landscapes.

This situation also highlighted the question of administrative leadership, the issue being the definition of political-administrative leadership in the context of cross-sectoral (horizontal) coordination. While the energy department would seem, logically enough, to have the lead in implementing this policy, it does not have control over the instruments needed to steer projects: land-use planning and zoning instruments are in the hands of territorial-development departments, and EIA procedure is the responsibility of environmental departments. On top of this, the absence (in most cases) of a cantonal wind-energy strategy means that cantonal energy departments struggle to adopt an organizational strategy (▶ 7 Strategy) allowing them to oversee the implementation of the wind-energy programme and arbitrate conflicts between the various stakeholders involved in the construction of wind farms (▶ 18 Project management).

The proliferation of KEV projects against a backdrop of major regulatory loopholes in this emerging industry led to a sharp rise in the number of appeals lodged by local residents and by nature-, landscape- and environmental-protection organizations (ENGOs) from the mid-2000s onwards.

70 This mainly concerns the Jura arc (especially the summits) and the Vaud plateau.

71 Negative planning indicates the (relatively limited) perimeters where it is not desirable to develop wind farms, implying that all the rest of the territory is suitable for hosting wind turbines. Positive planning, on the other hand, indicates the areas (also relatively limited) that are particularly suitable for the siting of wind farms, which in this case implies that the remainder of the territory is not suitable.

In response to the conflicts that implementation of the wind-power programme has generated, public authorities have endeavoured to strengthen regulations (▶ 5 Law) in two ways: first, since 2008, by making EIAs compulsory for wind-turbine projects; and second, since 2014, by bringing wind-farm projects into cantonal structural planning in the form of *positive* plans (indicating the relatively limited perimeters within which wind farms can, or should, be developed).

As a result of the requirement for wind farms to carry out an EIA—which opens the door to the right of appeal—since the early 2010s there have been increasing numbers of objections and then legal action by ENGOs and local residents. This involvement of the courts ("judicialization")—incidentally, sometimes sought by developers whose project has been rejected—has led to the development of a substantial body of case law produced by cantonal courts and the Federal Supreme Court (FSC).

In response to this phenomenon of litigation, which considerably slows and, in some cases, completely stalls the construction of wind-farm projects, in 2016 political decision-makers revised the Energy Act. The new law enshrined the principle—initially developed in the case law of certain courts—of the national interest of renewable energies in general, and wind-power generation in particular. This recognition in federal law of *the national interest of RE* will, in turn, affect the balancing of interests in court decisions (notably those of the FSC) and confirm the shift in case law in favour of wind power. The FSC's decision rejecting appeals against the Sainte-Croix wind-farm project[72] bears out this observation.

From the point of view of the actors involved, much of the conflict surrounding wind power stems from the broad span and heterogeneity of the groups impacted ("third-party losers")— local residents, ENGOs, neighbouring municipalities and/or cantons—for whom no form of compensation (ecological, financial, quality of life, etc.) has yet been provided. This is not the case in other areas, such as hydroelectricity (water royalties paid to the concession-granting communities) or nuclear power (free electricity delivered to the municipalities close to power plants).

It should be noted that the tensions surrounding the transition to renewable energies have recently been heightened by the unfortunate convergence of the (supposedly temporary) reduction in national energy-production capacity (following the decision to abandon nuclear power) and the effects of the Russo-Ukrainian war, which could strongly destabilize energy supply in Europe and Switzerland. Fears of an energy "crisis" have led to attempts—now underway (2022), particularly in the Federal Parliament—to prioritize energy-policy objectives over those of environmental protection (protection of ecosystems, biodiversity and landscapes).

Against this backdrop, the major challenge facing public authorities, and public organizations in particular, is how to manage the growing contradictions between

72 See the judgment of 18 March 2021, 1C_657/2018, 1C_658/2018.

the necessarily ambitious objectives of the energy transition on the one hand and those of environmental-protection policies on the other. This is mainly a matter of endeavouring to prevent the push to develop RE from undermining the protection of ecosystems, biodiversity and landscapes. Put another way, the goal is to prevent the energy transition—a key component of the ecological transition—from paradoxically overriding the environmental-protection policies patiently put in place over the last fifty years. This situation would also contravene a number of articles of the Federal Constitution.

The aim of this contribution, then, is to show how different dimensions or components of the IDHEAP model can be mobilized to meet the challenges of generating wind energy in compliance with environmental policies.

Figure 23.1 Examples of components that can be mobilized to meet the challenges of wind-power generation (in bold in the figure)

The IDHEAP model rightly emphasizes the importance of *law* for the conduct of public action. In this contribution, we consider law from the angle of its two most common functions in public-policy analysis (Dente 2009): (1) law as a *system of rules* resulting from the main constituent institutions of the Swiss political system, namely federalism, direct democracy and the principles of concordance and subsidiarity, a system that structures all the different stages of a public-policy process (objective law, "the" law); and (2) law as an *action resource* allocated, with varying degrees of equality, to the various (groups of) actors in a public policy (subjective law, rights) and which can be mobilized in various strategies, notably judicialization. Implementing the wind-power programme requires finding the best means of both *horizontal* (cross-sectoral) and *vertical* (multi-level governance) coordination, as well as the best *governance* system likely to ensure that the programme is implemented in compliance with the fundamental objectives and principles of environmental law. This governance system must in turn be translated into a *political strategy* by the political authorities as well as an *organizational strategy* internal to the units responsible for implementing the wind-power support programme. Ultimately, the construction and operation of wind farms requires a *project-management* system to coordinate the various stakeholders and their interests, and to ensure that a balance is struck between construction *cost* and *time* and infrastructure *quality*.

23.2 Key points of governance, law, strategy and project management

23.2.1 Governance

Federalism of execution and direct democracy are the two main institutional rules of the political system that have a significant bearing on implementation of the wind-power programme. The programme is clearly the result of an initial federal impetus and framework, but responsibility for its implementation falls both to the cantons (structural planning and EIA) and the municipalities (land-use planning and construction permits). In addition, local planning is often the subject of referendums. This institutional context requires efficient coordination between institutional levels (*vertical coordination*).

Beyond this, implementation of the wind-power programme is strongly subject to a number of *institutional rules* specific to the field of environmental policies. Chief among these are the causality principle (polluter pays), the principle of balancing interests, the EIA procedure or the right of appeal of ENGOs, all of which come into play in the procedures of wind-farm planning and construction authorization. Managing the inter-sectoral tensions that are likely to emerge thus requires effective coordination between the energy and environment sectors (*horizontal coordination*) in particular.

The challenge of administering the wind-power programme is therefore that of finding the best *territorial-governance* arrangement to allow both horizontal (cross-sectoral) and vertical (multi-level governance) coordination, as well as the best *sectoral-governance* model (legal and organizational form of project support) so that implementation of the wind-power programme can be guaranteed.

Territorial governance favouring vertical and horizontal coordination

The difficulties in implementing wind-power policy are partly due to major shortcomings in cantonal supervision of implementation of the federal KEV instrument. This instrument was introduced by the federal authorities at a time when the cantons had no ad-hoc legal basis or planning tools to oversee the number of projects and their siting. Initially, the cantonal authorities concerned (mainly in Western Switzerland) had to make use of land-use planning instruments (structural and allocation planning) that were not really suited to energy infrastructure planning. Wind power thus serves as an example demonstrating the importance of *preventive vertical coordination* between federal and cantonal authorities so that the effects of federal instruments at the cantonal and local levels can be anticipated, as in the case of the introduction of KEV. Coordination of this type is already possible at the parliamentary level through a prospective material legistics approach (Flückiger 2019) and/or a regulatory impact assessment (*ex ante* evaluation) (Varone *et al.* 2020) of the expected cantonal- and local-level effects of instruments introduced at federal level.

Similarly, the administrative units in charge of implementation should set up mechanisms to supervise and support the often-random emergence of local projects, so as to limit their number, avoid deadweight and ensure optimal geographical distribution. Such arrangements could take the form of positive structural planning and/or federal sectoral planning drawn up in close collaboration with the cantons concerned[73].

At cantonal level, the arrival of wind-power projects has often revealed the limits of *horizontal-coordination* arrangements between the units responsible for energy, environmental protection and land-use planning. Leadership and the distribution of responsibilities between these three units in political-administrative arrangements (PAAs) (Knoepfel *et al.* 2010: chap. 5.3) are not always clearly defined. Similarly, bringing wind-power infrastructure into the EIA regime has necessitated refinement of procedural rules, and has posed a number of interpretation problems that have opened the door to legal disputes with opponents of wind farms.

The cantons concerned should therefore set up PAAs specifically dedicated to the wind-power programme in order to preventively identify inconsistencies between bodies of law. This would forestall the emergence of projects that catalyse contradictions between legislations and turn into legal disputes. For example, the planning of wind-power projects in protected areas such as federal landscape inventories, forests and protected biotopes could be avoided. In these PAAs, the tasks, competencies and resources allocated to the various organizations, as well as the procedural rules governing the main administrative instruments, must be explicitly defined. Similarly, the leadership and responsibilities of the various administrative units must be clearly established and respected.

Lastly, as the case of hydropower (DETEC 2021) has recently shown, a promising approach for *combining vertical* and *horizontal* coordination and thus reducing

73 Article 89 of the Federal Constitution (SR 101) does not explicitly assign responsibility for renewable energy planning to the Confederation. This means that introducing a federal sectoral plan for wind power would probably require a constitutional amendment.

the risk of legal disputes is to set up "roundtables" to bring the main stakeholders together to identify the most efficient energy projects (those with the best ratio between *environmental costs* and *energy benefits*). These roundtables are established on the initiative and under the responsibility of a government member in charge of the policy domain, and follow an ad-hoc methodology agreed upon by all participants. A roundtable dedicated to wind power could also provide a forum for negotiating ecological, social and/or financial *compensation* to foster acceptance of wind farms by those negatively affected. Such quasi-corporatist arrangements for negotiating wind-farm planning could be developed at both federal and cantonal (or even regional or local) levels.

Wind-power *sectorial* governance

The mode of governance, that is, the configuration of the network of actors involved in wind-power generation, can vary substantially from one wind farm to another. Four systems of project governance seem to dominate the Swiss wind-energy sector. Wind-farm projects can thus be carried out either by (1) private (often local) developers, (2) sometimes in collaboration with a municipality, (3) public entities in the form of a consortium of (inter-)communal industrial services brought together in a limited company with wholly public capital, or (4) public-private limited companies (mixed corporations) with a majority of public capital. While there is no definitive theoretical argument for or against any of these governance systems (▶ 8 Governance), empirical observation seems to show that completed projects or those in progress fall almost exclusively into categories (3) and (4). In the current context, the main criteria for successful wind-farm governance are: mainly public ownership and capital, the creation of an ad-hoc project developer in the form of a public limited company whose shareholders are mainly local and cantonal public actors, and close collaboration between this entity and the cantonal administrative units (energy, land-use planning and environment departments). The advantage of this type of governance is that it ensures dual public control over the management of wind-farm projects: on the one hand, through public policies (wind-power programme, land-use planning and environment); and on the other, through ownership of the project developer (i.e. the limited company). This indirect presence of the cantonal and local public authorities in the project's capital and project development helps to alleviate economic pressure on the developer in the event of high transaction costs resulting from the high level of conflict and frequent litigation involved in projects.

The case of wind-power projects would seem to confirm the principle set out in the contribution on governance, namely that "with higher transaction costs, the hierarchical coordination mechanism becomes preferable, with its powerful means of control and its internal mechanisms for conflict resolution and decision-making in unforeseen situations" (▶ 8 Governance). All the evidence suggests that a "get things done" governance model (external contracting or public-private partnership) currently has little chance of success.

23.2.2 Law and the judicialization of wind-power policy

The difficulties of implementing wind-power policy, in both Switzerland and many other countries, highlight the crucial role of law as a resource for action that is mobilized—in different forms—by a multitude of actors, both public and private, to achieve often conflicting objectives. The courts (both cantonal and federal), judges and case law thus have a significant influence on the development and implementation of the regulatory regime for this new activity.

Public organizations must therefore take into account the highly dynamic and as yet unstabilized nature of the regulatory framework for wind power. Only by reconstructing the logics at work behind the dynamics of setting up this regulatory regime will administrative units be able to, first, understand the evolution of the structures of constraints they face and, second, transform them into structures of opportunity and develop anticipatory implementation strategies likely to lead to success.

In Switzerland, the gradual construction of the regulatory framework for wind-power activity involves processes of *influence* and *reciprocal readjustments* between (1) the public authorities' production of a strategic concept for the development of wind-power activity, (2) a partial and often largely insufficient translation of this conception into (federal and cantonal) *legislation*, (3) a significant amount of work (integrating elements of legislation and the strategic conception) on producing the *case law*, or jurisprudence, laid down by the various courts that have ruled on disputes concerning the construction of wind-power infrastructures, (4) the incorporation of central elements of this case law into revised legislation and, finally, (5) a change in case law as a result of these legislative revisions (Kodjovi & Bombenger 2019; Kuentz 2022). This back-and-forth dynamic between legislation and case law clearly shows how the law can be both a factor in stabilizing stakeholders' expectations through the shaping of institutional rules regulating wind activity, and a factor in changing this same regulatory framework as a result of judicialization procedures and case law.

In order to be able to act effectively in these two areas of law, public organizations need to hone their skills in the fields of litigation (e.g. anticipating disputes as far as possible by discouraging or prohibiting potentially conflict-ridden projects) and case law (e.g. systematically integrating case law into positive wind-farm planning procedures and into the balancing of interests when issuing building permits), and into legistics (e.g. promoting the "better-regulation" approach [▶ 5 Law] with the government and parliament). In the relatively frequent case of clear contradictions between bodies of law (notably energy law and environmental law), such skills should enable administrative units to develop solutions that best reconcile the fundamental objectives of different public policies without sacrificing their own fundamental objectives. This requires clear criteria for setting "red lines" (defined limits, lines not to be crossed) for each policy, distinguishing between what is negotiable and non-negotiable when balancing interests.

23.2.3 Wind-power programme implementation strategy

The difficulties encountered by the cantons in processing the flood of building-permit applications resulting from the introduction of KEV have highlighted the consequences of the lack of a genuine cantonal *political strategy* (on the part of both government and parliament) for implementing the wind-power programme. In particular, the lack of strategic planning (especially in the initial implementation phase of the programme) has contributed to the emergence of a range of projects that are very inconsistent in terms of land use, technically heterogeneous and overall, very poorly coordinated. This lack of political strategy explains the cantons' difficulty in developing a clear *vision* and *strategic positioning* on wind power, and an *organizational strategy* within the departments concerned (energy, land-use planning, environment).

Developing a clear, explicit and consistent policy strategy

Administrative units should therefore help political authorities to develop their *political strategy* in the field of wind power. At federal level, the advisability of drawing up a genuine sectoral plan for wind power (to identify the criteria for optimal wind-farm siting) should once again be studied in depth[74]. And not only from the perspective of legally opening up access to the territory for project developers, but also, and perhaps above all, as a collective learning process (*policy learning*) enabling the negotiation of sectoral interests (respecting the energy and environmental "red lines" mentioned above) in a perspective of multi-level coordination between Confederation, cantons and municipalities.

Formulation of a political strategy should enable administrative units, particularly cantonal ones, to develop their own *strategic positioning* on this basis; and then to develop an organizational and management strategy enabling them to mobilize administrative resources efficiently to implement the political strategy.

Translating political strategy into a clear, explicit and coherent cantonal action plan

Implementation of a political strategy, translated into the strategic positioning of cantons, should probably be based—following the example of the canton of Vaud—on formulation of an action plan (Knoepfel *et al.* 2010: chap. 5.4) that clearly and

74 Subject to resolution of the question of the division of competences between cantons and the Confederation with regard to energy-production planning (see previous footnote).

coherently sets out the spatial and temporal prioritization criteria for the construction of wind farms in the canton. The action plan should be distinct and more elaborate than a simple sheet of the cantonal structure plan, while being closely coordinated with the latter. It should also be binding on all stakeholders. In this respect, cantonal administrative units, particularly those responsible for energy, must take care *not to prioritize projects based solely on the interests and availability of developers*—that is, develop projects where there is a developer willing to do so (passive prioritization)—but rather encourage developer involvement where it makes the most sense to do so (active prioritization).

Cantonal action plans should prioritize wind-farm projects based on the best environmental cost/energy benefit ratio on the one hand, and conflict risk level on the other. On the basis of these criteria, a positive plan can be drawn up, and developers can be actively sought.

If they are to be successful, these action plans will probably have to be public, drawn up in collaboration with all stakeholders (possibly under the leadership of the minister in charge of the energy file), and strongly discriminatory from both a spatial and a temporal point of view. They should also provide for ad-hoc project management structures with a clear allocation of administrative resources to each project.

23.2.4 Wind-farm project management (strategic and operational)

In order to complete the wind-farm projects that are ultimately selected (e.g. as part of the cantonal action plan), project management must be efficient. It must combine *strategic* aspects (management of technical, legal and economic risks; reduction of social, political and environmental uncertainties; implementation of a compensation strategy) and *operational* aspects (management of human and financial resources, and deadlines; technical choices; coordination of the various stakeholders) for the entire project life cycle.

In a highly conflictive context like that of wind power, one of the central issues in project management is *risk management*. As suggested in the contribution on project management, risk management involves "identifying positive or negative events that could affect the success of a project. The next step is to assess the likelihood of these events, and then to implement measures to reduce the probability of glitches occurring. Finally, response protocols are prepared, in case a risk should materialize" (▶ 18 Project management).

Applied to the case of wind power, strategic management of a wind-farm project should, in our view, involve at least the following three operations: anticipate the risks of conflict and litigation, reduce uncertainties concerning the project's impacts, and set up a compensation system for actors negatively impacted by the project.

Anticipatory project management to prevent litigation

Conflict, and above all litigation, is certainly one of the main risks that project management must address. Such outcomes should be forestalled as far as possible and, if this is not possible, court rulings should be anticipated as much as possible.

A first step in this direction is to set up an explicit action plan, negotiated with all stakeholders (including potential opponents), which respects the "red lines" established in the planning process and clearly sets spatial and temporal priorities (see § 23.2.3 above).

In the event of a legal dispute, one possible strategy for administrative bodies could be to attempt to isolate or divide opponents of the project, to prevent them from developing coordinated strategies. To do this, it is advisable to: (1) separate negotiations with residents and other local groups from those with ENGOs; (2) provide for specific compensation for each of the groups adversely affected; (3) with regard to ENGO opposition, negotiate the main elements of the project (number, size and position of masts) as well as environmental compensation (possibly higher than minimum legal requirements) prior to the public inquiry.

Another strategic objective should be to isolate and dissociate, as far as possible, the various dispute procedures in order to prevent them from escalating (i.e. the interlinking of the various contentious dynamics) and to prevent opponents from federating into "advocacy coalitions" on a regional or even national scale (Blake *et al.* 2020).

More generally, analysis of implementation conflicts concerning policies with a strong infrastructure component and high social and environmental impacts highlights the existence of a *multiplicity of negotiation fronts at various institutional levels*. Administrative bodies should therefore be prepared to intervene simultaneously, and ideally in coordinated fashion, on a number of fronts, including social, political, administrative and media.

Should the risk of litigation materialize, it is advisable to anticipate court decisions as much as possible, by means of in-depth professional knowledge of case law and procedural rules.

Lastly, implementing these strategies requires good control of the "time" resource. Since, in politics as in many other areas of life, time is also power, it is worth developing a genuine strategy for managing this resource for political action (Knoepfel 2017). Experience shows that the winners are very often those who either *have time* at their disposal (to develop and implement their strategy), or have *control over time* (particularly that of other actors), for example by controlling the schedule and pace of proceedings. It also shows that opponents often have an advantage, since the drawing out of authorization procedures as a result of litigation works against the developers.

Reducing uncertainties about the social and environmental impacts of projects

The relatively recent development of wind power (at least in Switzerland) means that there is a great deal of uncertainty surrounding the nature of the issues at the heart of the litigation. Thus, as aptly stated by Kodjovi *et al.* (2020: 131): "[...] the emergence of new issues that are not regulated by ordinary law explains the difficulty that courts have in deciding on the merits of cases, because repositories of knowledge on these issues are built up as questions are asked and studies carried out. These repositories are only weakly validated by experience, since the real impact can only be known once wind turbines have been built." For the courts, such situations involve relatively complicated case-law work, hence the often very long duration of proceedings.

These uncertainties surrounding the impact of projects can be exploited for different purposes by the various stakeholders, for example to minimize their importance and consequences (developers), to block or otherwise increase the cost of projects (opponents) or to negotiate compromises (local public authorities).

To prevent such strategies from developing, the administrative units responsible for implementation should, as far as possible and as quickly as possible, reduce uncertainties surrounding the technical, environmental and social aspects of the project in the course of proceedings.

Providing compensation for losers (or those who consider themselves losers)

Experience in other energy sectors (e.g. nuclear power plants and hydroelectric dams) has shown the decisive importance of *compensation* in fostering the social acceptability of large infrastructures likely to generate significant negative social and environmental effects among local populations. Compensation can take various forms: social, economic and symbolic for local populations, ecological and landscaping for ENGOs or financial for local land and property owners.

Care must be taken to ensure that compensation is *equitably distributed* between the injured parties, particularly at local level. One of the conditions for effective compensation is therefore the ability to "communitize" its benefits. A particular difficulty with wind power as opposed to hydroelectricity is that, since wind is not an "object" (in the sense of the Civil Code), it is impossible to set up a system of "duties" (charges) that would allow local communities to be collectively compensated for the exploitation of "their" common resource (i.e. wind in this case), on the model of hydraulic royalties. In the current situation, the only real compensation is payment of a (very modest) rent by the wind-farm developers in return for building rights granted by a limited number of landowners to enable the siting of wind turbines. Individual compensation of this kind only increases the sense of injustice for the many more people who suffer inconveniences (views, noise, vibrations, etc.) without being able to benefit from financial compensation for building rights.

Administrative units, in collaboration with the legislator, should therefore develop *equitable collective compensation solutions* for all members of local communities who are being asked to sacrifice a (greater or lesser) part of their quality of life for the convenience of beneficiaries (i.e. consumers) who often live in cities far from impacted areas.

23.3 Future prospects and challenges

The energy sector has recently re-emerged as one of the strategic sectors for government action. Major revisions currently underway in Parliament (notably to the Energy Act) are aimed at strengthening and revitalizing the RE sector (in particular hydroelectricity, wind power and solar energy) in order to achieve the objectives set out in the Swiss government's Energy Strategy 2050. Unfortunately, this strengthening of RE is being achieved by revising the criteria for balancing interests, to the detriment of environmental, biodiversity, landscape and heritage-protection objectives. The proposed revisions include, for example, enshrining the principle of overriding public interest in RE in federal law, abolishing or streamlining EIA procedures (particularly for wind and solar farms), weakening the right of appeal granted to neighbours and ENGOs and allowing temporary suspension of minimum flows downstream of dams. This is a significant assault on the fundamental principles and main instruments of environmental, landscape and heritage-protection policies, and is likely to have significant consequences for ecosystems and the built heritage.

In this context, the role of administrative units at all institutional levels could be to develop the expertise needed to anticipate the issues involved in these trade-offs, and to support governments and parliaments in the difficult process of energy transition. In particular, they should develop and propose solutions for the strategic and operational planning of wind farms on a national scale, for the overhaul of procedures for balancing and arbitrating interests, and for the introduction of equitable collective compensation systems modelled on those of the hydroelectric and nuclear sectors.

Key concepts

- Balance of interests (*pesée d'intérêts, Interessenabwägung, ponderazione degli interessi*): the principle of arbitration between the interests of environmental protection and those of other sectoral policies.
- Environmental impact assessments (*études d'impact sur l'environnement, Umweltverträglichkeitsprüfungen [oder -studien], valutazione d'impatto ambientale*):

procedures for preventive (*ex ante*) assessment of the likely environmental impact of an infrastructure project.

- Judicialization (*judiciarisition, Verrechtlichung, giudiziarizzazione*): a propensity to favour litigation to settle disputes, particularly those arising from the implementation of public policies.
- Right of appeal (for environmental protection associations) (*droit de recours [des organisations de protection de l'environnement], Beschwerderecht [von Umweltverbänden] or Verbansbeschwerderecht, diritto di ricorso delle associazioni ambientaliste*): right conferred on local residents and landscape- and environmental-protection organizations to lodge an appeal under public law against an administrative decision (e.g. construction permit, operating permit, land clearing, etc.).

References

BFE, BUWAL, ARE (2004). *Konzept Windenergie Schweiz. Grundlagen für die Standortwahl von Windparks.* Bern.

Blake, K., Nahrath, S. & Ingold, K. (2020). Combining the Institutional Resource Regime (IRR) framework with the Advocacy Coalition Framework (ACF) for a better understanding of environmental governance processes: The case of Swiss wind power policy. *Environmental Science and Policy, 112*, 141–154.

Dente, B. (2009). The law as a policy resource: Some scattered thoughts. In S. Nahrath, Varone, F. (Eds), *Rediscovering public law and public administration in comparative policy analysis: a tribute to Peter Knoepfel* (pp. 33–44). PPUR.

Flückiger, A. (2019). *(Re)faire la loi. Traité de légistique à l'ère du droit souple.* Stämpfli Verlag

Knoepfel, P. (2017). *Les ressources d'action publique. Vers une nouvelle lecture du pouvoir.* Seismo.

Knoepfel, P., Nahrath, S., Savary, J. & Varone, F. (2010). *Analyse des politiques suisses de l'environnement.* Ruegger Verlag.

Kodjovi, M.-J., & Bombenger, P.-H. (2019). Évolution réciproque des jurisprudences et des politiques publiques de la transition énergétique : l'exemple éolien en Suisse. In *Droit et Gestion des Collectivités Locales*, Éditions du Moniteur, 135–172.

Kodjovi, M.-J., Bombenger, P.-H. Cherqui, A. & Savary, P. (2020). Situations de gestion environnementale de l'activité éolienne en Suisse occidentale – Proposition d'un modèle d'analyse et application. In R. Barbier, F.-J. Daniel, S. Fernandez, N. Raulet-Croset, M. Leroy, L. Guérin-Schneider (Eds), *L'environnement en mal de gestion. Les apports d'une perspective situationnelle* (pp. 115–134). Presses universitaires du Septentrion.

Kuentz, M. (2022). *La judiciarisation des politiques publiques : le cas de la politique éolienne.* Masterarbeit PMP, IDHEAP, Université de Lausanne.

Leroy, M., Guérin-Schneider, L. (Eds.) (2020), *L'environnement en mal de gestion. Les apports d'une perspective situationnelle.* Presses universitaires du Septentrion.

UVEK (2021). *Gemeinsame Erklärung des Runden Tisches Wasserkraft.* 13. Dezember 2021.

Varone, F., Bundi, P. & Gava, R. (2020). L'évaluation des politiques au Parlement : la fonction de catalyseur des groupes d'intérêt. *Revue Internationale des Sciences Administratives, 86*, 103–120.

References for further study

Commaille, J., Dumoulin, L. & Robert, C. (Eds.) (2010). *La judicisation du politique*. LGDJ.

Dupuy, C. & Halpern, C. (2009). Les politiques publiques face à leurs protestataires. *Revue Française de Science Politique, 59*(4), 701–722.

Key concepts index

Contributors

Laure Athias is Professor of Economics of Regulation and Public Economics at the Swiss Graduate School of Public Administration (Institut de hautes études en administration publique, IDHEAP) at the University of Lausanne. She has also been a visiting professor at the University of Bristol and a research associate at Yale University. Her research, publications and reports for public authorities and international institutions focus on improving the delivery of public services to populations, taking into account the impact of history, culture and values on the demand for and supply of public services. She also investigates issues related to the effects of private provision on public procurement, regulation and contractual design. She publishes in and reports for leading scientific journals such as *Social Science & Medicine* and *The Quarterly Journal of Economics*. She directs IDHEAP's *Policy Briefs* collection. She holds a master's degree in economics and management from European University Viadrina in Germany, as well as a master's and a doctorate in economics from Paris 1 Panthéon-Sorbonne University.

Giuliano Bonoli is Professor of Social Policy at the Swiss Graduate School of Public Administration at the University of Lausanne. His areas of expertise and research are pension policy, family policy, unemployment and workforce reentry. He has directed a number of national and international research projects. He is the author of several books and regularly publishes articles in scientific journals specializing in these fields. He is also called upon by the cantons to evaluate new measures and practices in the field of back-to-work policy. He holds a bachelor's degree from the University of Geneva, a master's degree from the University of Leeds (UK) and a doctorate from the University of Kent (UK).

Pirmin Bundi is Professor of Public Policy and Evaluation at the Swiss Graduate School of Public Administration at the University of Lausanne. His research, publications and consultancy work focus on the use of evaluation, evidence-based policy-making and how politicians evaluate public policy. He is also in charge of a research project funded by the Swiss National Science Foundation on attitudes towards federalism in Germany and Switzerland. He is the author of numerous publications in specialized scientific journals, a member of the jury for the Prix Seval of the Swiss Evaluation Society, and co-editor of the *Handbook of Public Policy Evaluation* (Edward Elgar Publishing). He studied at the universities of Berne, Copenhagen, UCLA and Zurich, where he obtained a doctorate in political science.

Yves Emery is Honorary Professor of Management and Human Resources Management at the Swiss Graduate School of Public Administration at the University of Lausanne. His research and publications focus on public human-resources management (HRM), with particular emphasis on issues of identity and motivation of public servants. His consultancy work covers a broad spectrum of issues affecting HRM strategies and processes in public organizations undergoing change. He has led several national research projects as principal investigator, the latest of which focuses on new ways of working. Author of numerous publications in leading scientific journals, he has also been deputy editor-in-chief of the *International Review of Administrative Sciences* and a member of the steering committee of the Swiss Society of Administrative Sciences. He studied at and obtained his doctorate in business management from the University of Geneva.

Flavia Fossati is Professor of Inequality and Integration at the Swiss Graduate School of Public Administration at the University of Lausanne. She has been professor of Social Policy at the University of Vienna and lecturer at the University of Zurich. Her research, publications and consultancy work focus on the integration of immigrants into Western societies, discrimination, and public opinion on social policies such as education, unemployment benefits and social measures during the pandemic. She co-directed a National Centre of Competence in Research project on The Migration-Mobility Nexus (nccr-on the move). The author of numerous publications in leading academic journals, she is co-editor of the *Oxford Handbook of Swiss Politics*, an extended version of the original published in German by NZZ Libro. She holds a doctorate in political science from the University of Zurich.

David Giauque is Professor of Public Management and Human Resources Management at the Swiss Graduate School of Public Administration at the University of Lausanne. He was previously a professor at and director of the University of Lausanne's Institut d'études politiques, a visiting professor at the School of Public Administration of the University of Victoria (Canada), and a lecturer in inter-university programs in human-resources management (HRM). His research, publications and consultancy work focus on HRM practices in the public sector, the conditions of engagement and motivation of public-sector employees, the work climate, new ways of working, culture, organizational climate and ethics. He has published numerous books and scientific articles on these topics in leading journals. He holds a doctorate in public administration from the University of Lausanne, including an academic year at the University of Montreal (HEC Montreal) funded by the Swiss National Science Foundation.

Olivier Glassey is Adjunct Professor of Public Management at the Swiss Graduate School of Public Administration at the University of Lausanne. He is head of the training programme and sits on the management committee of FORDIF (Formation en direction d'institutions de formation) and is director of the Observatoire romand de la culture. He also works as an organizational consultant for various clients in the public and para-public sector of French-speaking Switzerland. He holds a doctorate in information systems from the Faculté des Hautes Études Commerciales, University of Lausanne, as well as a "Create Entrepreneurship Diploma" from the École Polytechnique Fédérale de Lausanne.

Andreas Ladner † was Professor of Administration and Institutions at the Swiss Graduate School of Public Administration at the University of Lausanne. He was Director of IDHEAP from 2016 to 2020. His research, publications and consultancy work focused on the autonomy of Swiss municipalities, political parties, and the organization and reform of institutions and administration. He was responsible for monitoring Swiss municipalities and, at the international level, for the index of municipal autonomy. Among other things, he analysed the effects of voting aids on electoral behaviour and on various political issues in Switzerland. He co-authored *Size and Local Democracy and Patterns of Local Autonomy in Europe*, and co-edited the *Handbook on the Politics of Public Administration* and *Swiss Public Administration—Making the State Work Successfully*. He held a doctorate from the University of Zurich and a *venia legendi* from the University of Berne.

Vincent Mabillard is Professor of Public Management and Communication at the Solvay Brussels School of Economics and Management of the Université libre de Bruxelles (ULB). He is a regular contributor to public-administration training programmes, mainly in Europe. His publications focus on transparency and accountability in the public sector, on digital communication in government, particularly social media, and on place branding and marketing. His research has been published in many leading scientific journals and has won awards at international conferences. He holds a master's degree in political science from the Université catholique de Louvain and a doctorate in public administration from the University of Lausanne.

Tobias Mettler is Professor of Information Management at the Swiss Graduate School of Public Administration at the University of Lausanne. His research, publications and consultancy work focus on the digitalization of the public sector and its impact on society, oversight and governance, particularly in the fields of healthcare, demographic change and public welfare. He has been principal investigator on a number national and international research projects. Author of numerous publications in scientific journals, he is associate editor of *Information Policy*. He has been awarded a number of academic prizes in Switzerland and abroad. He holds a degree in information management and a doctorate in management from the University of St. Gallen.

Stéphane Nahrath is Professor of Public Policy and Sustainability at the Swiss Graduate School of Public Administration at the University of Lausanne. He was Vice-Director of the Institut universitaire Kurt Bösch from 2008 to 2014. His research, publications and consultancy work focus on environmental, energy and land-use planning policies, and on the sustainable management of natural and infrastructure resources. He has directed or co-directed numerous research projects, notably on the implementation of wind-power policy in Switzerland. His current work and publications focus on the circular economy, urban densification, the multifunctionality of hydroelectric infrastructures and the "new commons". He was co-editor of the journal *Espaces et sociétés* from 2018 to 2021. He studied at the Freie Universität Berlin, the University of Lausanne and the École des hautes études en sciences sociales (EHESS-Marseille). He holds a doctorate in public administration from the University of Lausanne.

Oliver Neumann is Professor of Strategy and Organization at the Swiss Graduate School of Public Administration at the University of Lausanne, and lecturer at the Bern University of Applied Sciences. His research, publications and consultancy work focus on innovation, the application of artificial intelligence, behavioural public administration and new, agile forms of organization. He is the author of numerous publications in scientific journals on public administration and information systems. He also has extensive practical experience in the public sector, particularly in the fields of sustainability and public transport. He studied at the University of Mannheim, the University of Konstanz, York University in Toronto and the University of Bern, where he obtained a doctorate in management.

Martial Pasquier is Professor of Public Communication and Management at the Swiss Graduate School of Public Administration at the University of Lausanne, and visiting professor or lecturer at various universities. He was Director of IDHEAP from 2012 to 2016 and was Vice-Rector of the University of Lausanne from 2016 to 2021. His research, publications and consultancy work focus on the governance and management of public and para-public organizations and on communication. He has been principal investigator on numerous research projects. He is the author of many publications in leading scientific journals and books published in English, French, German, Italian and Romanian, and is associate editor of the *International Review of Administrative Sciences*. He holds a doctorate from the University of Fribourg and a habilitation in business administration from the University of Berne.

Nils Soguel is Professor of Public Finance at the Swiss Graduate School of Public Administration at the University of Lausanne and was visiting professor or lecturer at London University College, the universities of Bath, Québec, Geneva and Fribourg and the École polytechnique fédérale de Lausanne. He has been Director of IDHEAP since 2021. His research, publications and consultancy work focus on public-sector financial management, fiscal and budgetary policy, economic analysis of federalism, municipal amalgamation, valuation of non-market goods and financing systems. He is the editor and publisher of the annual Comparative review of the Swiss governments' fiscal position. He chaired the Swiss Public Sector Financial Reporting Advisory Committee, the standard-setting body for all Swiss public entities from 2008 to 2024. He studied at University College London and the University of Neuchâtel, where he obtained a doctorate in political economy.

Mickaël Terrien is Professor of Regulation of Sport at the Swiss Graduate School of Public Administration at the University of Lausanne, and visiting professor or lecturer at the universities of Lille and Paris-Saclay. His research, publications and consultancy work focus on the governance and regulation of sports organizations in both the professional and amateur sectors. He is the author of numerous publications in scientific management journals, including some specializing in the field of sport, and holds several mandates with leading international sporting bodies. He also directs several training courses run jointly by IDHEAP and UEFA (Union of European Football Associations). He trained in economics and management at the École Normale Supérieure, Université Paris-Sorbonne and Université Paris-Dauphine, and holds a doctorate in strategic management.

Sophie Weerts is Professor of Public Law and Regulation at the Swiss Graduate School of Public Administration at the University of Lausanne. She has also taught as a visiting professor at the University of Geneva and Université Saint-Louis-Bruxelles, and as a lecturer at Université catholique de Louvain and Université de Neuchâtel. Her research, publications and consultancy work focus on the regulation of technologies and their impact on the legislative process. Her writings touch on a wide range of areas of constitutional law, administrative law and human rights. She obtained a doctorate in legal sciences from Université catholique de Louvain, after studying law and obtaining an additional degree in economic and social ethics. She practised as a lawyer at the Brussels Bar and was an expert on public-service reform and the modernization of public administration for the Belgian federal government

Table of content

IMPRIM'VERT®

Achevé d'imprimer en avril 2025
par Sepec Numérique – 01960 Péronnas
N° d'imprimeur : N36146250310